HOW TO GET GOVERNMENT CONTRACTS

HAVE A SLICE OF THE $1 TRILLION PIE

Olessia Smotrova-Taylor

Apress®

How to Get Government Contracts: Have a Slice of the $1 Trillion Pie

ISBN-13 (pbk): 978-1-4302-4497-4
ISBN-13 (electronic): 978-1-4302-4498-1

Trademarked names, logos, and images may appear in this book. Rather than use a trademark symbol with every occurrence of a trademarked name, logo, or image we use the names, logos, and images only in an editorial fashion and to the benefit of the trademark owner, with no intention of infringement of the trademark.

The use in this publication of trade names, trademarks, service marks, and similar terms, even if they are not identified as such, is not to be taken as an expression of opinion as to whether or not they are subject to proprietary rights.

While the advice and information in this book are believed to be true and accurate at the date of publication, neither the authors nor the editors nor the publisher can accept any legal responsibility for any errors or omissions that may be made. The publisher makes no warranty, express or implied, with respect to the material contained herein.

President and Publisher: Paul Manning

Acquisitions Editor: Jeff Olson

Developmental Editor: Robert Hutchinson

Editorial Board: Steve Anglin, Mark Beckner, Ewan Buckingham, Gary Cornell, Louise Corrigan, Morgan Ertel, Jonathan Gennick, Jonathan Hassell, Robert Hutchinson, Michelle Lowman, James Markham, Matthew Moodie, Jeff Olson, Jeffrey Pepper, Douglas Pundick, Ben Renow-Clarke, Dominic Shakeshaft, Gwenan Spearing, Matt Wade, Tom Welsh

Coordinating Editor: Rita Fernando

Copy Editor: Teresa Horton

Compositor: Bytheway Publishing Services

Indexer: SPi Global

Cover Designer: Anna Ischenko

Distributed to the book trade worldwide by Springer Science+Business Media New York, 233 Spring Street, 6th Floor, New York, NY 10013. Phone 1-800-SPRINGER, fax (201) 348-4505, e-mail `orders-ny@springer-sbm.com`, or visit `www.springeronline.com`. Apress Media, LLC is a California LLC and the sole member (owner) is Springer Science + Business Media Finance Inc (SSBM Finance Inc). SSBM Finance Inc is a Delaware corporation.

For information on translations, please e-mail `rights@apress.com`, or visit `www.apress.com`.

Apress and friends of ED books may be purchased in bulk for academic, corporate, or promotional use. eBook versions and licenses are also available for most titles. For more information, reference our Special Bulk Sales–eBook Licensing web page at `www.apress.com/bulk-sales`.

Any source code or other supplementary materials referenced by the author in this text is available to readers at `www.apress.com`. For detailed information about how to locate your book's source code, go to `www.apress.com/source-code/`.

To my husband Michael Taylor, my kids Julia and Caleb, and my mom and dad

Contents

Foreword

I have been fortunate to serve my country in both the public and private sectors, giving me a firsthand perspective of the internal discourse and processes that govern and affect decision making and subsequent action.

In my experience, I have found that the true obstacle to achieving excellence in government contracting and forming effective partnerships between the government and industry lies in the difficulty found following the regulations and processes of the contracting system.

In some respects, the sequence is straightforward. The government needs services that the contracting agency or individual contractor can provide. There exists both a problem and one or more effective solutions. This process, unfortunately, can get complicated when the needs of the government are not well articulated or the responding contractor does not understand or properly assess them. Security concerns can sometimes add yet another layer of complexity.

Initiating a federal government contract competition for an agency represents a step-by-step procedure of following the four layers of regulation that involve the U.S. Code, the Federal Acquisition Regulations, the specific agency's contracting regulations, and the subagencies' policies. These four layers are necessary to safeguard the government from impropriety, empower best practices, and customize guidelines for that individual agency. Additionally, the procurement officer has to sort through the complexity of understanding the technical requirements, determine the actual needs of the government, and tackle the challenge of translating all of this into a succinct yet thorough Request for Proposal (RFP).

From the industry perspective, when the opportunity requires extensive resources or sophistication, small businesses and less experienced contractors could be placed at a disadvantage and might not able to compete as effectively.

Building a bridge that explains the government contracting process from an industry perspective in a clear, understandable methodology remains not only desirable, but essential. This book does exactly that, with step-by-step processes, tools, and techniques. In addition, Olessia's essential guide will empower you beyond learning the mere mechanics of how to win your first contract or write a persuasive proposal. Instead, you will learn how to successfully grow your business in the government market, whether you are new to contracting or a seasoned enterprise.

From learning the ropes of the government market, preparing in advance for the proposal, communicating with the right government decision makers in legal and ethical ways, to preparing and delivering your compelling proposal and establishing a foundation from which to grow, this book will serve as your effective guide to understanding everything about the government procurement process. Carefully crafted by a successful contractor in her own right who has won nearly $19 billion in government contracts over the last 18 years, Olessia fills her book with insider insight, proven methodologies, and useful actionable lists to empower you to understand the process, win new contracts, and dramatically expand your business.

If winning a government contract to help the government meet its mission stands as your goal, this book is now your most valuable teammate. Having worked on both sides of the fence, I know how satisfying it can be to achieve these results. As Americans, we are an incredibly optimistic society. What we believe, we achieve. This book helps provide the processes and insider perspectives to make that happen.

Now all you have to do is go out and do it.

The Honorable Jay M. Cohen

Rear Admiral—United States Navy (retired)
Principal, Chertoff Group (present)
Former Undersecretary for Science and Technology, U.S. Department of
Homeland Security (2006–2009)
Former Chief of Naval Research (2000–2006)

About the Author

Olessia Smotrova-Taylor, AF.APMP, president and CEO of OST Global Solutions, Inc., has 18 years of experience in business development, communications, and marketing, including 12 years in contract capture and proposal management. She led winning bids for four out of the five top government contractors, winning more than $19 billion over the course of her career. She consults and teaches others how to get contracts with the government and large commercial organizations, as well as developing processes, tools, and Bid & Proposal Academy courses that enhance business developers' abilities to win business. She serves as the President of the Association of Proposal Management Professionals (APMP) National Capital Area Chapter. She is recognized as an APMP Fellow for her contributions to the field of capture and proposals—the highest honor in the business development profession. Prior to supporting a number of Fortune 500 companies and small businesses as a proposal consultant and growing her own company, she worked as a business developer for Raytheon and Lockheed Martin and wrote for the Financial Times of London.

Acknowledgments

Deep gratitude to my family: my husband Michael Taylor for providing inspiration and for taking care of the kids alone while I was working on the book. Thanks to my kids for putting up with many weekends and evenings without their mommy, and especially for my daughter Julia's constant encouragement. Thanks to my mom for bringing by delicious treats, and for my dad's constant help and support.

Thanks to my entire team at OST Global Solutions, especially Alex Brown and Julia Pochekueva, for putting in long hours as I was working on this book, and for their many words of encouragement. Also thanks to Betsy Kolmus for her editing, formatting, and coordination help.

I am especially grateful for those who have contributed to my professional development. Special thanks to my mentor, Amie Hoeber, for encouraging me to start my company and supporting me over the years. Thanks to Peter Hinz for enabling me to build the foundation of professional skills in business development; to Barbara Best who introduced me to the beauty of performance improvement, processes, and systems; to Malcolm Visser who lent perspective on work–life balance and supported me through hard times; and to George Connell and Tim Hannigan who believed in me enough to let me run capture of complex projects early in my career. Thanks to Marina Naumova, who has been a dear friend, supporting me with advice and anything else I needed to persevere, and who has also served as a model of a true professional. I have been blessed with knowing many masters of this profession, and there is not enough room to list all of them, but I am eternally grateful for their wisdom, knowledge, and generosity over the years.

Finally, thanks to Apress: Jeff Olson for the book idea, Robert Hutchinson for his wise editorial guidance and an unbelievable work ethic (I got e-mail replies back from him at 6 am on weekends within minutes!), Rita Fernando for her polishing of the narrative, and the entire team that made this book a reality.

Introduction

The U.S. federal government is the largest customer in the world, with its contracting, grants, and loans budget exceeding $1 trillion annually. Interestingly, only a small percentage of all U.S. businesses participate in this market, and even fewer reach true success and make it big. What is the point of knowing how huge the federal pie is if, by getting only a contract or two, you can enjoy just a few little crumbs that fall off the table where the established federal contractors eat?

The only point of building a business with the world's largest customer—as opposed to just any customer—is to leverage the potential for massive growth. The latest Washington Technology's Fast 50 list shows small-business federal contractors' compound annual growth rates over the period from 2007 to 2011 running as high as 437 percent—which is astounding in the current economic environment.

Not everybody reaches this level of growth, of course. Many struggle for years and never get to enjoy this level of success. They lack a system that brings all the information together and outlines a roadmap for winning multiple large contracts. With this book, you don't have to wonder how it's done anymore.

I show you not only how break into the federal market, but how to use a replicable system to achieve the triple-digit growth rates that the fastest growing companies in the government market boast. This way, you will get a slice of the trillion-dollar pie, instead of mere crumbs, adding millions of dollars to your annual revenue streams.

Aspiring government contractors face three major barriers on their road to success.

The first barrier is simply being scared of the proverbial red tape that allegedly surrounds government contracting. This book will demystify government contracting for you and dispel the fear of the unknown. It will help you weigh the pros and cons of entering the government contracting market, and disclose the secrets of what it really takes to succeed.

The second barrier is learning the ropes of how to break into the federal contracting arena. The information contained here will help you find the right customers and opportunities in more than 80 agencies, run successful capture pursuits to position yourself ahead of the competition, and write winning proposals. My experience working for two out of the top five government contractors, Raytheon and Lockheed Martin, consulting at such industry leaders as Northrop Grumman and IBM, leading winning capture and proposal pursuits for dozens of other prominent government contractors, and teaching advanced courses to thousands of business development professionals from nearly every top-100 federal contractor, has helped me develop a streamlined system to win and grow federal government contracting businesses organically. I share with you this step-by-step system here. You will learn exactly how the most successful companies do it, using professional-grade tools and techniques.

The third barrier is not knowing the secrets of how to thrust your company into an aggressive growth mode and create a true bid engine with high win rates. This holds true even for established government contractors. In this book, in addition to sharing with you the streamlined business development, capture, and proposal processes, I outline the strategic steps the fastest growing government contractors take to reach triple-digit growth rates.

This book is organized in an easy-to-follow way. The first two chapters help you get oriented in the government market, learn the rules, and get started in government contracting. Chapter 2 also shows you how to leverage small business status and socioeconomic programs, whether yours is a small or large business.

Chapter 3 shows you how to start winning contracts in the federal arena, and walks you through strategies for penetrating the federal market for the first time, finding perfect customers for your portfolio of offerings, and feeding your pipeline with high-probability deals.

Chapters 4 through 10 focus on how to win procurements before they go public by wielding the secret weapon called capture—which the most sophisticated government contractors use correctly to ensure success. These chapters cover everything from creating strong and lasting relationships with your government customers and "wiring" the federal opportunities to yourself legally, to gathering the right information to develop actionable intelligence to position yourself to win, developing a viable win strategy, outdoing your competition, creating the right team, and developing a winning solution well before RFP issuance.

Chapters 11 and 12 walk you through the process of writing a winning proposal. They offer an insight into the exact reasons why some proposals win, and many don't. They will help you read government RFPs correctly to understand what the government is looking for, and they walk you through the intricacies of the proper proposal development process. These chapters will also guide you in producing compliant and compelling proposals that will lead you to the highest probability of winning.

Chapter 13 covers techniques for aggressively growing your government contracting business and building a bid engine that will catapult your business to tens of millions of dollars and beyond.

Throughout the book, I offer links to valuable resources you can consult to expand your knowledge. I also tell you about the tools professionals use to achieve success in the federal market.

Although I run a thriving government contracting and consulting company and it might seem counter to my business interests to divulge all these secrets, I am freely sharing my professional knowledge in this book because I have a larger mission. Government contracts are extremely important to our daily lives, safety, and even global security: It is not just any kind of business—it's a business where you can make a difference.

My ultimate motivation for writing this book is to create better contractors for the government. The process of doing a great job on a contract starts during business development stages. Thoroughly preparing in advance and writing an outstanding proposal means that you have thought through and planned out your postaward work better—which translates into better performance.

It is true that the government market is extremely lucrative. But it is a win–win scenario when good contractors make money by doing an outstanding job and grow into larger and more capable contractors—while our government and ultimately our country benefits as well.

Come journey with me through the intricacies of federal business development, and build a thriving multimillion- or even multibillion-dollar business!

How Lucrative Is Government Contracting— and How Tangled Is the Red Tape?

Government contracting has long been covered in a shroud of mystery for many people unfamiliar with how it works. You have probably heard of the proverbial red tape that goes along with government contracting, especially when someone tries to sell you their expertise. Have you wondered what "red tape" actually means? Should you even try to enter this market? And if you did, how would you succeed in it?

Let's Demystify Government Contracting

The modern expression *red tape* comes from the venerable practice of tying bundles of official documents with red tape, observed by government bureaucracies since the 16th century in Europe and since the 17th century in America. In the 19th century, American Civil War veterans' pension records were bound with red twill tape. The expression stuck. Media, politicians, popular TV shows, and even musicians have used the expression on both sides of the Atlantic Ocean to refer to government bureaucracies. No wonder it sounds terrifying, even if it has become a cliché. Essentially, it has to do with getting tangled in endless procedures, rules, approvals, and forms while wasting time in attempting to navigate the highly bureaucratic and complex environment.

Paradoxically, government contracting is a booming trillion-dollar industry in the United States alone. If red tape is so prevalent, why are there so many who are able to navigate this industry? There is indeed a lot to learn about how to work with the government. The good news is this: the red tape is a thing of the past. The labyrinth of government contracting is not that complicated after all—if you have the right guide. Once you understand the basics, which this book will help you do, getting your first government contract and subsequent government contracts will seem rather straightforward. The key to success is getting the right information and guidance.

Before we venture further, let's look at the pros and cons of whether you should do pursue government contracts in the first place.

The Pros of Entering the Government Contracting Market

By mastering U.S. government contracting, you are can enter a world of endless possibilities and exponential growth. Let's look at some of the characteristics of government contracting.

Market Size

With an annual budget exceeding $500 billion for contracts alone, the U.S. federal government is the largest, wealthiest customer in the world. It purchases more than 13 million different products and services, including everything from staples to janitorial services to spacecraft. Whatever you sell, someone, somewhere in the government probably needs—and most likely already buys.

In fact, it is not only the federal government that purchases goods and services. You can also sell to state, local, municipal, and tribal governments, as well as the educational institutions market. Each offers a budget-rich environment. Then, there are governments of other countries that buy in a somewhat similar manner to the U.S. government, and large commercial companies that have modeled their procurement processes after the best practices borrowed from the feds. If you are an empire builder and want to continue to grow your company to become a *Fortune* global company, you can start in this market and logically expand to other markets that operate in a similar manner.

Stability

Conservative people tend to flock to accounting and finance because this field is stable. As long as there is money, people will need someone to count it. It means the ultimate in job security. Those who make it into government contracting (mostly by accident) realize that it can be just as stable. Think about it: as long as there is a government in the United States, and it doesn't become a huge totalitarian machine where every single job is accomplished by an employee on direct government payroll, there will be a need for contractors. Procurement rules might change, but the need to get goods and services from the private sector to enable the government to do what it does will remain.

Even in countries with huge totalitarian governments that own most of what there is to own in the country, the governments need contractors. They are chosen based on different criteria, of course, but nevertheless, all governments have a need to buy from the private sector.

Barring complete calamity and the fall of all governing systems, contractors will continue to exist—and flourish.

On a serious note, there is an occasional debate whereby some in Congress argue that we would all save money by insourcing the jobs now performed by contractors. *Insourcing* means taking the person a private company had to spend time and money to hire and develop and, without any compensation to the company, offering that person an equivalent position as a government servant. Insourcing had a hard impact on industry a few years ago, and it devastated many small businesses. The government slowed down after a public outcry, but many companies still report that this practice is alive and well.

Here is why the government toys with and occasionally acts on the idea of insourcing. Some "govies" (an endearing slang term referring to government employees as opposed to contractors) tend to believe that contractors are paid nearly double to do the same job as their government counterparts. But people in the know understand that the comparison is not apples to apples. In the end, it would be devastating if our government did away with the contractors and insourced all the jobs they do. In fact, it would end up costing more money. What supporters of insourcing fail to count is overall government compensation, downtime, reduced efficiency, training costs, and so on.

Most important, they would be doing away with the innovation, skills, agility, and competitive spirit of the private sector—and would be bloating the size of the government unnecessarily to boot. Hopefully this country never lets that happen. In the meantime, you can expect a relatively stable U.S. government market for the goods and services you are now selling.

Recession-Proof

Even in an environment in which most budgets are shrinking and fiscal cliffs come and go, the government market has been relatively stable through economic ups and downs and political deadlock. The recent negative impact has been mostly on contractors who have been supporting the war efforts in the Middle East and the space exploration programs. The rest of the industry has seen relatively small overall shrinkage and pronounced growth in such areas such as information technology, cybersecurity, and prevention of waste, fraud, and abuse.

The more mission-essential the work, the more indispensable are the services that your company can provide and the more recession- and austerity-proof is your field.

Timely Payments

With few exceptions, the government pays you on time, with net 30 guaranteed payment terms, or even better. It is unlike private industry, where net 45 or net 60 terms are commonplace and payments sometimes slip for several months. Timely payment helps your cash flow—you don't have to spend as much money on credit. Besides, credit is easier for those working in the government field to get. That's because there is a cottage industry of banks that understand how to hedge their risk through the use of Small Business Administration (SBA) guarantees. Analyzing a company's contract history shows such banks that contractors can pay loans back reliably.

Competitive Edge in the Commercial Arena

The U.S. government, because of its procurement rules that foster competition, numerous regulations, and a constant effort to reduce "waste, fraud, and abuse," created an environment where contractors had to come up with more sophisticated ways to win business. Government contractors, especially those in the services and solutions arena, are in general better at what's called complex sales. A *complex sale* is one that doesn't rely on a handshake and a relationship to close the deal. Instead, the contractor has to create a sophisticated solution, engage in complex preproposal preparations, then write an engaging proposal that addresses *every* need of the customer, present the solution, and then iron out all the details through negotiations.

In the commercial arena, many business developers have not been exposed to the rigor and processes government contractors have had to employ (although the smart ones are certainly learning and embracing the information). For those who come from the government field, winning commercial contracts is sometimes like taking candy from a baby.

By mastering U.S. government contracting, you gain the skills to open up a world of possibilities that far exceeds an already huge customer's budget.

Open to Entry

There are industries that are hard to break into, but, contrary to popular belief, government contracting is not one. The biggest barrier to entry is neither lack of capital, nor being later to market. It is simply lack of knowledge. This is perhaps one of the most unforgivable sins, of course, because the knowledge of how to do well in this field is readily available and is somewhat inexpensive. Most of the information is in the public domain and, unlike in most fields, courses offered are quite affordable. Perhaps the only hard part is navigating in the sea of information and figuring out what's true and what isn't—something this book is going to help you do.

Unlike other industries where being large and powerful is an advantage when entering a new market, it's just the opposite in government contracting. Tiny size and economic and social disadvantages can be strengths. The U.S. government favors minorities, women, service-disabled veterans, companies operating out of economically disadvantaged areas called HUBZones, Native Americans, Native Hawaiians, Native Alaskans, the disabled, small businesses with limited economic means, and many other groups. There are hefty set-asides and helpful programs specifically for small companies, SBA loans, and a variety of resources for small businesses to succeed. All you need to know is how to use these services to your advantage, and the contracting world will be open to you.

Not as Hostile as Other Sectors

It is true that there are industries that are tainted by corruption, favoritism, and a general dog-eat-dog attitude (think of the fashion industry, some technology markets, and manufacturing). Of course, the government field is vast, and there is a fair amount of rivalry, but in general, the whole atmosphere is far different than in many industries.

For starters, there is a lot more teaming between companies to win a contract. The percentage of contracts that companies win in partnership with others is significantly higher than those won on their own. Companies are forced to play nice with each other, or no one would ever team with them.

Because of the need for teaming, companies as a general rule are not as secretive about their processes as they would be if they could keep everything in house. It is common to have your teammates locked in the proposal room together working shoulder-to-shoulder and sharing strategies and techniques to make the document better. Companies with nasty reputations get a bad name quickly and rumors spread quickly.

Companies pride themselves on ethics—and ethical behavior is even more strictly regulated in government contracting than in the commercial world. Ethical violations can cause companies to lose the opportunity to do business with the government entirely. For example, if a business developer in a government contracting company finds proprietary information from a competitor, sound policy is to report it to their legal team, which then has to decide whether the company will exclude itself from the competition. That, of course, is nearly unheard of in the commercial field.

A majority of government contracting companies believe in what they do— they are in this field because they are proud of making a difference and providing a good public service. Although there are many people who just look to make a buck, and don't care, a great majority actually do find meaning in their work.

Clear Trend: Less Corruption and Greater Transparency

Certainly there are exceptions (and we tend to hear about the bad more than the good), but the U.S. Federal Government is less corrupt than most governments. Relationships are important, but not in every case. In fact, most of the time one can form these relationships the first time around, and continue building them by providing truly outstanding service.

As someone who was in the United States for less than a decade, barely 30 years old, and nine months pregnant, I arranged, with the help of my mentor, a meeting with a senior official from the Office of the Secretary of Defense in the Pentagon. I was responsible for winning a large contract, and I wanted to secure this meeting to make sure that certain requirements were changed in the $1 billion procurement. The government official I met listened and initiated the desired adjustments, which happened to be in the best interests of both the government and the company I was supporting. If a young woman with a tiny network could do it, and find the right person to make the introduction so that I could make my pitch, anyone can. You just have to know the topic really well, and know people who know people. Six degrees of separation means you can work miracles.

It is even possible to win a proposal without knowing the customer or the customer knowing you. The probability of winning is lower, but there are enough companies that have done business this way for years. Ultimately, they achieve a healthy size.

The government works actively to be transparent and expose any waste, fraud, and abuse. Different initiatives abound: the General Services Administration (GSA), one of the major players in the government procurement arena, has recently launched a System for Award Management (SAM.gov) designed to combine at least eight existing federal procurement systems into a single database. It not only provides a single place to register as a government contractor and look up other contractors, but also includes a database to expose "bad" contractors by integrating the Excluded Parties List System (EPLS) database. There are also places where you can look up every federal contract, such as the Federal Data Procurement System (FPDS). Immensely useful web sites such as USAspending.gov and FEDspending.org offer all kinds of statistics and details on government contracts, subcontracts, and grants. There is even an initiative underway to make public past performance records that show how well or how badly a company is doing on a project.

One can ask for all kinds of documents via a Freedom of Information Act (FOIA) request, including competitors' cost and technical proposals. You might think that this is a negative, but with a more level playing field, the theory is that a better company truly dedicated to service will end up better off.

In a nutshell, the federal market is an exciting field for those "in the know"—and this book will help you join their ranks and even become one of the best.

The Cons of Joining the Ranks of Federal Contractors

Now that you are all excited about the federal market and its many opportunities, let's infuse a bit of reality into the rosy prospectus you just read. You need to know many things that might lead you to decide against pursuing government contracting. Here are some of the downsides.

There Is a Lot to Learn

Not to belabor this, but there is a lot to learn. Don't think "So what?" until you truly understand how much. You will be drinking from a fire hose of information for years. If this excites you, you are in the right field. If this scares you, find another occupation.

You won't need to know only about your field of discipline—the actual specialty of your company. You won't just need to know how to run a profitable business. You will need to understand the government and specifically your unique set of potential customers. It's time to dust off your civics textbooks. Should I also mention the acronyms and jargon? You will know you speak "government" well when you can easily understand this sentence: "GSA awarded an 8(a) STARS II GWAC with two constellations that include industry partners with CMMI and ISO credentials, with TORFPs posted on eBuy."

You will have to learn the rules. This is the core of the proverbial red tape. There is no single set of rules in government contracting (see Chapter 2). There is a widely used set of rules, the Federal Acquisition Regulations (FAR), but in addition, each agency has its own regulations. Some agencies do not follow the FAR, and most agencies interpret the FAR in their own way. There are also precedents, just like in the legal system. The good news is that you don't have to learn them all at once. You will have to learn the basics, but then you can absorb a lot of these rules as you go along and look up all the applicable clauses on a contract-by-contract basis. In the beginning, you will have to rely on professionals a lot to tell you what is acceptable and what is not. You will also have to triple-check yourself to see if something that you do is allowed. Later on, as your revenue grows, you can hire a professional contracts manager who will interface with the government contracting officers and speak their language to give you the upper hand in negotiating with the government.

You will also need to run your business like a government contractor rather than one working solely in the private sector. That will mean employing different financial systems subject to Defense Contract Audit Agency (DCAA) audits; for example, complying with government regulations regarding employees, using different pricing approaches, and following a set of rules that you will need to pick up from an accounting team that specializes in government contracting.

Finally, you will then need to learn how to win business like a pro. This book will be a huge help, but you will need to take your learning further on a continuous basis using the resources provided at the end of the book.

It Is Hard to Focus

Many beginning government contractors (especially if they are running emerging businesses) don't know if they want to be a fairy princess or an astronaut. You have many decisions to make: Which agency do you want to work with? What are you good at? What services or products do you want to provide? Have agencies bought your types of services or products in the past? Will they buy them in the future? How steep is the competition at that agency? What's the best way to market yourself to them?

Although many understand the need to focus, there is a reason why they don't. When you need to keep making money to keep your lights on, any type of contract for any agency seems attractive. You will tend to want to list more specialties than you are able to deliver in your capabilities statement. You might go and sell anything anyone will have from you, just to stay solvent. In the middle of all of this, a thought might cross your mind: maybe there's a better way to go. Well, some companies make a decent living for quite a while, and some have been rumored to have grown using this approach, but everyone has had to focus at one point or another. Those who specialize in everything are masters of nothing, and others—buyers—aren't blind to that fact. The sooner you can focus on just two or three government customers and your core competencies, and overcome the temptation of being "omnivorous," the better. If you keep going at it for a few years without a clear strategy, you could find yourself in a rut, and you will fold as soon as your socioeconomic status (if you have one) runs out.

Some "Govies" Can Be Difficult to Deal With

Working with a government customer can be a royal pain if you don't luck out with a good one. You might just find your government customer an intelligent, reasonable, dedicated person who is truly trying to make a difference and work in the interests of the project. Or you could run into someone with a, let's say, difficult personality, not to be reasoned with. This person might be resentful because you are paid more than he or she is, or maybe this someone simply despises all contractors.

In commercial contracting, you can usually make a mistake with regard to your performance without having it affect your company's future. It's different in government contracting. Having contracting officers document negative past performance on your permanent record, which is available to other contracting officers, is not a joke. One or two "black eyes" will cost you all the future business you might have had with the government. Remember the transparency that is of such importance with the government but can be lacking in the commercial sector? It is a double-edged sword. Your poor performance on one project will be known government-wide to all agencies—and most likely even to competitors chomping at the bit to take your place. Getting what's called a "cure letter" might prevent you from winning any future contracts, because you will have to explain why you got it in your proposals for years to come. So, you have to please your government customer—or else.

Contracting officers just naturally have a propensity to be rule-oriented and focused on making sure you don't misstep. Their agenda sometimes is at odds with what your personnel believe would help in the success of the project. They seek to reduce costs, avoid any "scope creep" (the expansion of the job to be done that requires extra payments), and ensure that no rules are broken. They want to make sure that you have flawless reporting on the job's progress, although they might not understand all the technical complexities and nuances of what you are grappling with. Trying to explain some of the challenges could be met with a lack of sympathy. Your government project manager is typically easier to deal with than your contracting officer.

A contractor told me a story about a contracting officer who is all about efficiency and making sure that people don't slack off on their jobs. He instituted a clock-in, clock-out procedure for professional information technology (IT) staff working at a government facility. Now he is trying to figure out a way to monitor keystrokes. The contractor is afraid that people will start leaving in droves; good IT people in Washington, DC are generally in high demand and don't need to put up with micromanagement. If people leave, then the contractor will have a real problem satisfying the contracting officer. The contractor's recourse (e.g., complaining to the higher-ups at the agency) is limited because he is afraid to rock the boat and upset the contracting officer. The contractor is at this point just working with his people and trying to introduce some incentives (which will cost him extra money) to keep his IT staff from bolting.

Not all cases are this extreme. Still, when dealing with government personnel, you will have to develop amazing diplomacy skills. You will have to deal with people where they are—not where you want them to be. Whenever you assign personnel to deal with the customer, you will have to make sure that they have great people skills and customer chemistry. They have to be there any time, answering phones even when they are in meetings or at dinner, and available at a moment's notice to address any issue—or to provide a simple status update.

There are far more good experiences working with the government than bad ones, but with the government you must always be on your toes. Be prepared to do an outstanding job.

It's Not a Get-Rich-Quick World

You might have already run into a set of people preying on those not in the know and trying to sell government contracting as a get-rich-quick opportunity. They will claim that getting a government contract is easy, and that they can share some clever techniques where you make money drop-shipping items you never lay your hands on, or claim all you need is a GSA schedule. They play on your natural greed, getting you excited to get your share of Uncle Sam's money. They urge you to exploit tens of thousands of contracting opportunities with the government—with their masterful help (usually requiring minimal effort on their part). They use aggressive marketing pitches and "insult selling"—making you feel incompetent for not having already gotten into something this obviously lucrative that's been in front of your nose all along. They might even promise high win probability, failing to mention that the majority of the federal market is fiercely competitive, and you need to really know what you are doing to win contracts.

Before they separate you from your hard-earned dollars, let's set some realistic expectations. First and foremost, government business will not make you rich quick. It's likely that it will take 18 months for you to get up and going—and then a few years of earning good "past performance" reports painstakingly to join others' teams as a subcontractor, or even become a primer contractor directly to the government. Yes, there are programs whereby you might be able to get a contract quick if you qualify—but these contracts usually don't enable you to create much leverage. In other words, you will most likely be placing yourself and a bunch of others on those contracts, creating quite a bit of work. You will have to do a lot more business building during your "free time" late at night. If you are selling product, it's no better—you will need to get a GSA schedule to sell to the government, and then you will have to actively market and do relentless legwork to realize any money from it. You will do well if you do all the right things you learn in this book but—just like any business—it will take you time to implement your plan.

Here is a reality check: according to Grant Thornton reports year in and year out, government contractors make a very modest profit on services. Profit is the fee on top of labor rates, benefits, overhead, and general and administrative expenses. It used to be that you could charge as much as 20 percent profit for your efforts. Now, even in hostile environments such as war zones, contractors make only 16 to 18 percent, and this markup is going down. On regular services contracts, 12 percent profit used to be acceptable. Then, it was not to exceed 8 percent. Now the numbers are plunging below 5 percent. This is an average—meaning that some charge more and others charge less—but few are truly impressed with these numbers.

Some companies involved in the war effort came up with a way of charging nearly zero profit so that they could keep their personnel until the next war erupts. They are pleased to just be breaking even.

The government also has negotiated large Blanket Purchase Agreements (BPA) with vendors for commodities so they can buy them cheaper than retail—achieving significant savings. The rules for selling products to the government through a GSA schedule state that you are required by law to offer the lowest price to the government, which means lower than any sale that you have or might run.

How do government contractors stay in business? Well, some of them treat it as a game. As you proceed into the contracting world, you might find that there are certain ways of making the profit higher even though it doesn't show up high on your cost estimates. Companies use various strategies. For example, they might bid low but get well in the follow-on years (the so-called "option" years) of the contract. They try to document the scope with excruciating precision so that when they work on a fixed-price contract, they will be able to add money to the contract, by what's called engineering change proposals, if any request from the government deviates from the agreed-to scope. Some companies make an art form of bidding blended rates—or average rates representative of the labor category—and then back-fitting personnel into the rates where they claim one margin on paper, but in fact, make a whole other margin. This is especially true when they use more junior personnel.

Some companies claim one margin on a fixed-price contract, but end up making a higher margin and keeping it. The government could force them to return the money if they feel that they made excessive profits, but many companies are able to get away with it. Some companies do things that are less than ethical. For example, some don't staff projects to the level that was agreed to in the contract, while billing the government for the fully staffed service. Others resort to bait-and-switch tactics.

Some larger companies are more adept at using a variety of techniques as they hire savvy contracts managers who know the system inside out. Other large companies pick a favorite contract type and stick with it to keep margins higher. Most smaller companies, on the other hand, pride themselves on being able to serve the government without a single change proposal and come in within or under budget through greater efficiency. They don't dare play games.

The government wises up more and more to various techniques used by contractors to make money, and it closes the loopholes. It is akin to asymmetric warfare. There are fewer and fewer tricks that are not known to the government as it learns—but then the institutional knowledge goes away as some of the more experienced folks retire. Different contract types become popular and institutionalized and then die down as others emerge after someone figures out a way to make more profit—or fail because the contract type is too restrictive to accomplish the real work. Meanwhile, the business of some contractors—provided they are not using much gaming— doesn't grow even though they provide stellar services.

For now, you don't need to worry about the exact margins you stand to make and loopholes; just know that there is often more to profit than meets the eye in government contracting. Experienced government contractors have done quite well for themselves. Although there is no longer any of the legendary gold plating that the 1980s were known for, there is still a way to run a profitable government contracting business with integrity. The secret is getting a consultant to help you develop a true cost strategy and a winning approach, and then taking a look at a contract to ensure it is structured so that you don't lose (and actually make) money.

As you can see from the cons we just considered, it is not an easy decision to venture into the government contracting world. You will have to invest in continuous learning, write complicated proposals, and generally work hard at building your business. If this is okay with you, then read on to learn more about this vast field of opportunity.

Bird's-Eye View of the Market

The government market is vast. You can get a great snapshot of the federal market for contracting (competitive and sole source) at www.USAspending. gov. This site provides trends in total federal spending through dynamic interactive charts. At $500 billion, U.S. federal government contracts spending is still in the record-high range compared with the spending level of a decade or so ago, when it hovered slightly above $200 billion.

Who Are the Buyers in the Government Market?

Most federal agencies to which you are going to sell belong in the executive branch of government. These 15 cabinet-level agencies are as follows:

- Department of Agriculture (USDA)

- Department of Commerce (DOC)

- Department of Defense (DOD)

- Department of Education (ED)

- Department of Energy (DOE)

- Department of Health and Human Services (HHS)

- Department of Homeland Security (DHS)

- Department of Housing and Urban Development (HUD)

- Department of the Interior (DOI)

- Department of Justice (DOJ)

- Department of Labor (DOL)

- Department of State (DOS)

- Department of Transportation (DOT)

- Department of the Treasury (Treasury)

- Department of Veterans Affairs (VA)

There are also 69 independent agencies and government corporations that also report to the executive branch.[1] This large list includes the Central Intelligence Agency (CIA), the GSA, the National Aeronautics and Space Administration (NASA), the Office of Personnel Management (OPM), and many others. Some of these agencies, such as the Federal Aviation Administration (FAA), are exempt from the FAR and have developed their own sets of rules for contracting with the "industry" or the "private sector"— as the government often calls contractors. These terms are opposed to the terms "government" and "public sector" by which government customers refer to themselves.

Boards, commissions, and committees include 68 entities. They have a somewhat limited ability to purchase services and products, but they are not to be discounted. Examples include the American Battle Monuments

---

1   You can see the full list of executive branch agencies at www.usa.gov/Agencies/Federal/ Executive.shtml#vgn-executive-departments-vgn.

Commission and the Broadcasting Board of Governors, which governs stations such as the Voice of America. There are also four quasi-official agencies, such as the Smithsonian Institution, that are not government per se, but have similar reporting requirements.

The legislative and judicial branches buy from contractors as well. For example, the U.S. Congress might require furniture, renovation services, or IT support. The Library of Congress might need security services. A variety of courts under the judicial branch require services and commodities. The full list of those agencies can be found at www.usa.gov/Agencies.shtml.

In addition to the federal government, state, local, and tribal governments also fall under the definition of the public sector. Often it is easier to start working with the state and local governments rather than federal agencies. It is an entry point for a new business or a business that has been established in the commercial world and is just starting to venture into the government market.

The state governments sector includes all 50 states, the District of Columbia, and five U.S. territories (American Samoa, Guam, the Northern Mariana Islands, Puerto Rico, and the U.S. Virgin Islands). (Find out more about state governments at www.usa.gov/Agencies/State_and_Territories.shtml.)

The local government sector is huge, including county and municipal governments in towns, cities, and counties across the nation. You can find a list of links to these governments at www.usa.gov/Agencies/Local.shtml.

The tribal governments sector is also large and procures everything from professional services to commodities. You can see a list of tribal governments at www.usa.gov/Government/Tribal_Sites/index.shtml.

You also need to know about additional delineations in the government contracting world.

The entities reporting to DOD are often called the defense sector in the government vernacular, or the military, and all the other agencies are considered civilian agencies. The defense sector is vast. As part of DOD, there are the following larger entities that contain multiple departments, agencies, commands, services, and offices:

- Office of the Secretary of Defense
- Air Force
- Army
- Marine Corps
- Navy

- Joint Chiefs of Staff

- Combatant Commands

- Inspector General

- Defense Agencies

- Field Activities

- Joint Service Schools

You can see the extensive listing of these military entities at www.usa.gov/Agencies/Federal/Executive/Defense.shtml. Do note that some of these entities, such as the Army Corps of Engineers, do a lot of civilian work for which they have separate budgets.

It is also useful for you to know that some of the federal agencies are considered "big" or "major" from a contracting budget standpoint, and some are "small."

All 15 cabinet-level agencies are considered major. Big military branches or "services" within DOD are huge customers in and of themselves, and include the U.S. Army, the Air Force, and the Navy. The following are some of the additional budget-rich agencies:

- GSA

- NASA

- National Science Foundation (NSF)

- Nuclear Regulatory Commission (NRC)

- OPM

- SBA

- Social Security Administration (SSA)

- U.S. Agency for International Development (USAID)

This means that you can focus your entire business development effort on one or two agencies; it's quite possible to build a multimillion-dollar or billion-dollar business in that way. As mentioned, the government world is a relatively stable and safe environment in comparison with the general market—it is not as unwise here to put all or most of your eggs in one basket. In this way, your past performance references are always more relevant to new bids. There are plenty of highly successful companies that are focused on one sector such as the Intelligence Community (IC), and only a few agencies within that sector.

Although it is *always* wiser and safer to diversify your portfolio, you might want to start by specializing and going deeper rather than wider.

The small agencies are nothing to sneeze at either—they issue plenty of contracts and buy a lot from the private sector. You can take a look at the President's budget to see how much money they spend under "Other Independent Agencies" at www.whitehouse.gov/omb/budget/appendix.

How to Become a Pro at Winning Contracts Consistently

The companies that win government contracts consistently don't do it by accident. They use an actual system that produces repeatable successes. Every company that would like to win business from the government has to set up a system that has five critical elements. Let's go over each element in detail.

People

You might start as one person who is responsible for winning government contracts. This is not a problem—you can join the ranks of many who have started at one point or another and are still the only one writing proposals, even as their company has grown to a nice size and they have the capital to afford professionals. I once met the CEO of a 1,200-person business who still was the company's best proposal writer—he had a 99 percent win rate. (He'd lock himself in a hotel room for a week at a time with a few six packs.) It was possible because the company was focused on a single set of offerings and wrote for the same set of customers.

Many companies reach a point at which they have to start maturing and growing their business development, capture, and proposal capability. It usually happens when they have a constant volume of bids and they are looking for a more efficient way to develop proposals and win consistently. They want to scale up, grow aggressively, and create a true business development engine.

If you are a small company, the next phase of the business development team, beyond just you, could consist of one or two people, with technical personnel roped in as needed for subject matter expertise. This formula works when this team has to go after a handful of bids a year, but as you start growing aggressively and you need to crank out four, five, or ten proposals a month, you have to figure out how to scale intelligently. At that point you will need personnel—employees or consultants—that will include the following types of professionals.

- **Business developer (also called account manager or account lead)** to identify customers, foster and maintain trusting customer relationships, and find government contracting opportunities.

- **Capture manager** to chase each opportunity after the business developer hands it over, to increase your probability of winning it, and to do all the preproposal preparation—before the official request for proposal (RFP) ever hits the street.

- **Proposal manager** to run your proposal document development like a project—because proposals are so complex that it might take a whole team to put a winning offer together.

- **Proposal coordinator** to run your smaller proposal efforts, or to help the proposal manager run larger ones.

- **Proposal writer** to write and edit proposal sections, while working closely with the subject matter experts who have the knowledge of all the technical details but aren't necessarily the best writers.

- **Graphic artist** to develop your graphic concepts into professional-looking, attractive graphics that will make your proposals easy to understand.

- **Editor** to ensure your proposals are error-free and polished.

- **Desktop publisher** to format your documents for a professional appearance.

- **Price-to-win expert** to figure out what price your competitors might offer—and what price you should offer to beat them.

- **Price strategist** to develop the strategy to get to the price-to-win number.

- **Pricer and estimator** to support the cost proposal development effort.

- **Subject matter experts**, most likely your project personnel who bill directly to the government, pulled away from their regular work to provide specialized subject matter expertise for developing technical and management solutions.

- **Contracts manager** who will make sure that you comply with all the contractual language consistent with the FAR, and who might even negotiate your teaming agreements with the subcontractors.

- **Recruiter** who will quickly identify personnel and get their resumes and commitment to bid on your proposals.

- **Orals coach** to train your team on how to create and deliver winning presentations, if you target customers who favor orals and demos.

- **Management team or executive (at a director or vice-president level)** to oversee all the personnel and make sure that you are juggling your resources appropriately, and also to implement all the other aspects of business development.

As you can see, it takes many types of proposal professionals to help you win consistently. Don't despair. Most highly successful government contracting businesses started small—with one person wearing all of the hats and fulfilling all the roles. It will be up to you, as you grow, to know when to gradually add others to the team—to avoid burning out yourself and others.

Processes

The processes by which you are going to do business are another important element in your ability to win government contracts. In the world of sales and marketing, government is by far the most complex kind of sale you will ever make. Government requirements and rules are Talmudic: they are very detailed and occasionally self-contradictory. The government acquisition process is structured with multiple steps, and it takes time. Often, RFPs are won before they ever hit the street. Without a system that you can follow to prevail over the competition in this tough environment, you will struggle every time, winning little while overworking and stressing yourself out.

On the other hand, with a good set of processes and systems, you will inevitably succeed. Your systems will include process books, procedures for winning business, checklists, and templates that you can apply to make everything easier. The benefits of using processes are many: you will do more in less time, win more because of the improved quality of your proposals, delegate tasks to people with efficiency and ease, train staff, grow your business development organization, drive continuous improvement, and even build value in the company for a later sale if you would like to.

First and foremost, you have to understand the big-picture process of how you can go about winning business with the government, and then all the steps that go into each individual part of this process. Figure 1-1 shows the nine-step business development life cycle we have developed at my company to help our clients win government contracts.

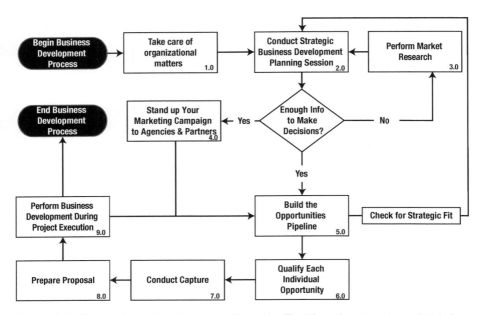

Figure 1-1. Full business development life cycle. The life cycle is iterative and includes nine steps necessary to win government contracts. (Courtesy of OST Global Solutions)

Step 1.0 is there to help you set your company up to do business with the government. When you are just starting, you have to get your registrations and formalities right. Even companies that have been in business with the government for a while have had issues with this step. Sure, they have done the basics, but when was the last time they updated their registrations and information? Is the information provided current, and is their company easy to find in the databases where they are supposed to register? You will need to revisit Step 1.0 continuously as you grow and your capabilities and status change.

Step 2.0 is about strategic business development planning, and should take place every year or even six months. Many companies ignore this step. As a result, they go after business haphazardly, don't focus on a set of customers and areas of expertise, fail to set goals and budgets, and fall into a trap of getting seduced by pop-up opportunities that might have nothing to do with the plan but seem attractive at the moment. Others make a mistake of writing the plan once, and then leaving it to collect virtual (and physical) dust while they are engaged in the routine day-to-day operations. This plan should be your beacon in the normal confusion of the fast-paced life of a government contractor.

Step 3.0, market research, will help you focus your efforts on the right customers who are more likely to buy the services or products you offer. Market research goes hand-in-hand with your strategic business development planning and is somewhat iterative. For you to plan, you need to know which vertical markets you are going to enter. This leads you to more market research, which then provides feedback into the planning process.

Step 4.0, marketing to the government, follows all the preceding steps and takes place simultaneously with the pipeline development process that we will discuss shortly. It takes place after your strategic planning session, once you have decided which customers you are going after. It is related to the overall effort of attracting customers to your company and creating awareness of your brand and offers. Modern government marketing is not the same it was a decade ago—or even five years ago. In addition to traditional methods such as personal visits to government decision makers, you now can take advantage of modern techniques such as social networks, webinars, training events, search engine optimization, and others.

Step 5.0, pipeline development, is the natural outcome of your market research. Now that you know which agencies and which areas you are going to explore, you will need to zoom in and develop a list of opportunities that you are then going to narrow down further and further as you learn more about them. These opportunities will be in the near term with an RFP or a sale coming up in one to six months, the midterm (with an opportunity expected to open up in the next six months to one year), and the long term (from one to five years out). Some of the large and important opportunities might then make it into your strategic plan (Step 2.0)—and you might start calling them strategic bids or "must-win" opportunities.

Step 6.0, opportunity identification, is the final step before you narrow down the field and begin focusing on each individual opportunity. As you sort through opportunities in your pipeline, you will narrow down the list to a select few. These are the opportunities in which you will have serious interest. Then, you will be ready to start chasing each of these individual opportunities to stack the deck in your favor.

Step 7.0, capture management, which we cover in great detail in this book, is the longest and the most important step in the business development life cycle. Capture is positioning your company preproposal to win a specific opportunity. A proposal usually has a short deadline, whereas capture could take months or years of engaging with the customer, learning about their needs, developing a strategy to beat the competition, finding the right team, and preparing an innovative solution. It prepares you to write a proposal in style, and then win the contract because the customer is excited to get it and to award the contract to you.

Step 8.0, proposal preparation, is managing the development of a winning proposal document to deliver it by the deadline. Government proposals are complex multivolume documents that require a lot of work. Proposal development is an iterative process that usually involves multiple contributors and a set of reviews to check quality and progress. Here are some of the most important characteristics of a winning proposal, the majority of which stem from a well-run capture effort:

- Matching the solution with the customer's requirements, wishes, and vision.

- Great process that gets you to the deadline without undue stress and allows you sufficient time to polish your document.

- Targeted features and benefits, with a clear value proposition.

Step 9.0, business development during implementation, refers to your ability to get even more work (and money) after you have won a contract. Once you have a government contract, the ground is ripe for adding scope (what is called an upsell in sales). It is actually a good thing for the government, because it eliminates another formal acquisition process. The formal process is rife with all kinds of headaches—from doing tons of paperwork to labor-intensive evaluation to risking protests

Once you have won a government contract or two, your people who work on the project with the customer can serve as your eyes and ears if you train them correctly in the capture process. They can find out about the need for additional work, and then tell the government customer that they will send someone to talk to them—usually your account manager with your subject matter experts. The account manager and subject matter experts will meet with the government representative, carefully learning about the requirements. They can then use this information to submit a white paper or an unsolicited proposal. This can often result in adding scope to your existing contract. This is easily accomplished through a change order process. It is such a profitable route that some companies get as much as 50 percent of their revenue from it!

Your staff on the ground can also tell your business developers about other requirements they are hearing about that might not lend themselves to adding scope. These are new additions to your pipeline—but these additions are infinitely more valuable than others because you get to hear about them early. They are from an existing customer that bought from you before and trusts you more, and you already have a connection with a satisfied client.

There is another reason implementation is an important part of the business development life cycle. If you do well, great things happen—you get to upsell, you get to find out more information about other pursuits, and you get to be in the inner circle. You also generate a great past performance, which is the track record that you can leverage in your next proposal.

On the other hand, if you don't do well, you tarnish your record with the government very quickly—and this record proliferates from one customer to other government agencies through past performance database records. It is very important that once you have won a contract, you do a great job. Do whatever it takes to deliver and please your customer. The government considers past performance indicative of future performance.

Technology

You will need a variety of tools for effective business development. Some people still think a computer, a whiteboard, and a shared drive are enough to run things well, but there is absolutely no reason to be stuck in the last century. Here are but a few examples of technology tools you can use to make your business development process more effective.

- **A collaboration workspace** such as Microsoft SharePoint, Privia, or Central Desktop—where you can house your business development documents, run capture and proposal efforts, or even house your pipeline of opportunities.

- **A customer relationship management (CRM) system** such as Sales Force to keep track of your contacts and opportunities.

- **A web meeting** capability such as Microsoft NetMeeting, Webex, GoToMeeting, or even the business version of Skype to run meetings and brainstorming sessions, and work on documents together virtually.

- **Software** such as the latest version of Microsoft Office, Adobe Acrobat Professional, or the full Adobe Creative Suite, and such neat efficiency boosters as acronym finder software, editing automation tools, and mind mapping tools.

Collateral

Collateral is the library of materials and templates you will have developed that will save you time in developing more. This valuable reference resource should include, at a minimum, these elements:

- Proposals you have won and lost, together with their RFPs
- Past performance information, with kudos from the customer
- A database of resumes for personnel you use in bids frequently
- Management, subcontracting, quality, and transition plan templates
- Common win themes
- Contact lists for everyone who could be involved, including consultants you could call if you are short on resources
- Price-to-win information
- Any golden nuggets such as your company's accomplishments and certifications
- Graphics
- Templates

A big task will be to keep this collateral up to date—so you might want to designate someone to do so for you. Initially, however, just having all these documents organized and easily retrievable will be a tremendous help.

Training

This book is the first part of your training—showing you the ropes of exactly what it takes to win government contracts like professionals do. After you are well on your way to winning government business, you will be training everyone on your team how to sell your company, find new opportunities for bidding, and write effective proposals.

Running a company that trains contractors in how to win government business, I have noticed that training is one of those things many business owners don't want to invest in. I find it ironic that people will keep losing multimillion-dollar bids, one after another, but refuse to invest a few thousand dollars in a training course showing them and their employees exactly how to do it all better. Smart people and companies in the services arena should invest nearly 10 percent of their annual profit in training and development. This book is an important step in your investment in winning government proposals the smart way.

These five elements that the pros combine to consistently win government contracts—people, processes, technology, collateral, and training—will be critical to your own success in the government market. The chapters that follow show you the ropes of government contracting, but you will need to blend these five elements in harmony to ensure continued growth of your company.

Get Started in Government Contracting

To win government contracts successfully, you must have a basic understanding of the rules and peculiarities of the market. Then, you must register your company as a federal contractor to begin the process of pursuing contracting opportunities.

Rules of the Game in the Federal Marketplace

Let's look at some of the definitions and elements you need to understand before you register as a federal contractor and begin competing for government contracts.

Fiscal Year

You might already know from political debates that the government fiscal year starts on October 1 and ends on September 30. This is a very important bit of information from a business development point of view, not just for politics or accounting. Government buying patterns change throughout the quarters, impacting federal contractors. Government procurement tends to pick up in the first quarter, slow down in the second, start slowly back up in the third, and really heat up around the fiscal year end—between July 1 and September

30. The reason for the end-of-year upswing is that agencies have to spend their allotted funds within the year or risk getting their budget reduced (unless they find a way to reallocate the funds). This is a powerful motivating factor. Knowing these patterns can help you prepare for your business development activities accordingly.

Budgeting Cycle

Government buying activities also correlate with the Congressional approval of the budget. If an approval comes early in the cycle, everything works as planned; if it is late, government tends to buy differently than it normally would, and you might end up bidding on a contract differently against a different set of competitors.

A budgeting cycle starts with the U.S. President's budget strategy roughly one year before the scheduled Congressional approval. Federal agencies submit budget estimates in accordance with the strategy to the White House Office of Management and Budget (OMB). After OMB's review and estimate, the President reviews and finalizes the budget, and submits it to Congress by February. Six weeks later, the Congressional committees report their budget estimates to Budget Committees.

By April 15, the Congressional Budget Resolution is supposed to be approved, and within one month, the House and Senate should begin consideration of annual appropriations (spending) bills. Within another month, a conference committee is supposed to hash out the differences between House and Senate versions of the annual appropriations bills. Ideally, Congress should have approved the annual appropriations bills and sent them to the president by June 30. The President must turn them around in two weeks and transmit a midsession review of the budget to Congress. By the start of the new fiscal year on October 1, the new budget is supposed to be implemented. If this doesn't happen, as has been the case in recent years, the government has to start the new fiscal year without an approved budget.

In this scenario, to prevent a government shutdown, Congress approves a series of continuing resolutions to keep government going until there is an agreement on the budget. Sometimes a final budget is not passed until halfway through the fiscal year, seriously affecting government contractors.

There are other reasons why you have to understand the budgeting cycle:

- You need to know how much money the President has allocated in the budget for each agency for the year, and you can check the Congressional budget item by item to see how much each program gets, and in what time period. This is an important input into your price-to-win analysis. Bloomberg Government (http://BGov.com) studies show that the President's budget is largely accurate, despite popular opinion to the contrary, with 85 percent of the line items intact after Congressional approval.

- As you get more sophisticated, you might want to influence the budgeting process both from the bottom up (when the users generate the requirements and agencies submit their budgets to the President roughly two years prior to scheduled budget approval) and from the top down (when you can engage with Congressmen and their staffers on Capitol Hill to ensure your program gets sufficient funding and doesn't get cut).

As already discussed, you can find the President's budget on the White House OMB site—the appendix contains all of the detailed information (see www.whitehouse.gov/omb/budget/appendix). The President's budget information might help you in figuring out the budget the government has allocated to larger programs, under which the contracts you are chasing might fit.

No Single Procurement Authority

There is no single authority in the government that issues contracts and buys for the government. Each government agency and even different parts of those agencies manage procurement their own way. It gets so confusing that the government at times has trouble tracking its spending and avoiding duplication of effort and resources. Although it has gotten much better at it, the government has yet to get a clear picture of all purchases across the board.

Rules

Just as there is no single procurement authority in the government, there is also no single uniform set of rules by which every government entity abides. As already discussed in Chapter 1, however, the FAR is the most important set of rules for you to know.

The FAR is a set of procurement regulations for acquisition that has been around since 1984 and is continuously updated. It has the effect of statute law. You can find the FAR clauses at www.acquisition.gov or http://farsite.hill.af.mil. Every time you encounter a FAR reference, make it a habit to look it up and see what it says. Gradually, you will become well versed in this complex regulation.

The FAR was created and gets amended by an interagency group consisting of DOD, GSA, and NASA officials. It takes from 1 to 15 years to implement a desired change into a law that makes it into the FAR. Each regulation, originating from legislation, executive orders, or even private citizens, has to pass through months, and often years, of scrutiny. An interagency team prepares draft language, and then a team of 15 analysts examines it and presents it to the civilian and DOD councils. After considering all the views, they arrive at one version of the rule that gets published for public comments. It then requires additional reconciliation, OMB approval, and signatures from the administrators of DOD, GSA, and NASA, before it gets published as a final rule.

The government then has to understand how to implement the rule. Each rule has to have a set of implementation guidelines. It takes a while to develop these, and it is not enough to just read the FAR—you have to know how it is implemented by each agency if there is no central guideline because each agency has its own take on the FAR interpretations.

You have to have a general understanding of the FAR regarding what is allowed and what is not allowed in the government world, and also which FAR rules apply to each specific procurement (they get published or referenced in each solicitation). In the beginning, you might want to recruit the help of a proposal consultant, a contracting specialist, or a government contracting attorney to read the contract documentation and interpret the FAR rules correctly.

Each agency has its own set of regulations specific to that agency, in addition to FAR. (You can get a good list of these rules with all the links at the FAR site at http://farsite.hill.af.mil.) For example, the VA, just like the rest of the 15 cabinet agencies, has its own set of rules in addition to the FAR— the Veterans Affairs Acquisition Regulation (VAAR).

DOD uses the Defense Federal Acquisition Regulation Supplement for the Department of Defense (DFARS) *in addition* to the FAR, as well as a companion resource called Procedures, Guidance, and Information (PGI). These documents are available electronically at the Defense Acquisition Regulations System (www.acq.osd.mil/dpap/dars/index.htm). The Army (which is part of DOD) also follows the Army Federal Acquisition Regulation Supplement (AFARS) in addition to all of the other DOD rules.

SBA has a wonderful web page dedicated to learning about all the government contracting rules, with a slew of courses that you can take for free at www.sba.gov/content/federal-acquisition-regulations-far.

As I already mentioned in Chapter 1, although there is a lot to learn, the good part about being a government contractor is that the knowledge you need is easily accessible. You just have to know where to look.

Government Procurement Methods

The government can buy products and services from contractors in a variety of ways. The form in which the procurement takes place depends on multiple factors such as the issuing agency, what they are buying, the dollar value of the procurement, and the amount of time the government has at its disposal based on the urgency factor or time left until the money expires (and is no longer in the budget).

The government can engage with industry through multiple methods that you need to know about to be able to sell to the government. The most important methods are covered next.

Micropurchases (or Purchases Under the Simplified Acquisition Threshold (SAT)

The government can buy commodities under $3,000 and pay for them using a government credit card (a purchase card) the same day, or via a purchase order in more official situations.

There are a few exceptions to that amount. If it is for acquisitions of construction subject to the Davis-Bacon Act, the amount is $2,000; if it is for acquisitions of services subject to the Service Contract Act, the amount is $2,500.

For acquisitions of supplies or services to support a contingency operation or to facilitate defense against or recovery from nuclear, biological, chemical, or radiological attack, it is $15,000 inside the United States, and $25,000 outside the country.

No formal written quotes or proposals are required; a govie can simply give you his or her card number to charge.

For amounts between $3,000 and $25,000, three informal quotes (via e-mail or a simple estimate) are required, and the government can still pay with a credit card or through a purchase order.

The SAT is $100,000 instead of $25,000 if a procurement office or agency has achieved certain electronic commerce capabilities and is on the Federal Acquisition Computer Network (FACNET). For example, DHS is on FACNET, so the $25,000 limit doesn't apply to them; their limit is $100,000 instead.

DHS also has other special exception limits given the nature of its work. DHS nuclear, chem-bio, or radiological procurements have a hefty $250,000 SAT inside the United States, and $1 million outside the country. It is understandable that when you deal with something that could cause devastation or wipe out the world's population, you don't want the government taking the time to go through the formal quoting process to pick a contractor.

A purchase for more than $25,000 (or exceeding the higher SATs where applicable) requires a formal procurement process with public notification on www.FedBizOpps.gov. FedBizOpps is a site where the government posts (or at least makes a valiant attempt to) all contracting opportunities. We discuss later where to find the contracting opportunities not posted on FedBizOpps.

A majority of purchases under the SAT go to local vendors, those who actively sell to the government where they are located. I have gotten calls from govies who found our company on the Web and got us under contract without us making any business development efforts whatsoever. But don't bank on that. You should actively pursue the work because hoping that your phone rings one day is not a strategy. The government makes a great amount of purchases under the SAT, and small businesses especially shouldn't disregard this avenue.

GSA and VA Schedules

GSA schedules, also referred to as the Federal Supply Schedules (FSS) or Multiple Award Schedules (MAS), are lists of prequalified suppliers in their respective areas of discipline, who will have submitted their price lists and other qualifying information to the government in the form of a GSA proposal. GSA vets companies to provide to the rest of the government a wholesale supply source for millions of products, services, and solutions. According to Bloomberg Government analysts, as of 2011, roughly 7 percent of all government contracting is done through GSA schedules.

GSA includes a Federal Acquisition Service (FAS) and the Public Buildings Service (PBS). If you are a construction company, you might want to include PBS as one of your customers.

Basically, any company in good standing that is registered as a government contractor can apply to obtain a GSA schedule. Note that it is not always advisable to get a GSA schedule, nor is it required to sell to the government, contrary to what many unscrupulous businesses around government contracting might tell you. According to GSA's own statistics, less than half of GSA schedule holders get anything out of their schedule, and 5 percent of the GSA schedule contractors win 80 percent of all business.

It takes about six to nine months to apply to get a schedule, it is valid for five years, and you can extend it for three years up to three times. You also need to make at least $25,000 in the first two years using the schedule to keep it, and continue making at least $25,000 annually thereafter. Do note that 60 percent of GSA schedule holders don't meet the minimum sales requirements to keep the schedule.

Having a schedule makes it easier for some government customers to award a contract to you. Remember, you are already prequalified as a good vendor, so all the government needs is to receive a quote (a shorter proposal) from you and two other companies to award a contract. You will, of course, need to offer a deep discount from the price list you have provided to the government initially. Do not waste time and money getting a GSA schedule, however, if your target government buyers prefer to award contracts through other mechanisms and don't use GSA schedules.

■ **Note**   You don't need a GSA schedule if your prospective government buyers prefer other methods to contract with the industry.

The GSA maintains a useful and informative web site, GSA.gov, that will tell you much of what you need to know about the schedules. You can even look up your competitors there, but be aware that their pricing will not be what they actually offer to the customer. They will issue discounts of 15 to 25 percent or more.

VA schedules represent about 2 percent of federal contracting dollars according to BGov, and are for companies supporting the VA health care system. You can learn more about VA schedules at www.fss.va.gov.

Variety of Competitive Procurements Above the SAT

Large procurements above the SAT threshold represent the lion's share of government contracting dollars. You can prepare for and submit competitive proposals in response to the requirements contracts. A *requirements contract* is a contract where you get a single award, and for an agreed-to amount, deliver a specific set of services, products, or solutions.

Requirements contracts employ a variety of solicitation types, including the following:

- **Request for proposals (RFP):** A traditional form of solicitation for professional services, systems, and solutions where proposals are complex, and where negotiation is part of the process. A proposal usually includes several volumes or parts that cover technical and management approach, past performance, and price.

- **Request for quote (RFQ):** A solicitation for a fixed-price, nonsealed bid contract. A government entity often uses RFQs as a way to check into the possibilities for acquiring a product or service and doesn't always award a contract based on an RFQ. The government might issue a purchase order in response to an RFQ that a contractor then has to accept.

- **Invitation for bid (IFB):** A request to submit the technical proposal, and if it is deemed acceptable, then submit a sealed, fixed-price bid. IFBs are mostly used in construction services or situations where the requirements are very clearly defined. The process of opening sealed bids is public: bids with the firm fixed price are opened and are often posted on a whiteboard for all evaluators to see. The government might even invite the bidders to the opening. Usually, the bid that comes in at the lowest price wins automatically.

You could also participate in *multiple-award* competitive procurements that are called multiple award contracts (MACs). They are also referred to as indefinite delivery indefinite quantity (IDIQ) contracts, so I use the terms interchangeably. Similar to GSA schedules (which also happen to fall in the IDIQ category), different agencies create their own contracting mechanisms to prequalify a pool of vendors.

There are different varieties of IDIQs. You might encounter such acronyms as enterprise-wide acquisition contract (EWAC), which is a single-agency IDIQ; a government-wide acquisition contract (GWAC), issued by only four government agencies (GSA, NASA, NIH, and DHS) to provide IT services to the entire government; an indefinite quantity contract (IQC) typically used by the USAID; and multiple award task order contracts (MATOCs) and single award task order contracts (SATOCs), used by the Army Corps of Engineers for construction services. These are all types of IDIQs, one of the most popular forms of government contracting these days. I apologize for throwing a bucket of acronym soup at you, but as I already mentioned, it is part and parcel of doing business with the government.

To submit a proposal to win a MAC, you respond to an RFP, just like when you submit a proposal for a single-award contract. Once you win, however, you won't make any money, besides a minimum guaranteed amount (which is rather small).

You will, however, now qualify to bid on task orders (for services) or delivery orders (for products) to win multiple actual contracts that make you money.

You will now only compete against those companies who also got the "hunting license," and not the rest of the world.

There are nearly 1,200 nonschedule MACs as of 2012, and their quantity has tripled since 2006, according to BGov analysts. Agency MACs represent roughly 16 percent of government procurement dollars, more than double the value of GSA schedules.

Using IDIQs to grow your company deserves a book all to itself. There are additional resources available, however. My company, for example, teaches exactly how to do it in our one-of-a-kind course, Winning Multiple Award and Task Order Contracts, so you can find everything you need to know to become wildly successful in this arena.

The reason IDIQs are popular with the government is that the 2008 National Defense Authorization Act required all contracts worth $100 million or more to be issued competitively using MACs, rather than single-award contracts. This way, the government gets to buy what it needs faster—in 2 or 3 months rather than the usual 6 to 18—and has better buying power, among numerous other benefits, such as the reduced possibility of protest by the losing vendors.

Once you get on an IDIQ vehicle, you have to put a slew of measures in place to maximize your task order wins. You will need to designate someone to actively develop business to identify task order opportunities before they ever hit the street, and put together resources, processes, tools, and collateral to prepare highly competitive, page-limited proposals. The length of a task order proposal is usually 5 to 20 pages, and the turnaround time typically ranges between 5 and 14 days. It makes it harder on the contractor to prepare, but easier on the government to evaluate the proposals.

IDIQs are hard to master and tend to require an initial investment before they begin making you money. They are worth it, though, because they can foster triple-digit growth.

MACs also include a subcategory of agreements: BPAs and basic ordering agreements (BOAs), and so on. BPAs and BOAs can also happen to be single-award agreements, but that is rare. An agreement is different from a contract, because a contract guarantees a minimum amount for an award (however small), and an agreement doesn't guarantee a single dollar. It simply defines the terms that enable the issuance of task orders or delivery orders, including pricing. For example, BPAs are a GSA contracting mechanism. GSA schedule holders can bid on BPAs, and BPA pricing can be 17% to 20 percent below GSA schedules and commercial pricing. To make any money on a BPA, you will need to get orders, which means competing again, and offering lower pricing than your competitors. BOAs are a similar mechanism employed by agencies other than GSA.

Becoming a Defense Logistics Agency (DLA) Wholesale Supplier

If you are in the business of manufacturing weapon systems or spare parts, or provide materials for humanitarian support and other endeavors, you should know that the DLA is in charge of logistics and spends billions on procurement. They could be a great customer for you through their EMALL. You can learn more and register at https://dod-emall.dla.mil. You should also register and search for RFPs. RFQs, IFBs, and submit bids on the DLA Internet Bid Board System (DIBBS) at https://www.dibbs.bsm.dla.mil.

Reverse Auctions

After they were proclaimed legal in 2005 by the federal government, reverse auctions have become an increasingly popular way for the government to buy commodities and simple services. A reverse auction is the opposite of a regular auction such as those on eBay, where a seller sells the item to the highest bidding buyer. In a reverse auction, the sellers (contractors) offer increasingly lower prices, trying to undercut each other for the bidder's business, in this case a government contract. One reputable web site for this type of bidding is Fedbid.com, a commercial entity that works closely with the government to run the auctions. All you need to do to qualify is be registered as a government contractor in SAM.gov, which we'll talk more about later. Some of the auctions will require you to have past performance with the government or commercial entities, and others will need just a simple quote.

Government agencies are adopting reverse auctions aggressively. For example, as of summer of 2012, the DLA decided to institutionalize the techniques it used to reduce material costs. The agency selected reverse auctions as its preferred method for price negotiations on *all* competitive contracts valued at more than $150,000! This is a radical departure from the more cautious reverse auction approach exercised to date, and covers complex services procurements rather than just commodities. DLA will either manage to pioneer a better way for the government to save money, or generate valuable lessons learned (translation: disastrous experiences) for other agencies on what not to do. Only time will tell.

One key to doing well in the auctions is to know your walk-away price. If a bid that someone else makes drops below that price, you should discontinue bidding, or you will risk losing your shirt, just like many gamblers do.

Grants

Grants are different from government contracts. The money awarded to recipient organizations represents financial assistance from a federal agency to carry out a public purpose of support or economic stimulation.

Twenty-six government agencies issue more than 1,000 grants that can amount to anywhere from a few thousand to hundreds of millions of dollars. These grants add up to a hefty $500 billion in average annual awards, almost the same amount available through government contracting mechanisms. In fact, between contracts, grants, and loans, the government has been spending more than $1 trillion annually. Although grants are not a subject of this book, a great resource for finding government grants you should know about is Grants.gov. Many concepts from this book apply to winning grants as well. It would be a big mistake to discount grants as a federal contractor, so take time to learn about them and explore various opportunities for your company.

Public–Private Partnerships (PPP or P3)

PPPs are an innovative way for the government to get the necessary services or infrastructure without having to invest a substantial amount of taxpayers' dollars. In a PPP, the government enters into a contract with a private company, so that this company can provide a public service or implement a project, while the company takes on the hefty financial, technical, and operational risk. In many cases, the company will make a capital investment, but will end up making money back in savings generated by this investment. For example, an energy performance contract (EPC) is a form of a PPP. An EPC is issued when an energy company assesses a government or other public-sector facility that doesn't use energy as efficiently as it should, and then installs at its own expense (or by getting third-party financing) a comprehensive suite of energy efficiency, renewable energy, and distributed generation measures. It has to guarantee that the savings produced by a project will be enough to offset the full cost of the project. Then, it pays for its own costs and benefits from the savings, and might even share the savings with the government. The government, in its turn, achieves the energy efficiency mandated by law even though it didn't have the money to make the upgrades. It gets facility improvements, "greens" its buildings, meets greenhouse gas reduction mandates, and might even avoid having to build additional power plants.

Research and Development (R&D)–Related Contract Vehicles

If you are in the field of R&D, you might run across such vehicles as broad agency announcements (BAAs). BAAs announce a topic of research interest with selection criteria and solicit proposals. Research announcements (RAs) announce grants or cooperative agreements for R&D firms. Announcements of opportunity (AOs) are a mechanism often used by NASA to solicit space mission proposals. For example, here is a recent AO excerpt:

> *The Explorer Program conducts Principal Investigator (PI)-led space science investigations relevant to SMD's astrophysics and heliophysics programs. Astrophysics Explorer investigations must address NASA's goals to discover the origin, structure, evolution, and destiny of the Universe and search for Earth-like planets.*
>
> Brief Scope: Explorer Science Missions of Opportunity

The Small Business Innovation Research (SBIR) program provides R&D grant support to small R&D businesses, starting with Phase I for up to $100,000, and Phase II for up to $750,000. You can find many R&D-type solicitations and announcements at Grants.gov. If you are in the field of R&D, it would behoove you to do some web searches to look up these terms and what they entail.

Priming versus Subcontracting

Of course, you don't have to start out with getting any of these contracts directly to do business with the government. Most government contractors start out contracting with other government contractors, not the government. They become subcontractors to *prime contractors,* those who have a direct contract with the government. After they learn the ropes and earn past performance, they can transition to priming themselves. Now that we have discussed forms of contracting with the government, let's discuss ways the government can issue a contract to you.

Competitions and Sole-Source Awards

When the government wants to award a single contract, and the amount of this contract is above the SAT, it will initiate a competitive procurement. This competition can be "full and open"—when any company of any size can compete for the work. It can also be a "set aside" competition for any small businesses or a specific small business category. I cover small business competitions shortly, as they deserve a separate discussion.

Another set of options govies have is to award work within a limited pool of vendors (in the case of MACs), extend the existing contract, or award the holy grail of government contracting: *sole-source*, noncompetitive contracts.

Sole-source contracts are cheaper and easier for the government to award, because awarding a competitive contract takes a tremendous amount of work, even more than preparing the cumbersome sole-source contract paperwork. Of course, sole-source awards are frowned on, and the current movement is to minimize their use. They are still alive, however, and you shouldn't discount them as part of your business development strategy.

The FAR has seven authorities for issuing sole-source contracts:

1. There is "only one responsible source." A company has unique research capabilities, supplies, or services that the government sorely needs; or the government needs to issue a contract follow-on while competition would lead to unacceptable delays; or there are other similar reasons.

2. There is an unusual and compelling urgency. There might be an emergency such as a major hurricane aftermath, or the country is in wartime (e.g., the notorious sole-source Halliburton contract awards in Iraq for several billion dollars).

3. In case of an industrial mobilization; engineering, developmental, or research capability; or expert services needed for the government from a specific specialist (e.g., an expert witness in court).

4. When an international agreement precludes competition or a foreign government covers costs of the contract, so they want their own company to do the work.

5. When company's products are authorized or required by statute; for example, purchasing brand items for commissaries on military bases. This clause also includes the all-important statutory contracts based on:

   • Federal Prison Industries (UNICOR).

   • Qualified nonprofit agencies for the blind or other severely disabled.

   • Government printing and binding.

- The hugely important sole-source awards under the 8(a) Program, HUBZone Act, and Veterans Benefits Act that we discuss shortly.

6. **National security.**

7. **Public interest.**

As long as you can do great market research and intelligently argue any of the preceding causes, you might have a great case for a sole-source contract. To issue a sole-source contract, you will have to help the government contracting officer prepare a sole-source justification that describes in detail why only the suggested contractor can furnish the requirements to the exclusion of other sources.

Many believe that you have to be a small business to get sole-source awards, but the majority of these awards go to large businesses. It is especially true for large consulting houses that work in acquisition support (basically playing the role of government contracting, technical, and scientific experts to augment the government) and know exactly how to do the paperwork to justify their continued presence at the agency. As long as their work is satisfactory and the customer is happy, they are there to stay.

Government Acquisition Process

For our government to buy anything competitively, it takes months or years of planning, decisions, deliberation, and assorted other headaches. Figure 2-1 shows what the government acquisition process for a typical procurement looks like on the government side.

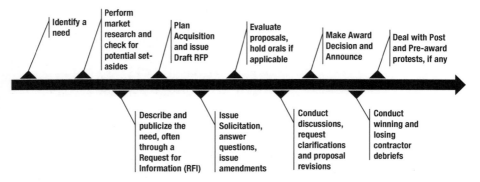

Figure 2-1. Acquisition process for a large procurement.

Each agency will have its own variation of this acquisition process, with greater detail. Get your hands on that process description, because it will help you tremendously. You can ask the government contracting officer for it, check with the Office of Small and Disadvantaged Business Utilization (OSDBU), or even search for this process on the Web.

As I keep reiterating, the earlier you learn about a contracting opportunity with the government, the better. Companies tend to win more when they identify an opportunity as soon as the government identifies a need, or better yet, they discover the need and point it out to the government. The later you learn about an opportunity in this life cycle, the less you can do to shape it in your favor and prepare for the proposal.

It is important to contact the government before it issues a draft or the final RFP, because after the full-blown acquisition process starts, the government will only communicate with you in writing through the contracting officer. It is also likely to make all your questions and comments publicly available to all bidders. Furthermore, some or all of your competitors have probably been talking to the government during the RFP drafting process, and the contract might end up getting "wired" so that only one or a handful of contractors is actually capable of winning the contract.

For example, one RFP came out requiring that a contractor have space within 10 city blocks of the client's facility by the time of submission (a week later)—a qualification that only one competitor had! That requirement was likely no accident. There's just no substitute for being engaged with the government. You can "wire" your own contracts just as easily, if you understand the acquisition process and how the government goes about issuing a contract.

How to Navigate the World of Rules and Acronyms

As you start in the government contracting arena, you will have to get over being intimidated by all the acronyms and an unfamiliar vocabulary. You have already been inundated with acronyms in this chapter, but it only gets worse.

Don't despair, though. You can quickly familiarize yourself with government speak. Luckily, most government publications come with glossaries, and you can also use a search engine to look things up if you cannot figure out the meaning of an acronym from the context (and it hasn't been spelled out in the text the first time).

Saturate yourself with exposure. If you're in the Washington, DC, area, listen to WTOP (103.5 FM), a radio station that covers government contracting (or listen online at www.wtop.com). Another great radio station is Federal News Radio at 1500 AM (www.federalnewsradio.com). Start reading such publications as *Washington Technology* (www.washingtontechnology.com). Get a subscription to BGov.com to receive their newsletters with the latest information pertinent to government contractors. Start paying attention to what you hear on TV about government contracting.

■ **Note** Pick up news about the federal government and contracting at www.wtop.com, www.federalnewsradio.com, and http://BGov.com.

The acronyms and government language are only part of the story. As I already discussed, government rules are complex, and add to the red tape mythology. Many rules are easy to identify, however. As you are considering bidding on some contracts, and start looking at RFPs, know that an RFP becomes a contract after award—and it has all the rules and terms that you have to follow listed in the document. Chapter 11 discusses how to navigate an RFP, but for now, understand that RFPs include numerous contractual clauses (or simply references to those clauses) that might scare you at first.

Look up the clause on www.acquisition.gov or simply type its number into the browser. Read the clause. Any time you deal with something unfamiliar, you need to go through a process of simplifying the information first by putting it in your own words. Initially, you might have to look up every clause one at a time and take a few extra hours to familiarize yourself with each of them. Ask yourself this: what is this rule or contractual clause really trying to say? Try to associate it with what you already know—if you can relate this information to something you have learned, you're ahead of the game.

After a while, you will recognize the same clauses throughout numerous RFPs, and they will become familiar. If something doesn't make sense, you can always ask a professional in an online forum such as LinkedIn groups to explain what it means, or even hire a consultant to help you through any discussions or questions to the contracting officer about the clauses that you find risky or prohibitive.

Also, know which government rules to comply with right away, rather than later, as you are starting your federal business. To become a government contractor, you will have to go through the list of registrations provided later in this chapter. You will also need to comply with rules listed in every solicitation on which you bid.

You don't need to invest in special accounting systems right away or get Defense Contract Audit Agency (DCAA) approval, for example. Your existing bookkeeping system might be just fine until you start going after prime contracts or sizable deals. You might need to comply with some labor regulations, Occupational Safety and Health Administration (OSHA) rules, environmental requirements, and other socioeconomic regulations—but many of them won't kick in until you get a larger contract—so you might have extra time to get ready if you are small. If you are larger and are venturing into government contracting, consider getting a consultant or a government contracting lawyer to help you sort through all the compliance rules.

Another important concept that might be confusing in government speak are the codes that you will be asked to get prior to entering the government market. There are three different codes—NAICS, SIC, and CAGE—that you need to know about right away.

NAICS, SIC, and CAGE

The North American Industry Classification System (NAICS) is the standard used by federal statistical agencies to classify businesses so that they can better understand the state of our business economy and compare it to Canada and Mexico.

NAICS was adopted in 1997 and has officially replaced the Standard Industrial Classification (SIC) system, which was less detailed or robust. You might still see, however, some government agencies request SIC codes from you, especially on older forms, although they are being phased out gradually. SIC is mentioned here only so that you don't get confused if a request for SIC comes up.

In addition to statistics, our government uses NAICS to search for businesses that it needs in particular areas of specialty (or to decide if they are eligible for bidding), and also determines whether a business is small or large for their particular industry. For example, a large business in consulting might not be considered large in IT. The government also uses NAICS for administrative, contracting, and tax purposes. That means determining the NAICS codes that best describe your company is really important in government contracting.

The NAICS numbering system uses a six-digit code at the most detailed industry level. The first two digits designate the largest business sector, the third digit is the subsector, the fourth digit is the industry group, and the fifth and sixth digits are the particular sets of industries. The most popular NAICS category is sector 54, Professional, Scientific, and Technical Services. Here is an example of how assigning the digits works:

54 Professional, Scientific, and Technical Services (general category)

541 Professional, Scientific, and Technical Services (more specific category, which doesn't change name in this case)

5412 Accounting, Tax Preparation, Bookkeeping, and Payroll Services (a more specific industry that falls into this code)

54121 Accounting, Tax Preparation, Bookkeeping, and Payroll Services (even more specific, but the level of detail at this NAICS code doesn't change; to this point, this code is similar across the United States, Canada, and Mexico)

541211 Offices of Certified Public Accountants (very specific code every CPA office would need to use)

541213 Tax Preparation Services (this is the code that covers tax preparers; for example, if an accounting office specializes in audits, they wouldn't use this code)

541214 Payroll Services (this is the code a company such as ADP, for example, would use)

541219 Other Accounting Services (this is the financial code auditors, for example, are likely to select, because this is a broader category)

You can use a handy web site to look up your NAICS at the U.S. Census Bureau web site (www.census.gov/eos/www/naics). Sometimes it helps to see more detailed descriptions of each NAICS code beyond its title, to determine where you fit. You can learn more at www.naics.com

---

▓ **Note** Find your NAICS number at www.census.gov/eos/naics.

The Commercial and Government Entity (CAGE) code is a five-character ID number to identify your facility at a specific location, and it is mandatory when you register to do business with the government. You will get a CAGE code automatically as you register, and you will need to make note of it for bidding on contracts.

Take Advantage of the Small Business Program

Companies can enter the government market when they are already established in the commercial arena, and have past proven commercial performance. They might even have capital to invest in business development. It makes it a little easier to get going. Many others, however, start out as small businesses with little past performance and few resources.

Being small in the federal market can actually be an advantage. The U.S. government favors small businesses over large ones. For starters, all contracts under $150,000 are reserved for small businesses unless there are none available.

■ **Note** All contracts under $150,000 are initially reserved for small businesses.

Additionally, there is also the important "rule of two": the government is required to set aside the entire contract for a small business or at least a significant portion of it, if there are at least two qualified small businesses able to compete for the contract.

In the course of the acquisition process that we have recently discussed, the government does a market study or requests information from an industry using a process called sources sought or request for information (RFI). If two or more qualified small businesses reply, and the government is satisfied with their stated capabilities (and a government small business advocate in the OSDBU is persistent in meeting small business goals and advocating for small business participation), the procurement will go to the small business, no matter how large the contract. Larger businesses, of course, will try to make sure they can be a prime contractor on this contract, and they will argue to keep this procurement as a "full and open" competition (meaning that it does not get set aside for small business primes only). They are, however, likely to lose that argument, given the new law.

You should note that the hardest place in the government contracting world is not being small. It is being midsize (or midtier in government speak)—just having crossed into the territory of "large business." Midtier firms can no longer take advantage of small business benefits and are not yet savvy enough or rich enough to compete with the behemoths.

This is why many large businesses incubate new small businesses and form strategic relationships with them. They can then take advantage of the multiple benefits available to small businesses when contracting with the government. They flip the relationship—now they become a subcontractor to a small business, instead of being the prime contractor—and still get to enjoy the benefits of the small business program.

Leverage Your Status

Having small business status alone is advantageous, but there is more to learn about the small business program. The most important question, of course, is how to leverage small business status, as well as socioeconomic programs, whether yours is a small or large business.

What's a Small Business?

Before we delve into the benefits of the small business program, let's first define what a small business is in the eyes of the U.S. government.

It would be too easy if you could tell right away if you are a small business or not, but that's not the case. Small business size is one of the more confusing areas of doing business with the government.

The reason size is a highly contested issue in the government is simple: the rules are complex, but size does truly matter. Based on size, you can participate in a variety of government programs such as the Minority Enterprise Development Program or SBIR Program, get SBA loans, and get exclusive contracting opportunities that are set aside for businesses of your size and socioeconomic category.

One reason size is so confusing is that the size of a small business can be determined by your average revenue (average annual receipts) from the past three years, or by the average number of employees. The definition is also different depending on what you do, based on your primary NAICS code, and what kinds of solicitations you are pursuing. These size standards change every few years.

You want to start sorting through the size issues with the SBA guidelines on size. Here is the easiest way to determine where you are. Pick your NAICS, and then look at the SBA table at the following web site to determine your business size and a threshold at which you will become a large business: www. sba.gov/sites/default/files/files/Size_Standards_Table.pdf.

You will see that even within the same group of codes, what the government considers large or small differs tremendously. For example, the 541430 Graphic Design Services size standard is $7 million. After a company reaches $7 million in sales, it is considered large and not eligible for all the SBA programs. But just a few codes down, 541512 Computer Systems Design Services, the size standard is $25.5 million—more than three times higher. It means that a company with the 541512 code can take advantage of the small business program much longer—and, if it is not in an SBA Small Disadvantaged Business (SDB) program, which I am about to discuss—maybe as long as it's in business, if it never goes over $25.5 million in sales.

The magic phrase in this whole size game is "set asides." The government sets aside billions of dollars in products and services that it prefers to buy from small businesses. For many agencies, it is a requirement, so being a small contractor therefore provides a competitive advantage.

With few exceptions, every solicitation will have its own NAICS code for size purposes. For example, if you are a small business under a $14 million NAICS code, but the solicitation that you are going after has a $7 million NAICS code, you are no longer a small business for the purposes of the solicitation. Even in the solicitations that are not set aside for small businesses, the NAICS code will show what size small businesses the large prime is supposed to subcontract with to satisfy its small business goals.

The size issue becomes complex when you consider the SBA SDB program. The government tries to prevent fraud and abuse of the program, so it has numerous rules surrounding calculations of your company's size. We go over some of these rules when we discuss teaming, but I would like you to ponder the following extreme example to gain an appreciation for size issues that could arise.

Even if you are a tiny company (sales under $7 million, with fewer than 500 employees)—relative to other government contractors—but your brother-in-law owns a large business, you might have to work hard to prove that you have separate finances, and your small business is separate from his, if your competitors decide to challenge it. They might argue that you could be "affiliated" with your brother-in-law for size purposes—meaning that your brother-in-law might be using you to benefit from the socioeconomic programs and you get a cut from it. It might be hard to prove otherwise.

There are also all kinds of rules that surround size determinations as related to teaming and joint venturing, which we discuss later in this book.

The U.S. government emphasizes "small business concerns" (the government term for small companies) participation in procurements. Every government agency has assigned socioeconomic goals, and each one is monitored on how well it meets its goals. Interestingly, less than 5 percent of all government contracts (if you count the number of contracts) go to large companies. The rest go to small businesses. Large companies, naturally, get the lion's share of the dollars, despite all the programs, as agencies sometimes fail to meet their socioeconomic goals. The picture will shift as more small businesses (and even large ones) become savvier at using the small business program—and as the SBA is getting more active at monitoring it.

Socioeconomic Categories

Small businesses fall into several categories, and some of them get especially favorable treatment from the government. The government sets statutory goals for the agencies overseen by the SBA, as detailed in Table 2-1.

Table 2-1. Business Types Getting Favorable Treatment from U.S. Government Purchasers. The government sets a goal of at least 23% of agency's contracting dollars to go to small businesses of various types, with percentage goals according to the type.

Socioeconomic Category	Approx. Percentage Goal Annually	Description
Small businesses (SB)	23%	Small business means it is owned by a person who just hasn't applied to join or doesn't fit into any socioeconomic category; e.g., non-Hispanic white male(s), nonveteran, not blind or severely disabled, living in a nondepressed economic area. A small business owner also owns and runs the majority of his or her company on his or her ownm instead getting someone else to do it. There are quite a few small business set asides, making this the largest category. All you need to do to qualify is to make sure that your company's size doesn't exceed the size limitation from the procurement's main NAICS code.

Socioeconomic Category	Approx. Percentage Goal Annually	Description
8(a) program	5%	The 8(a) Business Development (BD) Program is run by the SBA for companies it accepts into the program. The government prioritizes selecting acquisitions for the 8(a) program while SBA closely watches. A company enters the program for nine years (or until it grows over the size threshold in the primary NAICS), so companies go through all kinds of legal tricks to stay in the program for the maximum duration, and use every benefit that it offers. There are many, many 8(a) set asides, with regular 8(a)s eligible for sole-source awards up to $6.5 million for acquisitions assigned manufacturing NAICS codes and $4 million for all others. Indian tribes or Alaska Native Corporation (ANC), as well as the Native Hawaiian Organizations (NHOs), that are a subset of 8(a)s have an even sweeter deal. They are called super-8(a)s, and can have unlimited sole-source awards, and create additional 8(a) companies under them, among numerous other benefits. In an 8(a) mentor-protégé program, an 8(a) company can create a joint venture with a large company and still be able to go after 8(a) set asides as a small business. Given all the benefits, this program has been very popular, so the competition within the program has been extensive. Therefore, it hasn't been the magic solution for success, although it certainly helps a great deal.

Socioeconomic Category	Approx. Percentage Goal Annually	Description
Women-Owned Small Business (WOSB)	5%	The WOSB Program is otherwise referred to as 8(m) and is relatively new in its current form. It offers equal opportunity for women to participate in federal contracting and to assist agencies in achieving their women-owned small business participation goals. There is also an economically disadvantaged women-owned small business (EDWOSB) category for some of the NAICS codes where women are severely underrepresented. Currently, agencies are just starting to use the WOSB Program and create WOSB set asides.
Historically Underutilized Business Zone (HUBZone)	3%	The HUBZone Program offers federal contracting assistance for qualified small businesses located in historically underutilized business zones, to increase employment opportunities, investment, and economic development in those areas. The government tends to chase HUBZone companies hard as they are relatively rare in certain areas and the set aside goals are hard to meet. The government can award sole-source contracts of up to $6.5 million for manufacturing or $4 million for a requirement within all other NAICS codes. All approved HUBZone companies are listed at http://dsbs.sba.gov/dsbs/search/dsp_searchhubzone.cfm. It is a hard to qualify for this program, which has pretty strict rules when it comes to contract awards. Find out more about it at www.sba.gov/hubzone.
Service Disabled Veteran-Owned Small Businesses (SDVOSB)	3%	The SDVOSB program is for companies owned and controlled by service-disabled veterans and considered small under the NAICS code assigned to the procurement. There are many SDVOSB set asides (especially from the VA), but most important, SDVOSBs can receive sole-source awards up to $6 million for manufacturing NAICS codes, and up to $3.5 million for all other NAICS codes.

For agencies, the hardest goals to meet are the HUBZone and SDVOSB set asides—so they will scout hard for great businesses that qualify under those programs.

Large businesses benefit from the small business program despite being large. Even though they have to give away a portion of their money to small business contractors on one hand, they can certainly participate in a set aside competition as a subcontractor, and benefit from the money allocated to small businesses. There are rules for how much money they can get—for services, a large business subcontractor can get up to 50 percent, for specialty trades, up to 75 percent, and for construction, up to 85 percent.

A large business that's part of the SBA mentor–protégé program, a feature of the 8(a) program, can form a joint venture with its protégé small business. It then can go after small business set asides, as if the large company's joint venture with the small business were a small company. In other words, the leading U.S. government contractor, Lockheed Martin, could be considered small when in a JV as a mentor of to 8(a) company. It would be an awesome competitor to beat for the other 8(a) companies going after the same contract, if they don't have such powerful joint venture partners or teammates.

To sum up, you should carefully study the small business program at SBA by going to www.sba.gov/category/navigation-structure/contracting/contracting-officials/size-standards and exploring all the intricacies. Then figure out which program you can qualify for, and get the paperwork done to join the ranks of small business contractors. If you are large, start identifying great small businesses you can work with to get at the small business money.

Necessary Registrations

The final phase of the preliminaries to becoming a government contractor involves registrations. It is not really that complicated. The following checklist details the sequence for federal registrations.

Checklist for Starting Your Federal Business

☐ Obtain a DUNS number from Dun & Bradstreet (D&B). It is free and much faster to get when you indicate it is for government contracting purposes—look for a separate link on the D&B web site for that (www.dnb.com). Start building your credit record with D&B by ordering a credit builder program that will help you create a complete profile. This will help your credibility as a subcontractor and as a prime.

☐ Select your NAICS code(s). Often businesses have multiple NAICS codes, but don't try to list every possible one. Instead, select the ones that fit you best and have the right size associated with them. Look up the NAICS codes at www.census.gov/eos/www/naics. You might also have to get a SIC code(s) using the same link—it may be still required for further registrations (although it's been almost completely replaced by NAICS).

☐ Register at SAM.gov, which replaced the Central Contractor Registration (CCR) System and combined other databases in the summer of 2012.

As you register, have your DUNS number, NAICS code(s), and Taxpayer Identification Number (TIN) in hand. If you don't know, or don't have a Contractor and Government Entity (CAGE) code, skip that section on the registration form, and the CAGE will be verified or assigned through SAM.

To create an account:

- Go to https://sam.gov

- Click Create an Account.

- Choose Individual account.

- Provide the requested information and submit. In addition to all the basic data, you will be required to complete Representations and Certifications. Reps and Certs, which used to be called the Online Representations and Certifications Application (ORCA). ORCA is an e-Government initiative designed to replace the paper-based Reps and Certs paperwork that you have to submit with each proposal, usually as "Section K" in the RFP.

- Provide contact information for any mandatory points of contact required based on the information provided during registration.

- Once you receive the notification e-mail, click through the sam.gov link to validate your account.

- Log in at https://sam.gov with the username and password you created.

While you are registering, you should create a Marketing Partner Identification Number (MPIN). The MPIN will be used to provide you with access to other systems, such as Grants.gov and the Past Performance Information Retrieval System (PPIRS). Your MPIN will be your password for these systems, so you should keep track of it and guard it as such. This will be used on the next page as your signature to release your TIN to the IRS for validation.

Make sure that you describe your company well using the right kinds of keywords so people can find you in the SAM and the databases it integrates and communicates with.

☐ Determine your small business size standard based on NAICS code, and determine your eligibility for socioeconomic programs, as discussed earlier: www.sba.gov/contractingopportunities/officials/size.

☐ Select your Federal Supply Classification (FSC) Code if you sell products. The FSC Code is the most general description of your item. It is a four-digit number that is assigned based on end use. Therefore, it is possible for the same item to have more than one FSC Code if it is commonly used for more than one purpose (see www.dispositionservices.dla.mil/asset/fsclist.html).

☐ Check with the SBA and explore its web site to see what it can do for your business as far as services and SBA certification (www.sba.gov). You can also get some free business development assistance from the following sources:

- Procurement Technical Assistance Centers (PTAC) www.aptac-us.org

- Counselors to America's Small Business (SCORE) www.score.org

- SBA Small Business Development Centers www.sba.gov/content/small-business-development-centers-sbdcs

- SBA's Small Business Representatives www.sba.gov/content/procurement-center-representatives

☐ Sign up for e-mails from the Federal Business Opportunities site just to get familiar with what kinds of solicitations come out for your type of business: www.fedbizopps.gov. More about sources of opportunities and where you should look for them come later in this book.

☐ If you want to try your hand at reverse auctions, register at www.fedbid.com.

Once you are done with all the registrations and paperwork, you are set to start developing your government contracting business—and I'll explain how starting with the next chapter.

Break into the Federal Arena Without Breaking Your Neck

Getting started in government contracting is as tricky as landing a dream job straight out of college. Now that you have gotten through all the registrations and paperwork, you have to solve the puzzle of how you are going to get your first government contract.

The Chicken and the Egg of Past Performance

Getting into government contracting is a bit of a chicken-and-egg dilemma, because the government places a tremendous amount of emphasis on awarding contracts to proven entities that have performed on or completed government contracts successfully. As you are just starting out, you don't meet this criterion, by definition. It is a tad easier if your company is successful in the commercial arena—but only a tad—because if you have competition that's been working with the government for a while, it might be hard to beat it.

Think back to when you were looking to get your first job in your area of specialty without experience. The only way to get experience was by getting a job that you couldn't get because you didn't have the experience. The same scenario applies here—having no past performance with the government is frustrating, as even sole-source awards have to be justified somehow. You are at a disadvantage to those who have worked for the government or performed on government contracts before, and have contracting officer friends who can route some small jobs their way to get them started.

Strategies for Penetrating the Federal Market for the First Time

Let's discuss some strategies for penetrating the market that you can realistically employ if you don't already have extensive government connections, starting with the easiest and ending with the most difficult entry method.

1.   Start with being a subcontractor to an established government contractor. Because you don't have past performance yet, you might only be as valuable as your own and your colleagues' resumes. According to the government rules, your resume and the projects you have participated in while supporting the government (even when it was with another company) will count as your company's past performance if it's a brand new entity. When you "shop" for a prime contractor, it might be all about selling yourself to them, rather than promoting your company, which doesn't yet have any credentials. The trick is to resist simply being brought onboard as a W-2 employee of the prime contractor, and make sure your company gets the credit for the work completed. You'll also want to confirm that you will get past performance references from your prime contractor, because some primes don't provide references for past performance as a matter of policy.

2.   Go after state and local government contracts, which will count as government past performance. These are a bit easier to get than federal contracts when you are just starting out, especially if you have the right relationships, and your overhead is low, leading to the lower prices state and local governments universally favor. The right relationships matter in state and local

governments a lot more than in the federal market, although you cannot discount them anywhere.

3. Start with smaller contracts under the SAT in your area of expertise, and grow them into bigger opportunities. For micropurchases, the level of the required justification is low, and once you have done your job, you will have delivered a government contract successfully. This will allow you to gradually grow your ability to get prime contracts. If you make it easier to buy from you by getting a GSA schedule at this point, you could put yourself at a slight advantage.

4. Become a subcontractor on a multiple-award vehicle. In these situations, some primes are not as picky about selecting teammates and might bring you onboard regardless of your lack of experience. You can then drive some task order work your way.

5. Create a joint venture with someone you know well and use their past performance as your past performance. We will discuss how to do this in Chapter 9, which covers teaming.

Before you do all this, though, you will need to make sure that you find the customers who are perfect for what you have to offer.

Many companies start by sitting down and creating a long laundry list of every possible service and product they can offer to the government, and then finding a NAICS code to match every item on that list. Go ahead and take an excursion to FedBizOpps. Put in a keyword that matches your area of expertise. Click on any larger-dollar opportunity and check the Interested Vendors tab. You are likely to find companies that list every NAICS code under the sun after their name. They always look suspicious, unfocused, and, quite frankly, small.

It is very tempting to claim to be omnivorous. I was once in a business planning session for a startup where the owners listed everything as their core capabilities that they had ever done or even thought about. Once I forced them to dig a bit further, it turned out they didn't even know the basic terminology in many of the fields that they listed. After some debate, in which they fought me by arguing that they had more chances if they spread the net wider, they agreed to focus on three areas of expertise. Even those three areas were too many, as they weren't mutually supportive or related, but this was a way to compromise at the time. Later on, the company ended up doing only one thing, and branching out subsequently into some areas that weren't even on the initial laundry list.

You are much better served figuring out first what it is that know how to do best, and doing some market research to figure out how to focus your efforts.

How to Find Perfect Customers for Your Portfolio of Offerings in the Vast Federal Market

The government market is vast, so you need to set aside at least a few days to get your bearings and figure out who needs what you have to offer. To help with this somewhat tricky endeavor, here is a step-by-step checklist you can use to perform simple, streamlined market research. It will enable you to identify which customers you are going to target.

Market Research Checklist

☐ Before you get started with your market research, identify your company's NAICS codes and keywords for products and services that you offer—at least for the areas of business that you are required to grow. If you are still soul-searching after your initial registration process, check the NAICS codes again and refine your analysis (www.census.gov/eos/www/naics).

- Start with a keyword search on USAspending.gov, to see which agencies buy what you sell. For example, you could search for "marketing communications." Remember to use quotation marks if you use multiple keywords. See what contracts show up in the results. Make note of the contract titles and numbers that look especially interesting.

- You will also see what companies are winning these contracts. Make a note of them, because these are your potential competitors or teammates.

- Run a similar keyword search on FedBizOpps.gov to see what kinds of opportunities and awards have been issued by which agencies. On FedBizOpps, you will find even more details about the contracts' scope than USAspending.gov, so you can zoom into the kinds of work you might be interested in bidding on.

FedBizOpps is a perfect place to learn about upcoming opportunities for educational and planning purposes and figure out what types of opportunities exist for companies like yours. You are not yet looking for something to bid on, but the information on the solicitations is representative of the patterns of your potential customer agencies. You can see who buys what, how they do it, and how much and how frequently they buy. Don't get too excited if you happen to see something that looks exactly like what you are trying to bid on, though. FedBizOpps is pretty much useless to you for bidding purposes because most of the opportunities that appear there have been discovered already by your competitors. They have been planning for them for a while, throughout the entire acquisition process we discussed in Chapter 2. Rarely do you stand a chance of winning if you pick an opportunity off a website as public as FedBizOpps late in the game, once a draft RFP, and especially the final RFP, has been issued. It has probably been "spoken for" or "wired" by some company that has taken its time to prepare.

FedBizOpps is immensely useful, however, for research, to download the long-anticipated RFPs, for registrations when required by the contracting officer, for getting notifications about amendments to the opportunities you are responding to, for marketing yourself as an interested vendor, for finding out about vendor outreach events, and for building your pipeline with opportunities that are in the early stages of procurement. You can find out from FedBizOpps about opportunities that don't yet require proposals, as when the government issues an RFI, or announces "Sources Sought," or notifies of a "Presolicitation."

☐ Determine which agencies pique your interest. Narrow down the list at www.usa.gov/Agencies.shtml. Do not overlook small agencies: they still have budgets and buy from contractors, and they might be easier to get into.

The USA.gov agency listing has links to the individual agency websites. Take a look at each one. What is the agency mission? This research should complete the picture of the agency for you, and help you narrow down your list of possibilities. Ideally, you want to see how you and your company would fit with the agency's culture and mission.

☐ If you are an IT company, look up information on different agencies' IT budgets on ITdashboard.gov, to see if your target agencies have money to purchase what you sell.

☐ Check the President's Budget at www.whitehouse.gov/omb/budget/ appendix to determine how much available budget the agency has and what it is for.

☐ Take a look at the Exhibit 53 for that agency, which shows its budget request, and Exhibits 300 with justification and detailed program information on IT investments, in order to get further details on ongoing and new programs. The easiest place to find this information is on BGov, but that requires a paid subscription. An alternative is to run a web search, and try to collect all the pieces of information from open sources.

Some agencies have plenty of money to spend on contracts and others don't. You might want to check USAspending.gov to see how much an agency contracts out and what kinds of contracts it issues.

Also at USAspending, check the percentage of the agency budget spent. Remember the government fiscal year; for example, some years certain agencies will have only awarded a small percentage of their budget by the beginning of the fourth quarter, which means that there could be heavy spending activity going on during the summer. Note that it may not be useful for DOD as its budget reporting lags for security reasons.

☐ With the narrowed list of the agencies that buy what you sell, have money, and are a good cultural fit for your company, do some analysis to hone in on a list of competitors and potential teammates.

- Determine the top contractors for an agency by running a search at USAspending.gov or FEDspending.org. You should be able to determine the top large and small businesses at an agency. Combine that information with the NAICS codes to narrow down the list to those who share the NAICS code with you.

- Look up these companies on the Web to see what capabilities they tout on their web sites, and which of them are most similar to your company.

- Rate yourself against the best practices in the market. Where do you stack up next to these companies? Is the biggest value you can provide the skills of your people, or unique products that are better than what your competitors offer?

- Decide how your capabilities and resources align with the potential customers' needs, as compared to your competitors, and if there are any gaps. If there are gaps, are you able to fill them? If so, how? This analysis should lead you to making some strategic decisions that you should document in your business plan.

☐ Now you need to determine how to engage with your target agencies. Every agency's web site has a procurement section—it might be titled "Doing Business With," "Business," "Procurement," or something similar. It should have a link to a web site where opportunities are listed, and it isn't always at FedBizOpps.gov. Go ahead and check it to see what kinds of opportunities are on the horizon. Do note that many agencies have a very specific way of doing business. For example, DOE has a whole online tutorial for vendors explaining how to work with the agency. Many agencies have their own web sites with solicitations posted electronically (they usually make it to the central FedBizOpps web site with a delay). For example, the Navy posts its solicitations on the Navy Electronic Commerce Online (NECO) site. The Army has a web site called the Army Single Face to Industry (ASFI).

Even some contracting offices have their own web sites. For example, the Procurement Network (ProcNet, http://procnet.pica.army.mil) is the Army Contracting Command–New Jersey electronic commerce home page for unclassified procurement actions, generally over $100,000.

☐ While you are at it, go ahead and register at these procurement pages as a vendor if they offer it as an option. It is absolutely not enough to be registered in the SAM.gov system and to hold a GSA schedule; you have to target each specific customer directly.

☐ Do some research to see whether getting on a GSA or VA federal supply schedule is worthwhile and decide whether you want to make an investment at this point, or if you are better off waiting. You should be able to answer the most important question: Do your target customers use GSA schedules to buy the types of services and products you offer?

If the answer is yes, then you should get it. If the answer is no or rarely, save the money and effort and get on MAC vehicles that your customer prefers and uses a lot. For example, DHS does not use GSA schedules often; it prefers its own IDIQ vehicles.

■ **Note**   Only get on the GSA schedule if you're going to use it. If you get it but don't use it, you may lose it, and it will be harder to get later on.

Many of the opportunities listed on the GSA web site through its eBuy portal do not get listed on FedBizOpps. You will only have access to eBuy after you get a GSA schedule, though—and only for the types of schedule that you hold.

☐ If yours is a small business, pay a visit to the Office of Small and Disadvantaged Business Utilization (OSDBU) at every target agency. You can find more information and a slew of other helpful resources for small businesses at the OSDBU web site (www.osdbu.gov). Once you identify a contact, you can talk to the small business specialist, who will be helpful in giving you the following information:

- An overview of how to do business with the agency.

- Information regarding any vendor lists to which you need to add your name.

- People to whom you should talk. This might include the following:

  - Contracting officers

  - Program managers

  - Top contractors' contacts—to team with or subcontract to. Especially if you are a new business or do not have past performance that's relevant to your chosen agency, this is your best route, because every large contract requires a certain percentage of work to go to a small business. Even if you are not a small business, subcontracting to a well-established company with this agency can get you in the door more easily.

- An annual procurements forecast for the agency, which will show with relative accuracy what bids are going to be issued.

- The agency's procurement policies and practices; for example, does this agency prefer small businesses, prequalified suppliers, GSA schedule holders, and certain MAC vehicles?

- Business trends and practices regarding contracting.

- An organization chart for your target customer organizations.

Many OSDBUs are so flooded with requests that they will not meet with you until you attend a conference they put together outlining how to do business with the agency—where they can answer most of your questions from the outset. They seek to reduce time spent answering the same basic questions.

Good OSDBUs can be your great allies if you develop a working relationship with them—they can be tremendously helpful and influential—so start building the relationship early on.

☐ It's now time to start identifying key government contacts. The agency web site should be your first stop. Check there for any organization charts, key decision makers' bios, and contact information.

- On FedBizOpps, you should study every opportunity, past or present, that looks interesting, and you will be able to see who the responsible contracting officer or contracting specialist is. Although you might not be able to discuss the opportunity in question in detail, you might be able to start a relationship with the contracting officer because he or she might oversee similar procurements in the future. Your main goal here is to remain focused and not just spend time visiting people who don't handle relevant work, as your time and resources are limited.

Check to see if any of the govies you are targeting are on GovLoop.com, a social network for the government and "good" contractors. You can "friend" them there and begin building a relationship, or join some online groups and network.

Speaking of social media, many government agency officials now have blogs where they might mention new opportunities and talk about the burning issues and hot-button topics. One example is the blog of the Department of Transportation secretary at http://fastlane.dot.gov. You can find a listing of social networking sites and groups, including blogs, at www.usa.gov/Topics/Multimedia.shtml. This is a way to connect, ask questions, and provide advisory feedback, which could eventually lead to appointments.

Another source is online databases. You have to pay for the online databases—and they can get very expensive—but the investment is worth it. Here are some of the paid online databases that you could use to get information on government contacts:

- **BGov (www.bgov.com)**: BGov will put your FedBizOpps and USAspending.gov searches on steroids, making your task of crunching data exponentially easier (with more accurate information to boot) and helping you find what you are looking for, even when it comes to task orders on MACs that are usually hard to identify. You will also be able to look up the most up-to-date contact information for government decision makers, and all the agency data, documents, and news neatly compiled in one place. It is an indispensable resource for your market research.

- **Carroll Publishing (www.carrollpub.com)**: Carroll Publishing combines a variety of online services, print directories, and organization charts that include more than 700,000 points of contact. It is touted as the largest and most current database for finding government decision makers, people, places, and programs. This is also where you can get agency organization charts and lists of officials and their titles, along with the reporting chains of command.

- **GovWin IQ (www.govwin.com)**: GovWin IQ covers intelligence on government personnel and organization charts, contracts, agencies, companies, task orders, and much more needed to win government business. It is the Cadillac of government contracting databases, and it is costly. The package that gets you access to the organizational charts and market research information can cost $100,000 or more a year.

- **TargetGov (www.targetgov.com)**: The TargetGov Government Buyers Guide helps locate officials in the federal, state, and local government agencies—and contacts in the major government contractor companies located in Maryland, Virginia, and Washington, DC. It is not as comprehensive as the resources already mentioned, but it doesn't cost as much either.

- It is always useful to shake your tree and see who in your network could make introductions without the databases if you are not cash-rich. I am always surprised how true the theory of six degrees of separation is.

☐ Go visit some contracting officers or preferably program managers and Contracting Officer's Technical Representatives (COTR) at DOD, especially if an OSDBU has pointed you in the direction of one. It is not that difficult to get an appointment, but you have to be persistent in calling them if they don't pick up the phone. Ask for no more than 15 minutes of their time to make it harder for them to turn you down.

Before you start visiting the government, do your homework and find out about the opportunities they are overseeing. You will need to read this book to the end to know how to prepare for these visits. Also, before you see them, you will need to know where each opportunity is in its acquisition cycle. Generally, you are allowed to talk with the govies about a specific procurement in the very early stages, but you are *not* allowed to talk when it is too late in the game—usually when a draft or final RFP has been issued and the government is now prohibited from discussing this opportunity with any vendor one on one. The government is *encouraged* to talk to those in the industry one on one, however, before the opportunity is an official procurement, in accordance with FAR clause 15.201. They need the feedback from you and any inputs—and you can talk to them freely.

When you meet with the govie, you ideally want him or her telling you about something new that is in extremely early stages of procurement for which you will have time to prepare and get an upper leg on the competition—because it doesn't show up anywhere in the publically available sources. I cover more about influencing the opportunity in later chapters. Let's first talk about finding the opportunities.

How to Create and Feed Your Opportunities Pipeline with High-Probability Deals

Every business needs a pipeline, which is essentially a list of all the opportunities you are chasing, with their associated values, dates when they are going to be released and awarded, all the key information about each opportunity, metrics to see how well you are progressing with the pursuit, and a variety of other information that will help you track these opportunities better and increase your probability of winning them. You can start your pipeline as a spreadsheet, and as it grows, you might want to select an appropriate pipeline tool. For example, you could establish a pipeline in Microsoft SharePoint 360, Privia, Salesforce, or Central Desktop.

Your pipeline has to have plenty of opportunities in it to become your engine of business growth. It will distinguish you from the competition by giving you an advantage, because you will work on opportunities early and systematically.

Filling a pipeline is a bit tricky in the best of circumstances, let alone when you are just learning how to do it and are just starting out. The good news is that I am about to show you how to do it, so you have a set of solid options you can implement right away.

There are at least eleven ways to find and develop government contracting opportunities. If you implement these methods, you will be better off than even many of the most established government contractors:

1. Subscribe to online business intelligence databases.

2. Register with customer procurement web sites.

3. Pay regular visits to the customer to build a trusted advisor relationship.

4. Leverage your workforce and partners to find out about new opportunities.

5. Solicit small purchases or get sole source awards.

6. Create new opportunities by writing white papers and unsolicited proposals for innovative solutions.

7. Team with a prime contractor as a subcontractor by crafting an irresistible value proposition.

8. Find prime contractors who have trouble staffing their contracts and offer your staff to fill vacancies.

9. Register with large government prime web sites as a small business vendor.

10. Leverage social media and other marketing techniques to attract partners and customers to you.

11. Network at trade shows and other events.

Unfortunately, many companies (even those that have been in the government arena for a long time) use only one or two methods to fill their pipelines, which is not enough. You need to mount a concerted effort. Pick at least a half-dozen of the aforementioned methods and implement them on a regular basis to jump-start your business with the government. Let's look more closely at each of these methods in turn.

Subscribe to Online Business Intelligence Databases

Learn about opportunities from online sources and databases early so that you have time to prepare for an RFP. There is a variety of sources, each known for different helpful capabilities. Note that many of these services are costly, but will offer a free trial membership. You can sign up for a free trial and take a few days off work to dedicate time to thorough research to fill your pipeline. You can sign up when you get a solid revenue stream and the membership can pay for itself.

- **GovWin IQ**: As already discussed, www.govwin.com is the high-end solution. Get it if you are serious about government contracting, as soon as you can afford it—and learn how to use it well.

- **BGov**: This site, at www.bgov.com, has pretty much everything you could possibly need, but it takes a little more skill than GovWin IQ to navigate through the information and use it to your advantage. The good part is that you can learn about opportunities from this tool that are not available through GovWin IQ, and you will get a headstart on most contractors who rely on GovWin IQ alone. For example, you can learn about MAC task orders that are about to expire, and can project their renewal so you can compete. BGov is relatively new, although it is built on the foundation of a much older and established pipeline tool, Eagle Eye. It integrates the entire procurement life cycle, instead of the much narrower scope of its competitors. It is dynamic and is getting better every week, with new capabilities added on the fly. It is a must for market research, business development, and capture.

Here are a few tools we haven't yet discussed:

- **Centurion Research Solutions**: Centurion (www.centurionresearch.com) is an alternative to GovWin IQ. It helps government contractors identify and track contract opportunities early in the procurement cycle. Centurion's claim to fame is its insight into pricing and price-to-win—it is perhaps even better than GovWin IQ's pricing intelligence.

- **ePipeline**: ePipeline (www.epipeline.com) is a decent online source for federal contracting opportunity research and business intelligence. It uses proprietary short- and long-lead contracting research to help business developers plan their pipeline, with a focus on IT; command, control, communications, computers, and intelligence (C4I); environmental and architecture/engineering and construction; facilities management; energy; and security, although they strive to cover the whole market.

- **Onvia:** Onvia (www.onvia.com) is a pipeline tool especially useful in certain industries, such as architecture and engineering, construction, operations and maintenance, and supplies. It has a good variety of state and local government opportunities as well.

Finally, don't neglect to scour free FedBizOpps for the purposes we discussed earlier in this chapter. Check out the Small Business Set Aside Alert (www.setasidealert.com) as well; it is a low-cost tool that might prove useful to you.

As soon as you can afford it, you should sign up for two or three of these tools to get the most complete view of the market. Initially you will set up automatic searches, but eventually you will have to hire someone to search these tools on a daily basis to fill your pipeline.

Register with Customer Procurement Websites

It would be too simple if FedBizOpps were the single place where the entire federal government posted opportunities over the SAT. Although this is the government's intention, agencies still will post many opportunities only on their own home-grown web sites, or submit them to FedBizOpps too late. As you know, on a proposal, every day counts, and you can't afford any delays.

For example, ASFI (https://acquisition.army.mil) has been known to lag posting opportunities and amendments on FedBizOpps by at least 24 hours.

Some agencies never post on FedBizOpps, or if they do, they do not post under their own name. Examples of these agencies include the intelligence community (IC), which includes a number of three-letter agencies; you will rarely, if ever, see any IC opportunities in FedBizOpps. For example, the National Security Agency (NSA) has its own web site called ARC (www.nsaarc.net). On FedBizOpps, you might see NSA opportunities contracted through the Army Corps of Engineers, but you have to know what they are by staying in close contact with your NSA customers.

Another example is the DOE Sandia National Laboratories supplier portal at https://supplierportal.sandia.gov/OA_HTML/snl/AbstractQuery.jsp. You must register on this web site as an interested vendor, and you will receive an e-mail notification whenever a new opportunity is added.

If a web site lets you register, go ahead and register. If it doesn't, bookmark it and put a regular "date" in your calendar to visit it to see if there are any updates

Pay Regular Visits to the Customer to Build a Trusted Advisor Relationship

1. Pay regular visits to the customer to build a trusted advisor relationship; anyone with good people skills and some training in business development can do this. You can learn more about how to do it from this book, and get additional resources from the free articles and training courses on business development and capture at www.ostglobalsolutions.com.

2. Leverage this customer relationship to find out about problem areas, hot-button issues, and things they truly care about to ultimately shape the new requirements in your favor for an assured win when an RFP comes out.

This area is the sweet spot of business development. It doesn't work fast, but it helps you win a lot of business. This is the "wiring" process, even though there is nothing underhanded going on.

Once you have identified the customer, you need to find out the following:

- What are the burning issues on their minds—their current needs and the problems they are working on?

- What budget are they working with, on what timeline, and what plans do they have for upcoming procurements?

- Are they satisfied with their current contractors?

- What solutions are they interested in? Do they have specific technologies in mind?

- What are the business trends at the agency when it comes to making decisions?

To become a trusted advisor, you have to put yourself in the frame of mind where you view your offerings from the customer's perspective—what's in it for them. Then, you provide the advice—even if it doesn't include buying from your company! You are not there to sell; you are there to solve problems.

As you learn about new procurements or even pitch an idea for a new procurement, you will have a way to subtly influence the solution by helping solve the problem. For example, you could help write the statement of work—as the customer struggles to formulate the requirements, you could help them along. Just don't get paid for it or you will create an organizational conflict of interest (OCI) and will preclude yourself from further bidding.

When you help write the requirements, two things happen:

- You learn more about the customer's hot buttons, true concerns, and deep needs and wants—you learn the story behind the requirements. In fact, you help write the story. Then, when you tell this story in the proposal, it is bound to resonate with the customer.

- You try to subtly shape the requirements in your favor. It might turn into a bit of a tug of war because the customer cannot risk a protest by making it too obvious that they are writing this RFP for a specific company. They have to make requirements as generic as possible to create a "level playing field." Your task is not to skew it so much to yourself, but to make sure that you can absolutely outshine others in every area of the requirements no matter what they do—and that there are no requirements in the RFP that you cannot fulfill with flying colors. Perhaps you could point out to the customer that some stricter evaluation criteria would be required, or a specific business model (where you happen to excel) would be more beneficial to them. Then, you can bid this vetted solution safely, knowing that it is the preferred one.

Leverage Your Workforce and Partners to Find Out About New Opportunities

Once you get your government contracting work going, you will probably have people collocated with the government at the government site. A team executing a project for an existing customer is your eyes and ears on the ground.

Find out from your workforce or even other subs working side by side with the customer if the customer has brought up to them a problem that's not related to the current project, or expressed a burning need outside of the current project's scope.

To get better at recognizing opportunities, it really helps to train your workforce. We have run a course, "Business Development for Project Personnel," with a lot of success, helping those who had no exposure to business development.

Once your project personnel notifies you of a potential opportunity, your next set of actions should be to go ahead and meet with the customer to get further details. Then, you can develop the requirements together with them, and write an unsolicited proposal to add scope to your current project or drive work to another vehicle where you can get work under contract quickly and help this customer. Because the government would rather bypass the complex procurement process, the customer might be amenable to adding scope to your existing contract. If it doesn't work out, you should explore driving this project to your existing GSA schedule or other MAC vehicles you are a prime on, to add scope.

When your company masters this process, you can generate hundreds of millions in revenue from identifying these hidden requirements. If you recall, this is the implementation phase of the business development life cycle discussed in Chapter 1.

Solicit Small Purchases or Get Sole Source Awards

When you learn through your marketing visits about an urgent need for products or services, and you don't have a vehicle by which this scope could be added quickly, you might want to examine other alternatives to a complex procurement process. Small procurements could add up to quite a bit while allowing you and the government to avoid the whole proposal process.

Remember that anything under $25,000—or often even higher thresholds—doesn't require much documentation. All you need is a quote, and the decision and payment are quick to follow.

By working with the contracting office, you can also break up opportunities into smaller logical pieces and have them sole-sourced to you. For example, what if you are an SDVOSB, and you find a $6.5 million project that the customer needs done in a jiffy. Well, you could work with the customer to divide this project into two natural phases that happen to be each under the $3.5 million threshold. You will have to proceed cautiously because there are certain FAR rules you could inadvertently break in the process, but it can be done with proper guidance. Then, this customer could award this contract to you on a sole-source basis.

Create New Opportunities by Writing White Papers and Unsolicited Proposals for Innovative Solutions

When you have an innovative and unique product or service, you can create new opportunities:

- Perform thorough market research to check that what you are selling is indeed unique and innovative, and the government is not already buying it from someone else.

- Determine whether your solution is different enough (and has clear benefits to the government) to warrant the headache of documenting a no-bid procurement.

- Find agencies and customers that would clearly benefit from what you are selling.

- Pay them some visits to find out about their exact requirements and hot button issues, and submit to them your white paper on the subject or even an unsolicited proposal. Make sure that your proposal follows the agency's format and process for unsolicited proposals. Familiarize yourself with FAR 15.6, the rule that applies to unsolicited proposals for innovative solutions.

- You need to make sure that there is a sufficient budget for your offering, because if it's not in the budget, no matter how much the govies like it, they won't be able to buy it. Sometimes there is some money left over, but often there isn't. If you guide your customer to submit a budget request as part of the regular agency budgeting process, it might take nearly two years. You will have to understand the budget approval cycle that we discussed earlier, and work with an expert who might have to navigate on Capitol Hill to push this budget through. Congressional earmarks are less common these days due to the ban, but you can still get people from on high interested and therefore get a budget line item to include funding for your solution.

Do note that earmarks and approved funding don't mean a sole source contract for you. They just mean there will be a budget for a specific purchase. I once worked with a company late in the game writing a rush proposal. This company had an amazing product and spent a lot of money on a consultant who leveraged his relationships and worked sheer miracles to create an earmark for them—but they missed some crucial steps in the solution development process, and made a fateful decision to submit the first rough draft of the proposal as the final version, because they didn't want to spend money on polishing and maturing the document. They felt that the project was theirs anyway. As a result, their competitor had much to thank them for. This competitor, instead of them, got the contract with the earmarked money, because they wrote a better proposal.

Team with a Prime Contractor as a Subcontractor by Crafting an Irresistible Value Proposition

You don't have to start out in a new market as a prime—in fact, the easiest way to penetrate the agency is as a subcontractor. You will have to build a business-to-business rather than business-to-government relationship. Building a business-to-business relationship is sometimes easier and less intimidating. It is simpler if you are a small business, but it still works if you are a large business with a small or large business prime.

Your task is to find a prime within the agency that's going after a contract that you couldn't prime as of yet but could execute some part of, and get added to the team. You need to ensure that this prime actually stands a chance of winning this contract; simply getting added to just any team is not going to help you much.

Unless you bring a tremendous value to the pursuit, you don't need a large work share from that contract. One or two people might be enough to start generating a past performance record. This is also a way to "plant the insiders" in the customer's territory if you are performing on site or somehow have an interface with the customer.

Whatever you do, take your time to carefully prepare for the meeting with the potential prime contractor. Study the target company. Study the opportunity. Study the customer and build your own relationship with them. Determine the target company's win probability.

Then, create a value proposition to them:

- Showcase your customer relationship if you have one.

- Show why you want to team with them; demonstrate the results of your analysis.

- Advertise what you can bring to the table: either complementary capabilities, past performance, or even your ability to do proposals or pay for proposal development. You can also negotiate a quid pro quo where in exchange for this workshare, you could provide workshare on another contract you hold.

Find Prime Contractors Who Have Trouble Staffing Their Contracts and Offer Your Staff to Fill Vacancies

Another avenue to find opportunities is to identify a "hurting" prime within the target agency. Your task is to find an existing contract holder that's actively advertising for positions. Do some research on them: How well are they doing? Do they have specific performance metrics for staffing personnel, and are they at 80 percent of being staffed when they should be at 95 percent, for example?

You can call their employees and ask questions directly, or through your strategic and teaming partners who might work with them. You might even visit with their government customer and ask the same questions. You also want to examine their web site to see if they are actively advertising for open positions that look like what this contract requires.

Try to analyze why this is happening. Did they underbid salaries? Are they having trouble finding qualified people at the low price ranges? Do they have problems with their management not treating employees well?

Do your homework to determine pain points, and then approach them with the resumes of your great people to add to their workforce by adding you as a subcontractor. Then, proceed to expand your footprint in the agency and build relationships with the customer.

Register with Large Government Prime Web Sites as a Small Business Vendor

If you are a small business, go ahead and register with large government primes on their web site procurement sections.

Develop a list of target prime companies that are leaders in your field, and then task an administrative person in your company with keen attention to detail to register you.

Next, get business development (BD) personnel names from FedBizOpps or GovWin IQ (on interested vendor lists or industry day or bidder conference attendee lists), and schedule appointments to talk to them. Also, find out the name and follow up with their procurement person.

Actively pursue being added to the team on opportunities that are up their alley to chase. You can find out what they might be chasing through GovWin, IQ, Centurion, or BGov, correlate the information on who is the largest subcontractor in an agency, what are the company capabilities and past performance, and what are the largest opportunities for that agency. This way you can make a safe guess that they are going to bid. Don't forget to create your value proposition when you approach the large prime.

If you are a large business, find out if you have a procurement section on your web site—and if not, add one.

Leverage Social Media and Other Marketing Techniques to Attract Partners and Customers to You

It is exhausting to always be marketing and trying to knock on the doors of potential clients and partners. What if you had *them* knocking on your door, offering contracting opportunities without your active prompting? I had that happen to our company more than once, so I know firsthand that this works and can promise this will work for you if you make the effort. Your task is to leverage modern marketing techniques.

The first order of business is to create a functional web site. These days, most adults check the Web first when they need a solution. Unfortunately, most web sites are like a leaf in a tree in the middle of a huge forest: they are impossible to find. Even if you know the web address, a web site won't do much for your potential customer. Most web sites are online brochures that do not engage your potential partners and clients.

You want to make sure that your web site works for you while you sleep (or most likely, when you work on something else). Instead of being an online brochure, your web site should do your prospecting, distribute marketing literature such as the capabilities statement and white papers, collect contact information from your prospects, recruit personnel, enable your customers to interact with you, and many other things.

I am not going to give you a course in marketing, but here is the minimum of what you need to do:

- Post your marketing collateral on your web site, including your capabilities statement (scrubbed for competitive information) and white papers, and use an auto-responder to capture the information of those people who decide to download your materials.

- Perform search engine optimization to get up in the search engine rankings.

- Drive government, partner, and talent traffic through social networks and blogs to your web site.

You also want to get engaged through social networking. Use groups on LinkedIn, GovLoop.com, TFCN.us, and Facebook to advertise your services by showcasing your professional expertise, and gradually build the relationships. Use Twitter, as now some contracting officers tweet about upcoming opportunities. I am not sure yet how Google+ will fare as far as its usefulness for business development purposes, but you should cover all the bases and monitor emerging venues. Marketing is a constantly evolving, dynamic field.

Regularly update your data on SAM.gov. Post yourself as an interested vendor in FedBizOpps and GovWin IQ opportunities, if it fits your strategy. Participate in GovWin, a free contractor networking companion of GovWin IQ. Post your presentations on Slideshare and similar business presentation services.

With the proper marketing exposure, you will have customers and partners contact you with opportunities, instead of you always having to do the legwork.

Network at Trade Shows and Other Events

Over the years, trade shows, conferences, and other gatherings have been notoriously useful for rubbing shoulders with government attendees in a more relaxed environment outside their offices. After the GSA Las Vegas conference scandal, however, the government has canceled dozens of conferences and enacted a host of travel reforms, and at the time of writing this book it was hard to predict what might happen. More likely than not, there will still be professional gatherings you can attend and network with the govies, although they will be a lot less extravagant than the ones in the past, and there will be fewer of them.

Govevents.com is a great source for learning about upcoming government events. You will have to decide which ones you will attend based on your industry, and who is coming, as the event organizers will brag about high-profile attendees.

Go ahead and schedule a number of appointments with these customers and partners ahead of time; see if they will, perhaps, have coffee, lunch, or dinner with you. Attend the networking breakfasts and mixers, seeking to approach them. You have to stay extremely focused to justify the expense of going to such an event. To get the greatest mileage from your investment, the secret is to target specific attendees and follow up relentlessly.

It might also be beneficial for you to join such organizations as the Small and Emerging Contractors Advisory Forum (SECAF), the Armed Forces Communications and Electronics Association (AFCEA), the American Council for Technology–Industry Advisory Council (ACT–IAC), the Association of Proposal Management Professionals (APMP), the American Small Business Coalition (ASBC), various Chambers of Commerce in the greater Washington, DC, area that are actively working with the government, the National Contract Management Association (NCMA), industry–government networking groups and organizations, and various military organizations.

Don't just join them; become active in these organizations by attending the events and joining committees and even their boards of directors.

Qualifying the Opportunities

When you apply the techniques we've covered for *identifying* the opportunities, and start serious business development and marketing efforts, you will very quickly find a myriad of opportunities. Your first challenge will be to examine each opportunity closer to see which ones *qualify* to make it into your pipeline.

You have to ask yourself if an opportunity looks promising. If you decide it is a "yes," you then need to find out more information to answer the following four basic questions:

1. What exactly is the opportunity?

2. Why do you want this opportunity? How does it fit within your strategic business development plan and how would it earn you money?

3. What is the current status? Where is it in the procurement cycle? How do you stack up per the initial customer and competitive analysis, and could you win?

4. What would the plan to proceed require from you?

Not every identified opportunity that initially piques your interest is worth pursuing. In the end, dozens of opportunities you have examined might turn into only a handful of decisions to go ahead and conduct a capture effort to maximize your win probability and write a proposal. This is why it is important to have clear criteria to eliminate the unworthy opportunities and to focus on the ones that have a high win probability.

You have to establish a formal process of vetting the opportunities and putting them through a set of filters to narrow down their number, instead of reacting to every single opportunity that pops up on the horizon. This will save you a tremendous amount of bid and proposal (B&P) dollars, and your precious time.

You will have to conduct a series of reviews to decide whether you should continue spending money to pursue an opportunity, or if you should stop throwing good money after bad. These reviews, called in business development vernacular gates, step reviews, or readiness reviews, must be spaced out strategically over the time period preceding the RFP release. You should document your opportunity's readiness status, win probability, and any other updates in the pipeline after each review.

It is also a good practice to review your pipeline weekly for a sustained business development effort. This way, you can keep a steady flow of opportunities that will feed and grow your company.

In the next chapter, we are going to discuss how to position your company to win the identified opportunities before they become publically known.

Win Procurements Before They Go Public

The first three chapters provided the groundwork for this chapter on the most critical step of the business development life cycle. In Chapter 1, you learned about the pros and cons of doing business with the government, what the government market looks like, the federal business development life cycle, and the resources you'll need to get started. In Chapter 2, you learned the rules of the game for winning contracts, how to decipher government jargon, what socioeconomic programs to sign up for to give you a leg up in the market, and a precise, step-by-step checklist for getting started. In Chapter 3, you learned the five strategies for breaking into federal contracting, how to do market research in the federal market, and the techniques for filling your pipeline.

Now that you know all of that, you are ready to move on to the next phase of federal business development, which is the secret weapon of seasoned government contractors: the capture process. You will learn the six components of capture to make winning a proposal a slam dunk, how to "wire" opportunities to yourself legally, and how to prepare for a proposal in style.

The Secret Weapon of Seasoned Government Contractors: Capture Planning

Government contractors who know how to play the game pay a lot of attention to preproposal preparation work and other activities aimed at raising your win probability, called *capture*. Essentially, capture is the equivalent of presales for commercial companies that deal with complex sales, albeit even more regimented. Complex sales is when you have to go beyond a handshake and a contract, have to position to win ahead of an RFP issuance, and then write a fairly complex proposal. The concept is old, but the term capture is relatively new, having gained recognition as a full-blown profession since the 1990s.

The goal of capture is to make sure winning is a slam dunk before an RFP hits the street, and to sustain a competitive advantage all the way through the award. According to APMP, a majority of capture and proposal industry veterans agree that prospects' buying decisions are 40 to 80 percent made before proposals are submitted. This is what wiring is all about!

You wouldn't try to write a proposal in the commercial world without selling yourself to the customer first, establishing a relationship, finding out about their needs, and figuring out who your competition might be. Unfortunately, in the government market, where sales is a dirty word (and a lost art) and there is more transparency through public access to bids, some people count on winning blind, without any preparation. They find an opportunity in an intelligence database that posts opportunities for bid discussed in Chapter 3, and just go ahead and write a proposal, hoping to win.

Some simply don't know they have to position themselves properly, and others don't do it because they think capture is for those with deeper pockets. Amazingly enough, these bidders do get lucky on rare occasions, especially if they know how to write good proposals and the work is truly within their core area of expertise. Most of the time, however, they waste precious resources with nothing to show for their efforts.

Bidding on government opportunities without proper capture planning is no better than gambling. It's like taking a few pool lessons, getting lucky and winning a few games, and then taking a suitcase full of $100 bills and going to a pool hall to play against the local pool sharks.

In government proposals, just like in the pool hall, there are those who know what they are doing, and those who know only enough to be a danger to themselves. Those who know what they are doing will work hard on capture, before the RFP ever hits the street, and will nearly always beat those who don't. The only time someone would get lucky and win a proposal without capture is when their competitors get lazy or complacent, and don't do capture either, so everyone is equally unprepared. They all hope to win— and hope, albeit useful, is not a strategy.

Capture is the art of winning the game before it officially begins. It starts when you are qualifying an opportunity, and technically ends with RFP issuance, which indicates the start of the proposal process.

In reality, this delineation is not clear-cut. Capture has to continue all the way through the proposal preparation, and even after submission, in the postproposal phases, up until the contract is awarded. The capture period for a regular requirements contract or an IDIQ contract can last up to five years, but on average takes about 12 to 24 months. It takes that long to convince the customer they need you and not someone else. According to an APMP survey, companies with high win rates (upwards of 70 percent) spend approximately 60 percent of their budgets on capture, and 40 percent on proposal development.

Capture as a discipline can seem complicated, but in reality it boils down to only three goals:

1. Limiting your competition or avoiding a competitive proposal effort altogether

2. Getting the customer to look forward to your proposal

3. Preparing as much as you can for a winning proposal

All actions have to serve these three goals, or they are wasteful.

Capture Goal 1: Limiting Your Competition or Avoiding a Proposal Altogether

The most important goal of capture is to stack the deck in your favor. Forget for now about proving you are the best among the most awesome competitors by writing a winning proposal. Let's think about how you can reduce the number of competitors from the outset, or even better, how you can avoid the competition and get a sole source award where you don't even have to write a competitive proposal.

Interestingly, when you are trying to reduce the competition, you are at odds with the intent of most government rules, but you are actually helping your customer.

Limiting competition is bad because competition is supposed to result in a more beneficial deal for the government, and better stewardship of taxpayers' dollars. It is a double-edged sword, however: competition delays much-needed services or products the government needs, sometimes for years, due to protests that companies launch when they have reasons to believe the competition wasn't fair, or when they simply grasp at straws and try to game the system. It also wastes taxpayers' money by forcing the government to go through a lengthy and cumbersome selection process in accordance with the FAR and other regulations. Even the premise of a better deal is questionable, as the best possible companies to do the job often lose for reasons that have nothing to do with their capabilities or value.

You can help your customers by saving their resources instead of spending them on competition. You could encourage them to add scope to another contracting vehicle you hold, or figure out how to get the work awarded to you on a sole-source basis, like we discussed in Chapter 2. You can also scope out the competitive landscape, and drive this opportunity as a task order to an IDIQ contract you dominate. Let's say you do well on a MAC with only five competitors, and tend to win a majority of the task orders. Then, the government could move this task order to that MAC to maximize the chances of selecting you as a winner.

Or how about making sure the procurement goes to a small business or even a specific type of set aside? For example, if you are an 8(a) company, can you limit this competition to 8(a) companies only? This way, you will not have quite as many competitors that have the right past performance and credentials to beat you. Or, you could check if this bid could be awarded to you within the $4 million threshold as a set aside, if you are certain no other 8(a) companies possess the right past performance. If you are an SDVOSB, you can get a sole source award up to $3.5 million if you can prove there are no other SDVOSBs immediately available to execute the scope. If there are other SDVOSBs, the procurement could be issued as an SDVOSB set aside. A similar approach also works for HUBZone companies.

Can you influence the contract type or selection criteria that are in your favor but would damage your competition? Can you neutralize competition through specific targeted statements and actions that would put other companies in a negative light? These tactics work especially well in early capture when acquisition strategy is still undecided and you can freely talk to the customer.

It is important to note that in some cases, capture efforts have to be shrunk into much shorter time frames—as when you deal with task orders or delivery orders on an IDIQ contract, or when you are simply late learning about a bid. In this case, you might find out about an opportunity past the point when you have a chance to engage with the customer. Sometimes it means that someone else made sure that they limited the competition, or this task order is added to their preferred MAC vehicle, and they have the highest win probability. In other cases, it could be that the government simply added this opportunity to the roster because they decided it would be quicker to award through a particular MAC. In this case, flip ahead to Goals 2 and 3 to start planning your capture strategy.

Capture Goal 2: Getting the Customer to Look Forward to Your Proposal

Your second goal is to get the customer excited about your company and looking forward to selecting you. To do this, you have to understand the customer's written and unwritten requirements, position yourself as a trusted advisor, as discussed in Chapter 3, and vet your solution in advance to make sure that your customer is in full agreement with you and looks forward to what you have to propose. Customer intimacy is the holy grail of capture.

Again, it takes a while to build relationships, because you can fit only so many meetings in just a few months—trying to see someone every week to build a relationship will get you a big stalkerazzi stamp on your forehead. Although it's not a full-time effort, it's a long-term one. This is why it takes years when it's done right.

Capture Goal 3: Preparing as Much as You Can for a Winning Proposal

If you couldn't avoid a competitive procurement, every action is about arriving in style to the proposal effort. At this point, it is not so much the actions that matter, but a pragmatic and practical state of mind.

For example, when you do research as part of your capture, every nugget of information you find has to shape an approach or a statement that will have a home in your proposal, or you are wasting effort. All the information you dig up should result in a specific section, paragraph, or sentence in a proposal, or directly lead you to figuring out how to add these.

This intensely pragmatic focus must be brought to bear on all your preparations to write your proposal. When you think of a competitor, think about how you will emphasize your strengths and subtly highlight their weaknesses in your proposal. When you pick a teammate, picture how you will describe the reason why they are on your team, and exactly how you will showcase their past performance. Don't pick them if you can't do it.

Also, remember to document every piece of information painstakingly. If it's just in someone's head, it doesn't exist or doesn't count.

Six Areas of Capture to Make Winning a Proposal a Slam Dunk

Now that you understand that capture is a necessary step in your ability to win government contracts, let's talk about what goes into it. You will have to take a close look at an opportunity you find, and decide if you are interested in it enough to dedicate some resources (your and your team's time and money) to chasing it, and begin the capture process.

Capture normally includes three phases, shown in Figure 4-1. In these phases, your knowledge will progress from general information about the opportunity to a well-prepared and positioned state right before the release of the RFP.

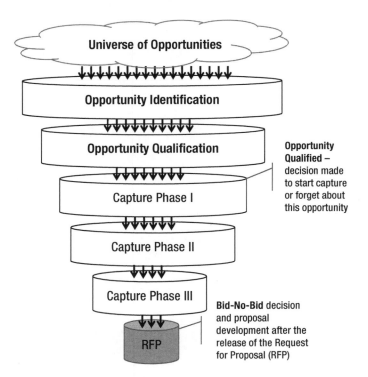

Figure 4-1. Capture phases. As opportunities enter the pipeline, and you qualify them, the capture effort begins. After the Bid-No-Bid decision, the capture continues in the background, in support of the proposal and postproposal efforts.

With capture, many companies make the mistake of focusing solely on the obvious: what are the company's capabilities and past performance, and what can the company propose in response to the customer's needs. They tend to miss the boat with the rest of the capture tasks because they either haven't had capture training, or they got lost in the process.

Capture has been represented to date as a sequence of a few dozen steps that includes development of numerous plans. Even for veteran proposal professionals, it makes it hard to think in terms of dozens of process steps and to-do lists. After struggling with it early on myself, I have developed a simple model.

This model, shown in Figure 4-2, does away with a hard-to-remember, bloated linear process, focusing instead on the essential capture areas and their interrelationships. Anyone can remember just a handful of areas and figure out how much progress has been made, whereas one can totally drown in a flowchart of capture activities expressed as dozens of steps.

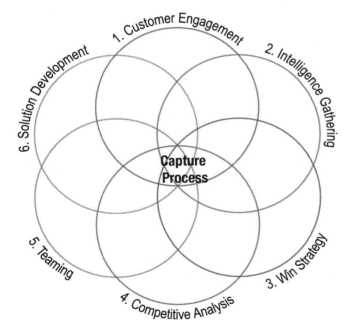

Figure 4-2. Capture process. The six capture areas make it easier to remember the key steps and measure your progress.

In this model, capture includes six fundamental areas that are completely interconnected, interlocking, and overlapping. If you miss one area, your preparation effort becomes incomplete in every other area, lowering your probability of winning by a factor of six. For example, if you omit Capture Area 3, Win Strategy, then your entire capture effort will be unfocused. If you omit Capture Area 4, Competitive Analysis, then you might team with the wrong companies that won't give you a leg up, your pricing could be too high, and you will miss an opportunity to proactively show the customer how you are better than your competition. Focusing on just six areas and not the granular steps will help you easily remember which parts need to progress on a weekly basis, and how the other areas are affected if you haven't addressed a particular area.

Remember the three capture phases we talked about earlier? After you qualify an opportunity and make the decision to proceed, you will enter into Capture Phase I. In this early phase, your goal is to learn as much about the opportunity as possible from the customer and other sources. Capture Areas I and 2 map to Capture Phase I.

Capture Phase II is where you will turn your knowledge into action. You will continue to focus on the customer and gather intelligence, while building a relationship with the customer (Capture Area I), defining your win strategy (Capture Area 3), and figuring out your competition (Capture Area 4). Based on your understanding of the customer's desires, your competition, and win strategy, you will also do research here to find the best teaming partners (Capture Area 5), companies that will help you win and accomplish the project's work scope.

Capture Phase III is all about solution development (Capture Area 6)—figuring out what exactly you are going to say in your proposal—before the RFP is issued.

When the RFP comes out, and you make a bid-no-bid decision, you will enter the proposal phase. Capture activities will not be over at this stage, but they will become even more granular and precise, as they will be subordinate to the proposal development effort. After the proposal is done, the capture effort won't be over, as there are some activities a company can undertake after bid submission.

In the remainder of this chapter, I briefly introduce the six components of the capture process in turn: customer relationship, intelligence gathering, win strategy, competitive analysis, teaming, and solution development. Each component will then be treated at length in Chapters 5 through 10.

Capture Area I: Customer Engagement

The sales process for the government is not that different from the commercial sales process: you have to have a relationship with the buyer. Companies that believe they can find an opportunity on FedBizOpps when the RFP comes out, submit a proposal, and win the contract are wasting a lot of money and energy. They might win something on occasion, but they won't realize the explosive growth other government contractors enjoy.

Just because the government is required to post its complex procurements publically does not mean that you should go ahead and bid on these RFPs or that this is a level playing field. There is always much more to the story than you see posted on FedBizOpps, paid databases, or an agency web site, because for a government customer it's impossible to express all their wishes and desires in a heavily regulated RFP format.

There is also almost always a human aspect to the equation. Government evaluators are much more likely to have greater trust in someone they know than someone they don't. You have to know exactly with whom to build the relationship, how to approach them, and how to continue working with them until the window of opportunity to communicate shuts and the RFP comes out.

From these relationships, you will gain an understanding of what keeps your customer up at night and what influences his or her buying process. In that process, you will have to build an effective rapport so that the customer knows and likes you. You can even use this relationship to influence the requirements or prevet your solution.

Capture Area 2: Intelligence Gathering

In government procurement, you and your competitors will be operating in a cone of silence. Despite the famous Myth-Busting and Myth-Busting 2 memos you can easily find on the Web (using these keywords), that educate and encourage the government to communicate with the industry, govies will try to reduce the number of opportunities for you to talk to them. They do it out of fear that something improper will happen, and they will get in serious trouble. In this environment, the best informed competitor wins.

To mitigate this problem, you will need to gather comprehensive intelligence from customers by educating them based on the information from the memos, and building a relationship with them (this is where the customer engagement and intelligence gathering areas of capture overlap), and also from a variety of open sources. Then, you have to document this intelligence in a way that is useful for those who will write your proposal. This intelligence fuels every aspect of your capture effort and your proposal response.

Capture Area 3: Win Strategy

Your win strategy is a comprehensive plan that prepares you to finish on top. It is a way of formulating actions that will move you forward in all aspects of the opportunity, leaving no stone unturned. It incorporates a priority-driven action plan with deadlines and responsible parties assigned to each task.

Win strategy starts with the analysis of customer's hot button issues (their important unstated needs to which they attach strong emotions) and stated requirements; this leads to the development of win themes and culminates with a gap analysis, enabling you to see where you have no win themes that match the hot button issues or requirements. When you cannot think of anything compelling that you could offer to the customer, and your customer has an unmet need, you must develop a strategy to be able to do it. Based on this strategy, you will develop actions to close the gap and finish ahead of your competition.

Capture Area 4: Competitive Analysis

The point of a competitive analysis is to identify your main competitors' likely strategies and shortfalls. You can then develop a way to outdo them through strategic actions, subtly and not-so-subtly exploiting *their* flaws in *your* proposal. You might even end up teaming with one of your competitors to increase your win probability. By the way, this is the reason you should never pick teammates prior to doing a competitive analysis, and why teaming (Capture Area 5) follows the competitive analysis, and not the other way around.

Keep in mind, however, that your competitors might be working just as hard as you to overcome their flaws in time for the RFP release. Your competitive analysis will therefore be a continuous process instead of a one-time activity.

Capture Area 5: Teaming

This area includes the development of a teaming strategy, identification of subcontractors or joint venture partners, negotiation of teaming or subcontracting arrangements, and forming a team of great companies before someone else snatches them up.

When forming team relationships as a prime contractor, try to secure exclusive agreements so your teaming partners don't also end up on other teams that will be bidding against you. When you are a subcontractor and join the team, you will have to consider whether you sign up exclusively or nonexclusively. Although it might seem like you are increasing your chances of winning by being on more teams, and there are some clear advantages to nonexclusive teaming, there are also serious drawbacks that we will discuss in Chapter 9.

Capture Area 6: Solution Development

This stage really enables you to prepare for the proposal in style. It includes the development of every part of the proposal in advance. It is a little tricky because you don't yet have an RFP, so it might feel like putting the cart before the horse, but don't despair. You can figure out the requirements from alternative sources to help you in preparing the proposal. For example, you might be lucky and have a draft RFP from the government. A draft RFP doesn't require a proposal response yet, but provides a way for the government to solicit industry feedback. It is often part of the government acquisition process discussed in Chapter 2. You might also have access to an old RFP for this or a similar bid in the past. If neither is available, you will have to postulate key requirements, which we discuss in Chapter 10.

After figuring out what the government might need, you will have to brainstorm on solution architecture and prepare your technical approach for every part of the scope; prepare your management approach; draft your executive summary; and stage numerous other materials, such as resumes, past performance information, and other artifacts in preparation for the proposal. This stage is extremely important because as you start developing the solution, you will find that you have many more questions that you can then get answers to through the other five components of capture.

Putting It All Together

After all six aspects of capture have been implemented, and you are into your proposal process, you can still take actions to address the six areas. The process never stops, it just intensifies and speeds up. You will need to verify facts, brainstorm, chase the right information, add a teammate to handle an area of scope you might have overlooked, and so on.

After a proposal has been submitted, you have to continue making a positive impression on the customer, building excellent performance record, watching your competition closely to ensure they don't undermine you, and providing other deliverables that might be requested by the government prior to award. In this way, your capture lead has to remain active and engaged throughout the process.

If you are looking to win more proposals, allocate more than half of your budget and effort to capture versus the proposal development. This will allow you to wire the opportunities to yourself legally, and then prepare a killer proposal that will blow your competition out of the water.

In the next six chapters, I treat in depth each one of the six components of the capture process introduced in this chapter separately, in relation to the other components, and in relation to the successive phases of the capture process. Chapters 5 through 10 will teach you all the techniques that seasoned companies use to win the game before the final RFP hits the street. Let's begin with the customer relationship.

Create Strong Relationships with Government Customers

Your first and most important task in capturing and winning federal contracts is to get the customer to want to do business with you. This chapter shows you how to create strong and lasting relationships with government customers, while considering the rules of interfacing with government personnel that you don't want to break at any cost. It also guides you through the process of gathering information from customers to gain insights into their written and unwritten requirements. This will help you understand what keeps them up at night and what influences their buying process.

Four Key Tasks for Interfacing and Building Relationships with Government Customers

Engaging the government customer boils down to four key tasks:

1. Building relationships.

2. Collecting information.

3. Influencing the requirements.

4. Vetting your solution.

Let's discuss these key tasks in greater detail so that you can accomplish them on your own as you carry out capture.

Key Task 1: Building Relationships

Your task is to build a relationship with the government customer to win a procurement. But where do you start? You need to focus on three aspects of this task:

1. Knowing when in the capture process to interface personally and most effectively with your government customers.

2. Identifying and differentiating the various types of government customers.

3. Earning trusted advisor status.

First Aspect: Timing

First and foremost, in the task of relationship building, you need to know that the government actually wants industry to approach government customers. FAR part 15.201, "Exchanges with industry before receipt of proposals," states: "Exchanges of information among all interested parties, from the earliest identification of a requirement through receipt of proposals, are encouraged."

The FAR then states that the purpose of exchanging information is to improve the understanding of government requirements and industry capabilities, thereby allowing potential offerors to judge whether or how they can satisfy the government's requirements, and enhancing the government's ability to obtain quality supplies and services at reasonable prices. The FAR goes on to express the government's desire to further increase efficiency in proposal preparation, proposal evaluation, negotiation, and contract award. The same law encourages one-on-one meetings with potential offerors.

You will find that despite this law, the govies are often worried about breaking the procurement integrity rules—so you will have to learn when to talk to them, and when not to. Generally speaking, you can talk to the government freely before they have developed an acquisition strategy (or the way they are going to run the competition) for a specific pursuit, and then the communications become increasingly limited and formal. Therefore, you want to start as early as possible before their doors shut.

In reality, your opportunity to interface with the government gradually diminishes as the acquisition life cycle progresses. For example, when the government identifies a need and performs market research, your chances of talking to them and their openness with you are the greatest. They will be willing to meet one on one, and tell you pretty much anything you need to know to win. Once they publish an RFI or Sources Sought, they might treat the meetings more officially if it is a large procurement; if it is a small procurement, you might still be able to talk to them freely. This will be especially true if you write a detailed response to their RFI with lots of useful advice on how they should run acquisition and what should be in the statement of work. I have seen lately that the government will meet with you only in an official setting after an RFI. They will no longer accept personal meetings. They won't necessarily disclose what they discuss with you with other bidders, but the contracting officer will be there to provide "adult supervision" to make sure that the government maintains a level playing field. This presents a tougher way to build relationships.

Once they develop an acquisition plan and possibly even issue a draft RFP, your opportunities to talk with them in private will all but disappear. In rare cases, they might still set up one-on-one meetings, but now you will be under the careful watch of a contracting officer, who is interested at avoiding protests at any costs, and will enforce the strictest possible interpretation of the rules. So, unless they have decades of government experience and know the rules really well, meeting participants are unlikely to be forthcoming with information that might give you a leg up on your competition.

With a draft RFP on the street, you will still be able to ask questions and provide recommendations in writing that they might or might not make public. More often than not, they will post a public Q&A response list.

There could also be a set of official vendor outreach events such as an Industry Day, or a site visit. This will provide an opportunity ask questions in a public forum, or even have a word with the govie at the end of the meeting. Keep in mind, though, that your competitors will be lurking, listening, and watching your every step.

After they issue the final RFP, the government will not meet with you and will not discuss any details of the procurement unless their vendor outreach event or site visit happens during the RFP phase (as is customary in certain industries, such as construction, and happens occasionally in other industries). You might still be able to weigh in on the RFP requirements, but now it all has to be in writing, addressed to the contracting officer, and published for the rest of the world to see. The customer is also likely to reject any major changes, as you should have proposed them long ago. Questions are often due by an early deadline, with little opportunity to digest the RFP. Everything is disclosed to all competitors to avoid preferential treatment.

On many MACs, the door is almost permanently shut for each task order. It is very difficult to get any information on the upcoming requirements before they turn into a formal procurement. Rules vary from contract to contract, so your capture cycle has to start even earlier.

There is always a way to go through the back door and meet with the government in an unofficial setting before the draft RFP or the final RFP are issued (or in rare cases, even after). However, this is usually done only through special relationships that already exist.

As you are building any relationship with a customer, you can only go and see the same person so often. You won't succeed in building a relationship if you only allot a couple of months to do it—it takes much, much longer, because your visits have to be spaced out over time. Your best bet is therefore to get to the right people early.

Second Aspect: Customer Types

Second, you will have to identify the right people to approach, so that you can build relationships with them. Generally, there are six types of customers that are involved in the procurement process. Knowing who they are brings you one step closer to understanding what drives different government players, how to build a relationship and influence them, and what they would like to see in your offer.

Buyers

Buyers give the approval to buy. In the government world, buyers usually are called the source selection authority (SSA). The SSA approves the final decision to award the proposal to you. Different people in the agency will serve as the SSA, depending on the size and importance of the contract. Most likely for the smaller bids that you will start with, the procuring contracting officer (PCO), or just simply the contracting officer, is often the main buyer.

When the SSA is not a PCO and is much higher in the chain of command (when a procurement is very large), he or she will not be weighing into the source selection decision. The SSA will appoint a PCO, who will oversee a source selection evaluation board (SSEB) or source selection team (SST). This board or team will review all the proposals, and make a selection recommendation. The SSA will either accept the recommendation (which is what's done in most cases) or veto it. A contracting officer is often assigned a contracting specialist, who might be your immediate interface and whose name is on the RFP as the addressee of your proposal. Sometimes the contracting officer and contracting specialist are one and the same person. The contracting officer acronym is CO in the civilian agencies, and KO in the military, so as not to be confused with another CO, the commanding officer.

COs care about making the right decision and how it is going to reflect on the agency and its professional performance. They care first and foremost about following the rules, and might not know all the technical details about the contract. Their biggest concern is to avoid protest. What they hate the most are the repercussions from breaking the rules, so they will want to make a relationship with you as official and arm's-length as possible. But they also hold the purse strings and control the buying process. Less experienced COs will also try to do the project at the lowest possible cost, so they will be the toughest negotiator.

Users

Users manage the use of your proposed solution. A user usually has the title of a program or project manager (PM) and comes from the Program Management organization, or is the contracting officer's technical representative (COTR) from the contracting organization. They oversee proper program execution along the lines of quality performance, on-schedule delivery, and staying within budget. They work in tandem with the CO, and on occasion have a bit of an adversarial relationship with the CO—as the CO will care about not breaking the rules, whereas the PM or the COTR will care about getting the project done properly. Users usually personally care about fulfilling the pressing need and how the proposed solution is going to impact their work and lives. They often create and drive the requirements. They want the work done and done well. They know that their performance depends on your success with the project. They have a lot of influence on the process because they have to live with the project and its results—and they are the most outspoken members of the evaluation team. You always want to have a relationship with the PM on the government side in addition to the contracting personnel, because these individuals could be either your biggest advocate or your biggest obstacle.

End Users

End users are your customer's customers. They benefit from your work, and your customer is interested in providing the best solution possible for their benefit. For example, on a large centralization effort of IT support for the U.S. Air Force, Air Force Base commanders are end users of the services. They have to be satisfied by the team of the KO and the PM, or they will complain loudly about the program, and it's never good to receive complaints up the chain of command.

There are tiers of end users as well. There are those who immediately experience the program's services, and those who might be a tier or two below them. You have to take all of their needs into consideration. The ultimate end user for DOD programs is always the Warfighter. For the civilian agencies, it will be the population the agency services. For example, retirees are one of the populations the Centers for Medicare & Medicaid Services (part of the Department of Health and Human Services) serves.

End user representatives could be part of the SSEB. You have to speak to their concerns as well as those of the CO and PM. Be careful, however, because end users usually want more than the government has money for. The opinions of the PM and the CO usually matter more than those of end users because they are more in tune with the available budget.

Technical Experts

Technical experts serve as the government's technical eyes and ears. Often, if they are not direct government employees, they don't have voting power during proposal evaluation, but they check if the solution is viable and can screen out technically inadequate solutions.

Technical experts are seldom government employees. They could be representatives from contractors hired for the purpose of helping the government, or borrowed from the national laboratories, think tanks, or test and evaluation organizations. They are the gatekeepers to check the technical accuracy of your proposal and vet the solution. They might deem your solution unacceptable and thus preclude you from winning; and they also care that you are compliant with the specifications.

Champions

Champion is a sales term describing someone inside the customer organization who wants your solution, likes you, and coaches you on how to navigate through the sticky wickets. The champion has to respect you, and be respected by the other buying influences in the organization as it relates to the specific pursuit that you are chasing. You have to actively work on developing at least one champion in the customer organization—and preferably someone beyond the representative from the OSDBU. The best champion to have is the PM or COTR, because they are usually extremely helpful in getting the right intelligence. The next best champion to have is the CO or KO.

Sponsors

Sponsors work at the highest levels and early on in the process. They could include personnel from organizations high in the chain of command such as the Office of the Secretary of Defense (OSD), and government oversight authorities such as Congressmen and staffers with various committees in the House and Senate.

Sponsors are involved in getting the right budget for the requirement, and like to make sure that the program gets executed well. Many times for large, high-visibility programs, working with the sponsors is extremely important. Although their level of involvement is low, it does carry a heavy weight. These days, sponsors are becoming more and more important, as the buyer and the users are becoming harder to reach and more aware of how contractors try to influence them. The pressure from the sponsor above often produces the desired effect with less effort and headwind.

You can find out who is who from several places. The most cost-effective places to find contacts will be the FedBizOpps.gov (contracting officer's names), the agency web site, and the small business specialist from the OSDBU. Among paid sources, GovWin IQ (www.govwin.com) is a good (but very expensive) source for information on the key players, but remember to always verify the information, as it can get out of date. BGov (www.bgov.com) will provide good government contact information once you know which agency is issuing the procurement; it has a huge database of the most up-to-date government contacts. You can get there Congressional sponsor information no other source has. Carroll Publishing (www.carrollpublishing.com) offers detailed organizational charts and contact information as well.

Third Aspect: Earning Trusted Advisor Status

Yes, selling to the government is different, but the first thing you need to remember to make it a bit easier is that you are still dealing with people. The government has its own rules, and the process is hard to navigate in the beginning. Government officials have their own culture and language, but all the universal rules for building relationships apply, with some interesting twists.

When you build a relationship with the government representatives, you have to take a multidimensional approach. You need to build as many of the relationships as possible. Your main government contact could up and leave after you invested all your time and efforts into building a relationship. For example, in DOD people frequently get reassigned after only a couple of years in the office. Therefore, you want to build relationships with as many people in the agency as possible.

You also need to create a contact plan using phone calls, visits, and, to a lesser degree, e-mails. Through this process, you will have to learn about the customer's pressures, key care-abouts, hot button issues, and needs. You will need to give them help— they might need you to consult for them on preparing the statement of work; or find out about state-of-the-art technology or different options to solve challenging problems on their projects. You will have to practice your active listening skills. The government universally despises salespeople, so your goal is not to sell yourself and your company; your goal is to become their trusted advisor.

You have to remember that to succeed with the government, you have to possess certain qualities and exude certain assurances that are absolutely essential to being considered a trusted advisor:

- You have to come across as squeaky clean honest and ethical—a "straight arrow."

- You care about them and the project more than your company, and you honestly believe that your company will be the best possible contractor for the job.

- You care about our country a great deal.

- You understand how this government servant's mission impacts the entire country.

- You are there to help and to solve their problems.

- You will always give them the best deal.

Finally, you have to also recognize they are human beings. This includes remembering their birthdays and their family members' and pets' names and knowing what makes them laugh.

Key Task 2: Collecting Information

When you are meeting with a government representative, your purpose is to listen. Dale Carnegie said that you can get a reputation as an extremely engaging conversationalist by mostly listening—and it holds true for working with the government just as much as it does in other aspects of life. This not only helps you form a great relationship with the customer, but becomes an information-gathering technique.

You should come to your meeting well prepared, having researched as much as possible about the customer and the agency's mission. Be prepared to talk about yourself, but only in the context of the customer. Then be prepared to ask open-ended questions about the procurement that you are chasing, getting the customer to open up and talk. Early in the procurement cycle it is much easier to get the government to be open with you.

Twenty Questions for Gathering Information from the Customer

Here are 20 question clusters to get you started when you are meeting with the customer. This is the most basic set of information you need to collect about the opportunity. As you learn more, you will of course elaborate, refine, and adapt these questions accordingly:

1. What exactly is the requirement? What is this project all about? What is the scope of the work?

2. What is the acquisition strategy that the customer is intending to use?

   - A regular single award requirements contract via an RFP?

   - A task order under a MAC? Which specific MAC?

3. Where is the customer in the procurement process? What needs to happen for the procurement to be issued? What is the approximate schedule for that? What are the issues that are still unresolved?

4. Is the contract or some portion of it going to be a small business set aside?

5. What type of contract is the customer likely going to use?

    •   Cost plus (and all of its varieties: fixed fee, incentive fee, award fee, etc.)

    •   Firm fixed price

    •   Time and materials

    •   Other

6. When would they like the project to begin in an ideal world scenario—versus what the reality will be given all the protocols they have to follow to get the procurement approved?

7. What are the key project milestones (start, other milestones, end)? What will the project duration be (a base and option years)?

8. What is the ballpark budget for this opportunity? Does this include the government personnel costs, or is this the contract cost? If government representatives are reluctant to answer this question, offer them budget ranges— for example, is it under $10 million, between $15 and $20 million, and so on.

9. Has this budget been approved and funded? If not, what are the milestones for approval and funding? What is the risk that the project will not be funded?

10. Where will this work be done? Would the personnel be required to be on the government's site or contractor's site?

11. Is this work that is being done already? If so, via what contracting vehicle (a MAC, a GSA schedule, or a requirements contract)? By what contractor(s)? Who is the incumbent?

12. Could the way the work is being done right now be improved?

13. Does the customer have a specific vision for solving their problem? Would they like some suggestions and options?

14. What is the customer's vision regarding a particular technology, methodology, approach, platform, or solution?

15. Who else in the customer's organization is or will be involved in this procurement? What will be their role?

16. Are there any facilities or infrastructure requirements?

17. Are there any special personnel requirements, such as security clearances or certifications?

18. Is there any specific challenge the customer is worried about? What keeps them up at night?

19. Would they like help with anything? A description of work requirements, for example? Different solutions for the problem, trade-off analysis, or anything else that would help them write the statement of work (SOW) for the RFP?

20. Has anything changed since the last visit or conversation?

You have to work those questions into the conversation naturally as the opportunities come up; don't turn this into an interrogation. Some of them will apply, and others will not. These are just a few examples of questions to get you started.

Starting is the hardest part. As you get the hang of it, and especially as your relationship with the customer grows, you will come up with more questions to ask that are specific to this opportunity. Be prepared not to get all this information in one visit. You might not get it all from one person either; you might have to meet with several people in the customer's organization to get full and credible answers.

Key Task 3: Influencing the Requirements

The best of the best of government contractors shape the requirements in the RFP to raise their win probability. They wire the contracts to themselves early on, and seal the deal with the perfect proposal. Wiring seems like something negative, but unless you are violating the procurement integrity laws, there is nothing unseemly or unethical in doing this, just good business for Beltway insiders. As I have already mentioned a couple of times, the good news is that you can wire the contracts to yourself as well.

The recipe for wiring an opportunity to your company is simple:

1. Build the relationship early and become a trusted advisor.

2. Find a solution that will benefit you and make it difficult for the competition to win.

3. Make recommendations to the government with the interests of the projects in mind first. In other words, you have to show how the solution you came up with *is in the best interests of the government*, and follows their rules (it cannot be obvious that

they are giving you preferential treatment and are limiting competition, or someone will protest).

You can shape numerous things about an opportunity.

Shape the Scope of Work

Help the customer define what tasks and objectives need to be accomplished to solve the customer's problem—and what metrics apply—to make them fit for your solution. You can also keep the scope under one procurement versus splitting it up across multiple procurements (and potentially different contractors) through "modular contracting."

You can dictate how the scope of work is going to appear, in a prescriptive statement of work versus a looser statement of objectives or performance work statement: Would you prefer a strictly defined scope of work, most likely issued under a fixed price contract with a very specific budget you could provide guidance on, and with which you could live? Or, would it benefit the project (and you) to have more wiggle room to execute?

Should some elements of scope be excluded because they are not to your advantage, and should others be included because they make it harder for your competitors? Would it benefit you if you had solid performance metrics you could apply, whereas the competition wouldn't hold a candle up to your metrics and ability to perform to those metrics?

Shape the Contractual, Procurement, and Evaluation Matters

Argue to the customer that it would be more beneficial if it were a firm fixed price contract because you know exactly how to estimate the job and come in lower than anybody else. Or suggest a cost-plus or a performance-based vehicle if you think it would be more advantageous for you.

Perhaps you could phase the work so that all the pieces fall into a series of smaller purchase orders under the $150,000 where all the work has to go to a small business. Maybe you could add scope to your existing contract with the same customer. If you have a MAC where you keep winning task orders, you could move that work to that vehicle so that you could win it easily. You could get the work as a single contract with options versus a series of successive contracts. Or, you could recommend a set-aside category based on your small business status. If you are a small business or a small disadvantaged business, it is a no-brainer to argue for a set aside, there just has to be another viable small business competitor in accordance with the rule of two and the procurement automatically has to become a small business procurement, as discussed in Chapter 2.

If you are an incumbent on an existing contract, or you know an area inside out, you might prefer a swift procurement process without a draft RFP, with the shortest possible time to write a proposal. If you are someone for whom the field or customer is new, you might want more time, a draft RFP, and a longer proposal process to have the time to react and develop a better offer.

You might also try leveling the playing field (or avoiding the same). Should certain incumbent documentation be released to the other contractors (including you) to make it more fair and easier for you to bid—and reduce the "unfair advantage" an incumbent has? If there is a library of documents set up, should it be done virtually for anyone to download, or should it be in a physical reading room with a strictly limited amount of time and no copying allowed? Should there be a site visit, a bidder's conference providing more detail about the project, or should these be avoided or reduced to a "give you no more information than we absolutely have to" event?

Most important, you can influence the evaluation criteria. How would you recommend wording the evaluation criteria so that your qualifications would score better? What criteria would be the most important, playing to your strengths, versus the least important that would point up your weaknesses? Would these criteria enable you to outscore your competition and emphasize the competition's weaknesses? You might not be able to influence the wording of the evaluation criteria, but you might suggest increasing the relative importance of those criteria where you would score highly, or decreasing the importance where you would not fare as well.

Argue for OCI considerations if you know that your competitors have been working on too many contracts with this customer and might have been exposed to information that would provide them an unfair advantage and compromise procurement integrity. Should some competitors be precluded from being able to bid through the RFP language because it puts them into a position of an OCI (or even a perception of such)? If you would not fall in that category, you might want to have an OCI disclosure requirement included.

Are you adept at orals? Orals are when you present your proposal in an oral form, with a PowerPoint presentation instead of or in addition to a written proposal. Orals can be challenging for newbies, and take a tremendous amount of preparation and practice, as well as staff readily available to put together and deliver the presentation. Those good at orals could beat those who aren't.

Do you have a model ready of what you are selling that could absolutely blow away the competition through an amazing demo? If so, go ahead and see if the government would add this requirement.

Also, you could influence the proposal page limits. Would a lower or a higher page limit be to your advantage? It is challenging to write a highly competitive proposal in just a handful of pages, but if you have mastered the art, it could be to your advantage to keep the page count of the technical volume to 50 or less. You probably would want your cost volume pages limited if you are an incumbent and when your proposal is judged on best value, and unlimited if you are a successor—to prevent a successor from proving their lower cost is realistic. If you do not have the skills and resources to write a huge proposal, you might want to reduce the page number to a manageable size.

Shape All Aspects of the Solution the Customer Requires

Shape the past performance, key personnel, and resume requirements. Quite simply, these are the areas where you should shine. If you have the right qualifications and people to bid, recommend that the RFP be more specific and prescriptive, or count these more in the evaluation criteria. If not, do the opposite.

Requirements for specific infrastructure, resources, facilities, certifications, qualifications, platforms, standards, and industry best practices are another area you could influence. If you can somehow work in the requirements for facilities that you have, or minimum level certifications such as CMMI Level 3 and ISO series, or any other specifics that would make sense with the project, try to do so. These might become less stringent during the Q&A session where some contractors could whine, but it doesn't hurt to try.

Do you have facilities in all the right locations? If so, make sure that these are required, and vice versa. Do you have the right infrastructure such as the DCAA-approved accounting system? This is a great way to discriminate even among large contractors. Do you have a lot of IT Infrastructure Library (ITIL) masters? Do you use specific platforms and technologies? Do you have a stable of Project Management Professionals (PMP) readily available? Do you have Lean Six Sigma black belts? Do you advocate certain tools that you have fully adapted to the environment and that are compatible with the customer's solution? You need to look at all of those areas and define the minimum requirements that would enable this project to be completed with a high degree of quality.

Set expectations for a very aggressive schedule if you are absolutely certain you can do it, and it might preclude other competitors from bidding or have their prices go up more than yours if this is the case. Or, you might want to make the schedule longer to argue that the schedule is more realistic and packs less risk to the government. Look to see if the schedule will fit well with other milestones or events. If you are an incumbent, you might want to reduce the transition and startup time, and if you are a successor, you might want that period to be longer.

Shape the Legal and Insurance Requirements

Do you have an invention or source code for the software and will to cede to the government the rights to your intellectual property? Or will you have the government license it from you? How would it impact you and the competition, and what language will favor your solution and preclude the competition from bidding?

See if you would like the customer to require any specific insurance to work in the war theater or a foreign country, or sizable bonding on a construction project. It might be the policy and funding you already have but would take time for others to obtain. You might want it included as a requirement. Are you willing to accept a bid bond requirement? A performance bond requirement?

Remember, as you are looking to shape and skew the requirements in your favor, the government is always moving in the opposite direction, looking to level the playing field. They don't want to make the procurement seem too biased in your favor, or they risk protests. There is nothing worse than a protest that triggers a GAO audit, draws attention from Capitol Hill with requirements to testify in front of Congress, and brings negative press. You have to take this into consideration when you shape the RFP: be strategic, be smart, and think for the government. You have a much better chance to create a clever solution by thinking through all the objections first, rather than being caught unawares and having to come up with a quick solution on a fly.

Key Task 4: Vet the Solution

Because you never want to surprise the government with a solution that's so original they might not understand it—or approve it—you want to run it by the government. For example, what if you decided to get the same job done with three people but they used to use ten people? Would they be happy or upset? Are they attached to the initial number of people for different reasons, perhaps because these people are doing a lot more work for them than is apparent from reading the SOW? Do these people report to different departments that like to have their own resource instead of sharing a person? See if they approve your solution, and tweak it with them if they don't. They might also at that time drop a valuable hint as to what they would ideally want it to be.

You might decide against running the solution by the government in a couple of situations:

- If you know that someone in the government is very close with your competition and they would most certainly disclose your solution to them.

- If there are too many other contractors involved and are running around your customer, who could leak this information to their strategic partners. People are people, and they tend to talk. You might want to carefully evaluate this risk. Although it is low, in some really large and strategic pursuits, you should exercise extra caution and decide what you want to run by the customer, and how, and what (if any) artifacts you want to leave with them.

Rules of Interfacing with Government Personnel That You Don't Want to Break at Any Cost

Marketing to the government is very different than marketing to commercial customers. With most commercial customers, you can wine, dine, and entertain them. Not so with the government. If you do, there are two outcomes: government personnel will either start avoiding you outright because they will know that you don't know how to work with the government, or they might be corrupt and accept your gifts—and when that gets out in the open, you will lose your government business in a big scandal. It's simply not worth it.

You have to know and abide by the rules. Government employees cannot solicit or accept gifts from any entity that does or seeks business with the government. A gift is any item with a monetary value, except for very modest items of food and refreshments, greeting cards, or plaques and certificates. There is a small exception: all gifts given in a year must not exceed a total of $50 in value from your entire company, and no single gift can be worth more than $20. You can give a personal gift to a govie if they were your relative before business-related contact was established, for example, but you cannot be reimbursed by the company.

If you go to lunch, it should be at a place where your government contact is able to pay for lunch out of his or her salary, which is probably lower than yours. Govies will normally offer money to you for their portion of the food, which you should not refuse. When they visit you at your facility and you offer food to them, put a donation jar there so that they can contribute a symbolic amount of money—otherwise they might have to do a tremendous amount of paperwork.

If you offer a discount to a government employee, make sure that it does not discriminate against other government employees. In other words, once you give a discount to one government employee, you have to give it to others as well. You can offer free training to the govie if it can be considered a "widely attended gathering."

So, as you can see, there is much to learn in the world of interfacing with the government and building customer relationships—but it is not as complicated as one might think.

The government will meet with you, but you have to start early—at least a year ahead of the RFP—to prepare in style. You can do many things in capture as a last-minute crunch, but building relationships is not one of them.

The next chapter shows how to extend the information dominance you establish by forming a relationship with the customer through other sources of information.

Intelligence Gathering

By following the guidelines in Chapter 5, you have been getting as much information as possible from your customer, but in the blind and silent world of government procurement, you also have to get intelligence from other sources. This intelligence-gathering process will enable you to bring something valuable to your customer as well, helping to make it a mutually beneficial relationship. Let's discuss how to get information like a pro researcher to position yourself with your customer and prepare to nail your proposal in style.

Public Bid Posting Doesn't Mean a Level Playing Field

The U.S. government is all about transparency: it posts bids publicly. Yet, just because most opportunities are posted for the world to see, that doesn't mean a level playing field.

You have to learn how to take advantage of other open sources of information, in addition to your customer intelligence (or instead of it, if you missed the window of opportunity to talk to the customer).

Our government releases unbelievably rich and useful information via the Freedom of Information Act (FOIA). You can request any unclassified document, including your competitors' contracts and even winning proposals—and get it!

The government also publishes information as to who holds contracts and subcontracts for what work. It indicates the contract value in the Federal Procurement Data System (FPDS; see fpds.gov) and other web sites we have already discussed, such as USAspending.gov. Government agencies also post a slew of information artifacts on the Web that are immensely useful in preparing proposals.

Don't ever rely on what you read in the RFI, RFQ, RFP, or any other customer document. You have to understand that only the driest, most basic version of the story about what government truly needs, makes it into the requirements. Often an agency doesn't know how to write an RFP properly and how to express its complex needs succinctly in a set of requirements. Sometimes the well-expressed initial set of requirements has to be simplified and changed based on multiple inputs from other key players or budgetary constraints—distorting the initial intent. Often it is impossible to determine the real intent behind the requirements because there is insufficient information. Only the person who knows the environment and the job can tell.

For example, once I got a call from a potential client who wanted to bid on construction of a child care center on a military base. They were interested in doing this because they had built similar two-story buildings before: how hard would it be to build a child care center? They were determined to bid. I started explaining to them that they had to know the story behind the story—that there is more to writing a proposal on that than just explaining the design build process they use and showing past performance ("Trust us, we've done this before!"). For example, did they know the site and its particular issues? They had missed the site visit that had taken place previously and hadn't visited the base subsequently. They didn't have any answers to develop a detailed solution. For example, they didn't know what kind of access they would have and hours for the workers to be at that facility. They also didn't know what kinds of specific needs the base personnel had regarding the building. The RFP only included the basics—such and such building for this many occupants. To win this bid, the client would have needed to have much more information to tell a credible story.

Presume that everything you will see in the RFP will be limited. It will not be sufficient for you to write a compelling proposal. Furthermore, as you know, the government, unlike most commercial customers, will worry about repercussions from violating procurement integrity, and will shut the door early on. This will especially be true on MACs: as soon as the government decides to issue a task order in the future, they stop discussions about it.

Unless you start way ahead of the game, you will be operating in a blind and silent world where you will have to use snippets of information to build a mosaic of the whole picture to compensate for your lack of knowledge. Even if you have contact with customers, they won't tell you everything—so you will still have to search for information to fill the gaps. In the government world, the best informed player wins.

Where and How to Gather Actionable Intelligence on the Internet

Intelligence gathering is research and detective work, where you painstakingly collect little pieces of the puzzle and put together as complete a picture as you can to help you make good decisions. Very quickly, as you learn about the opportunity and the customer, you will get into a full-blown intelligence gathering process that has multiple dimensions and information sources. As you find out more and more information about the opportunity, it will be like peeling an onion—there will be juicier, deeper, and thicker layers the further down you go.

You will need to formulate more pointed questions, and go back to the same sources or find new sources. It is an iterative process. You will probably never have enough information; the key here is to use your judgment and prioritize your efforts to get "the biggest bang for the buck."

Your first task with any opportunity that you have discovered is to figure out its background and history. There is a reason and a story behind every requirement, and not knowing them can and will hurt you.

You will first have to research how this requirement came about and how it evolved. Who or what was behind the genesis of this requirement? An agency's mission? End users' requirements? A specific person who saw a need? A program that listed this work as its necessary element? An existing procurement that is about to end? You have to investigate the requirement's source.

Then you have to figure out what key events happened to influence the course of the procurement. Were there any problems encountered along the way? Have they been resolved, or do they still linger? Were there any scandals associated with this opportunity that resulted in media articles, the much-dreaded GAO audits and Inspector General (IG) reports, or even more feared Congressional hearings?

Check which contractors have been involved with this opportunity from the start. Was this opportunity issued as a contract before? Was there a company that performed only for a year or two, and then the government got rid of them?

Find out if there are specific issues with the site, the nature of the location, suppliers, technology, or any other considerations that would be important in your solution development effort. Did any technical or management solutions fail or get rejected along the way? Have there been any regulatory snags with approvals or licenses?

You should definitely inquire about any "third rails" that you'd better not touch. A third rail is where electricity runs in an electric train—and it will shock and kill you if you touch it. Similarly, there are some things you should know to avoid when dealing with the customer, or else. You are better off knowing what these pitfalls are ahead of time.

As you answer all these generic questions, you will come up with the answers that might prompt you to ask more specific questions. The goal here is to become at least as knowledgeable as your customer is about this opportunity—and preferably more so. Knowing more than your customer could help you educate your customer and capture their interest. Knowing the "story behind the story" helps you shape your solution by taking into consideration all the nuances. You will also quickly make it into the "insiders' circle," which will help you secure a better team and find better solutions.

Your next step is to go granular and find out about every single requirement and its genesis. Don't overlook the big stuff, though: the larger context for the opportunity—the problems in the field in general—that could impact this opportunity. For example, if this is a project that services military families, you have to understand the issues surrounding the stresses that families have been put through with recent repeated deployments.

Research starts with the right questions, and the most important ones you can ask are these:

- What is it that keeps your customers up at night?

- What is it that keeps them going and gives meaning to their lives?

- What makes them proud?

- What causes them anxiety?

- What are their goals?

- What are the recurrent themes and words that you keep seeing in all the information that you find, pointing to a core need?

- Where does the contract you are pursuing fit in all of this?

After you ask these questions, you have to know where to look for answers. The information is out there. You just have to know how to search.

Paid Information Sources to Find Answers

Professional capture managers, just like business developers, save time by getting subscriptions to different data sources. They can be quite expensive, but it might be worth your while to get the information your competition is getting from these same sources.

My top five recommended sources for capture, just like for building your pipeline, are listed next.

BGov

In the capture context, BGov (www.bgov.com) is great because it's a news aggregation service among its many features. It includes news clippings from more than 30,000 sources—so you can enter your customer's agency and name, and will get a digest every time your customer appears in the media. Every interview with your customer will give you insight into his or her hot button issues. BGov also contains agency profiles and a comprehensive compilation of useful documents, so you can research all the GAO and IG reports to find out about important customer issues. You can use the available tools to find teammates, do competitive analysis, look up task order awards by a specific MAC, find business and agency contacts, read up on legislative insights indispensable for interfacing with project sponsors, and more.

GovWin IQ

To be on a level playing field, you want to know what your competitors know, and most likely, they will have access to GovWin IQ (www.govwin.com). Here, you can get your hands on FOIA documents and past contract information, see interested vendors, conduct a teammate search, use a small business directory with contacts, look up competitor rates, look up profiles for each agency, download organizational charts and agency contacts, purchase market research papers, look at task orders forecast, purchase capture reports GovWin IQ does on "popular" opportunities, and more.

Centurion Research

The information you can find on Centurion (www.centurionresearch.com) for capture purposes is also organized by opportunity, similar to GovWin IQ, with all the associated information, including pricing information, which tends to be less plentiful but typically more reliable than GovWin IQ's information. You can also find FOIA documents, including competitors' proposals, past contract information, and task order forecasts that Centurion touts as more proactive than what's available from other sources. It also tends to be less expensive than GovWin IQ, but has historically lagged behind in updates.

Hoovers

Hoovers (www.hoovers.com) is an excellent source for teaming and competitive analysis. It is a Dun and Bradstreet (D&B) directory of companies that will show you company summaries, decision makers' contact information, data on financial health of the companies, and even who their market competitors are.

Carroll Publishing

Just like for business development and market research purposes, Carroll Publishing (www.carrollpublishing.com) is useful for intelligence gathering to obtain detailed agency organizational charts and agency contact information, if you don't already have it from other places.

Researching on the Internet Like a Pro

You might not be at the point that you can shell out a few thousand dollars a year (or more than that for GovWin IQ) to pay for a subscription, so you might have to rely on web-searching. Know that most of the information that paid resources provide they get from open sources or by doing some legwork you could replicate. These services save you a lot of time, but you can still access most of the same information on your own.

Generally, an average person's web searching is limited to typing a few keywords into his or her regular browser—which for most is Google. Instead of doing that, master the keyword search. Don't just stop with the subject matter words that describe the customer and the scope of the opportunity. As you get to each tiny piece of information on this subject with each subsequent search, grab new ideas for other keywords you could use in your search.

For starters, it is useful to try dozens of different word combinations to pull up the right data. Patience pays off. Google also has a drop-down list of popular searches once you start typing a keyword—try these as well. To avoid manually sifting through pages of useless information, play with the advanced search functions to start setting more precise parameters for the search.

After you have run through a few general searches on Google, try the following resources:

- **Agency-specific web sites:** You can find customer-specific language and care-abouts, presentations, and mission statements, among other valuable artifacts.

- **Interviews and articles in specialty online magazines:** These enable you to speak your customer's language. Go ahead and search for articles on the topic of your pursuit. Articles are important because often you get to hear the voice of your customer. Journalists routinely interview government and corporate officials, and often you will find out exactly what keeps your customers up at night and what they care about the most.

For example, if you are an IT company, you should have the following IT-focused publications bookmarked:

- **Government Computer News:** www.gcn.com
- **Federal Computer Week:** www.fcw.com
- **Infoworld:** www.infoworld.com
- **Computerworld:** www.computerworld.com
- **Washington Technology:** www.washingtontechnology.com
- **Wired:** www.wired.com/techbiz

All you need to do is use the search function on these web sites for some keywords related to this procurement, remembering to search by the names of the customer personnel who might be involved in source selection, issuing agency's or company's name, and some opportunity-specific terms. Then go ahead and paraphrase or even regurgitate the customer's own words and ideas in your proposal, so that you speak straight to their needs and dearly held beliefs.

Here are some additional searches you should perform:

- **For programmatic issues:** When it is related to IT projects, search for the OMB Capital Asset Plans (Exhibit 300s) that show budgetary information and program performance metrics, and Exhibit 53s that report funding for the entire IT investment portfolio for each agency. For all customers, you need to check for the relevant GAO findings, articles, and news stories that concern the performance of your customer in managing the incumbent program and your competitors.

- **President's Budget:** This is where you find out how much money has been allocated to each program. Make sure that you understand which programs have been bundled together, and how to back out the government portion of the spending versus the contractor's portion. Historically, the numbers proposed and those approved by Congress have been pretty close, so you definitely shouldn't discount this resource.

- **Defense Budget:** The Office of the Under Secretary of Defense (Comptroller) provides insight into the defense budget (www.defenselink.mil/comptroller). This is where you can look up the defense budget items to get a glimpse of what your customers are working with while issuing procurements for specific programs.

- **Federal Procurement Data System (FPDS):** This is where you can find a lot of competitive intelligence and historic information on different contracts. This data is searchable in different, more flexible ways at USAspending. gov, and it is more accurate.

- **FedBizOps:** Here is where you can find out information not only on the procurement, but some information on its history.

- **SAM and D&B:** Here is where you find the information on your competitors. SAM is the system where everyone who does business with the government is required to register. D&B contains financial information on your competitors and potential teammates. Note that you will have to pay a fee for your competitors' D&B data.

After you are done searching through these web sites, you should try search engines other than Google, as each one uses different algorithms. They might yield different results in response to your keywords. Here are some alternatives for you:

- **Yahoo!:** www.yahoo.com

- **AltaVista:** www.altavista.com

- **Ask Jeeves:** www.ask.com

- **Excite:** www.excite.com
- **Gigablast:** www.gigablast.com
- **Bing:** www.bing.com
- **Teoma:** www.teoma.com

Metasearch sites allow you to conduct a search on several search engines or directories at the same time. After you enter your search, these sites will present you with the few best matches from multiple sites on a single page:

- **Metacrawler:** www.metacrawler.com
- **SurfWax:** www.surfwax.com
- **Dogpile:** www.dogpile.com
- **Ixquick:** http://ixquick.com
- **Kartoo:** www.kartoo.com
- **Mamma:** www.mamma.com
- **Search.com:** www.search.com

Government documents search sites and directories are helpful for navigating through government documents and publications:

- **USA.gov:** Do not forget that www.usa.gov offers a whole listing of government blogs (see Chapter 3).
- **SearchGov.com:** www.searchgov.com
- **About.com's U.S. Government Information Directory:** http://usgovinfo.about.com
- **GovSpot.com:** www.govspot.com

Remember that, no matter what you do, you have to make sure that all your efforts count. Your data has to be massaged into information, information has to gel into knowledge, and knowledge has to transform into actionable intelligence. In other words, any intelligence you gather that doesn't result in an action that leads you to writing a better proposal, or information that will go into your proposal, is a wasted effort.

Additional Information You Can Collect That's Necessary to Win

There are a multitude of other sources of information you can tap into to position yourself for a win.

Rumors and Stories

Rumors and stories are the unconfirmed second- and third-hand bits of information that you hear about the opportunity. They are extremely valuable. If you subscribe to the belief that there is no smoke without a fire, you should collect every rumor and then check it against everything that you know about this opportunity. Sometimes you might receive pieces of information that don't make sense alone—but make note of them anyway. As you continue going through the capture effort, other pieces of data could get added, and all of a sudden you might gain a powerful insight.

Of course, you should consider the source of the rumors. Rumors might get fed to you by your competitors, creating disinformation, so be careful and don't act on a rumor alone. Always check it against what you know. In fact, you might want to start your own rumors if a situation warrants.

Your on-site personnel and teammates who know a lot about the customer and overhear things are the best possible source of information. You have to take time on a regular basis to talk to your people who might already be working on a government contract for you, educate them about your opportunity and the ethics rules, and ask them to listen closely to anything that would provide insight into an opportunity. It is amazing what you find when you truly look.

Speaking of ethical information gathering, you can get your company in a world of trouble if you don't use the following rules of thumb:

- Never ask for or accept acquisition-sensitive information from the customer or others close to the customer.

- Do not fish for company-sensitive data from people that you have just hired away from your competitors (such as an incumbent)—and especially *do not* accept any documents from them that they might have brought with them when they left. They shouldn't have done that in the first place, and you should think twice about hiring this kind of person.

- Do not accept any kind of sensitive information like that from your employees, consultants, teammates, or subcontractors.

The general rule for the people who have left a competitor is this: They can tell you about the opportunity or a contract and about the customer and give you "soft" information, but they cannot tell you any of the proprietary information from your competitor—no matter how tempting it might be.

Customer's Presentations and Other Useful Artifacts

Your customer probably produced all kinds of presentations and documents that have useful nuggets of information that offer insight into what they care about the most when it comes to the contract opportunity you are chasing. Your job is to find these documents and sift through them to extract the right types of information.

Here is what you need to look for:

- **Mission statement:** Usually posted on the customer's web site and such subscription services as BGov and GovWin IQ. The agency's mission statement will tell you about the agency's priorities and what keeps them up at night—why they are doing what they are doing in the first place. You have to figure out how your pursuit fits into this larger mission.

- **Briefs, presentations, speeches, and papers:** You have to actively search for these artifacts on your project personnel's shelves and in their electronic files; on the Internet as part of a conference or a media event; or on the customer's web site. If your customer spoke at some conference, look for a conference attendee list to see if you know them or know someone in your network who might know that attendee and get a copy of the presentation, or even contact the conference organizers and purchase the materials from them.

- **Press releases:** These are available on the customer web site ("Press Room" section) or Internet search. Press releases usually discuss various contracts and events that might shed some light on the opportunity history.

- **Various reports and plans:** Check your customer's web site or those of your contractors and teammates that work at the government site. These documents can show you opportunity history, accomplishments, status of different projects, ideas, concepts, problems, needs, strategies, and the outlook for upcoming projects.

- **Congressional testimony and statements, IG, and GAO reports:** BGov offers a neat compilation of this information for each agency, or you can find it by scouring the customer's web site and other web resources. These information sources usually will point at the serious issues and challenges faced by the agency; see if you can relate these to your opportunity.

- **Budgets, annual funding, and availability of funds:** Check the President's Budget web site, USAspending.gov, Defense Budget, FEDspending.org, Exhibits 53 and 300, and the Program Objective Memorandum (POM) for each DOD customer. You can also ask the customer directly whether they have the funding and how much they have for the year versus total budgeted for the program. Glean insights from the paid sources such as BGov, GovWin IQ, and Centurion regarding the program value and spending history.

Information from End Users

When you are allowed to talk to and can reach the end users—people who are your customer's customers—you can get a lot of valuable information:

- How are they experiencing your customer's service (probably through the incumbent provider) and what do they feel about it?

- What are their key concerns and specific problems? What is it that they would need (from their perspective) for the service or solution to work better?

- What feedback have the end users been providing to the customer on the quality of performance, schedule, budget, and risk from the solution that has been offered?

All of this information leads to new intelligence, and new intelligence leads to further, more detailed questions you can ask that are specific to your solution.

Sometimes it will take you a lot of digging to figure out several layers of end users. For example, there are multiple layers between the combatant commanders (COCOMs) and base commanders and the ultimate end users, the warfighters. Each set of users will have its own set of concerns.

Your task is to understand what each set of end users cares about. You have to ask deep, probing questions with genuine concern for their preferences and needs. You need to convey that you really want to make a difference and solve their problems.

You will then have a chance to tout this understanding in your proposal, and this will show the customer that you can take care of their customers and make them look good in front of their customers. If there is an incumbent, and they are doing a questionable job, this is an opportunity to remind the customer of their pain by masterfully using this information in a dialogue with them, as long as the lines of communication are still open. This is also good fodder for "ghosting" later in the proposal. Ghosting is a way of subtly pointing out to the customer your competitors' weaknesses.

You might have some difficulties reaching the right end users who can provide you the information. You have to be creative, but it is worth it. As a general rule, don't ask permission from the CO to contact the end users if it is not expressly prohibited, because the CO might prohibit it "just in case." Proceed carefully, and don't make a lot of noise and fuss about it. Generally try to use stealth to get this information, as an incumbent might complain and others might talk, and your information lines will be cut immediately.

It is better to use people already on the customer's site to do some fact-finding for you, because they hear the rumors and have already earned the customer's trust.

Intelligence from Site Visits, Proposal Conferences, and Industry Days

The government uses industry days, proposal conferences, and site visits as ways to involve the industry and to maintain a dialogue to improve the government's procurement process. This is a great opportunity for you, so you have to be prepared for these events and get them to serve you to the max. Here is what you need to know to maximize the benefits from these events:

1. Send the right people—not the company leadership (unless yours is a very small company), but those best able to collect the right intelligence and ask technical questions. Usually it's the capture manager and the technical subject matter experts (SMEs).

2. Read up on the opportunity from your collected materials and do the initial fact finding. This will give you an ability to hear

things that go beyond the most basic data and read more between the lines.

3. Create a list of questions, especially specific technical questions that you might get direct answers to on the spot, which might otherwise never be answered in the RFP. Just be careful not to tip off your competition, because they will be listening.

4. If any documents get mentioned in the discussion with the customer or you notice any documents while you are visiting the site, request those documents for reading.

5. Ask for what you would like to be included in the solicitation and elaborate how it is in the best interests of the customer. This is another opportunity for a dialogue. *Just be aware that someone else from a competing side might make a great counterargument, so be careful what you publicly suggest.*

6. Look around. Who is there from your customer's organization? Write down the customer's names and positions. Count how many government people might be involved in this procurement directly as oversight or management vs. the evaluation team. The number of people involved in management is important to know for calculating the winning price; this way you will be able to back out the numbers for government personnel salaries from the total budget number to get contractor dollars.

7. As your customer is speaking, listen for the following "between the lines" information:

   • Customer's care-abouts: What do they want to see come from this procurement? Are there goals that they are looking to achieve?

   • What are the recurring themes they keep weaving into the points that they make? Pay attention for lessons learned from the past program, quality, certifications, sustainability, getting inputs on some questions that they have about the acquisition or scope of work, and so on.

   • Any buzz words they are using, such as quality system, ISO, PMP, ITIL, or performance metrics.

8. Look at your competitors and try to gather some competitive intelligence:

- Who is attending, and from what companies and divisions in those companies?

- Who might be teaming with each other: people from different companies who appear to be quite friendly and sitting or walking together?

- Are there any companies advertising that they are looking for teaming opportunities?

- Who could be your competitor's program manager candidate they brought in to "socialize with the customer"?

- Glance over the sign-in sheet that gets passed around and make some quick mental notes as to who is attending, and request a vendor list from the customer as part of the Q&A session, unless they already said they would post it.

9. If you are at a site visit, look at the site conditions and collect as much information as possible about the following:

- Work location

- Topography, layout, and physical characteristics (size, elevation, other)

- Equipment (government and contractor-furnished)

- Any other distinguishing factors that would be important to the nature of the work that you are looking to do

- Potential challenges posed by the site

10. Make suggestions to the customer during the conference that would be regarded by them as insightful, helpful, and proactive, again being careful to influence the requirements in your favor without educating your competition too much.

11. If you have a chance for any impromptu one-on-one time after the briefing is over, introduce yourself, "socialize" your key staff (such as your own PM), and—if the competition is not lurking around—reiterate your key messages.

12. After the event, while your recollection is still fresh, immediately document everything you have found out and observed, note the resulting action items, and share those with your management and your capture team.

Document Intelligence in a Capture Plan to Be Useful for the Proposal Team

It is vital that you document the valuable intelligence you collect, retaining both your conclusions and the raw data. The best tool for your Internet research is Microsoft OneNote, which most Microsoft Office users have but few know about. It will allow you to compile notes, save web pages, compile artifacts such as customer documents and reports, and save other data in case someone else would like to see the source. You can share this file with your team. They might be able to glean from it new information that you could have missed, as they might have different skill sets.

As you collect this information in OneNote, document your conclusions immediately in the centerpiece of your capture effort, the capture plan. A *capture plan* is usually a PowerPoint presentation where you can start compiling your intelligence in one spot—processing it into a coherent story and drawing your conclusions, which translate into action items. The reason the PowerPoint format is preferable for a capture plan as opposed to OneNote or a word processing document is that the capture plan's primary function is communication, whereas information organization is only its supporting function to make the communication possible.

The capture plan is your living, working document that describes the capture strategy and action items, but also provides a lot of detailed background information about the customer and the acquisition. It becomes the master repository of all information about the opportunity—the "bible" that holds all the details. When filled out, it can have as many as 75 to 120 slides, and might include all the preliminary proposal content, with document titles and links to the OneNote file for all the backup information. This is a document that can get everyone who is joining the pursuit entirely up-to-speed on the opportunity. Slides from this deck become part of the proposal kickoff package to get the entire proposal team on the same page, and will help you make a decision to bid or not to bid. Slides can be added or deleted as you see fit.

Appendix A provides a list of slides and the type of information that needs to be included in the capture plan.

The next chapter discusses how to develop a win strategy to focus your capture effort, develop an actionable plan, craft powerful win themes, and beat your competition through strategic actions.

Develop a Win Strategy

A win strategy is the glue that holds the whole capture effort together and the lens that focuses it in the right direction. Without it, your capture effort is meaningless. If you don't have a strategy for proving why your company should win, interfacing with the customer will only get you so far. Without a solid win strategy, you could do directionless intelligence gathering and competitive research for hours on end without results that will yield success. You might find teammates, but your team will be much weaker than if it were driven by a win strategy. Your solution and proposal will lack punch because there won't be win themes.

This chapter enables you to avoid this winless predicament by teaching you how to do the following:

- Distinguish yourself from the pack and avoid the trap of flaccid win strategies.

- Develop powerful proposal-level and section-level win themes that provide a conclusive set of reasons why the customer should select you and not your competitors.

- Turn your win themes into action items to outdo your competitors.

- Identify top-level actions that create a winning offer.

- Troubleshoot win themes.

How to Distinguish Yourself from the Pack and Avoid the Trap of Flaccid Win Strategies

All successful capture pursuits have to have a sound strategy, just like sports competitions or military campaigns. Win strategies help you run a pursuit in a way that distinguishes you from the pack. Essentially, you have to be able to tell what will enable you to win—your *win strategy*. Your win strategy has to be written in a succinct set of statements, reviewed regularly to make sure it is still accurate, and adjusted as necessary.

After defining your win strategy, you will implement a set of *actions* that will enable you to implement this win strategy, with clear priorities, deadlines, and targets assigned to each task.

Then, you have to state the *win themes* in your proposal that are reflective of your win strategy. Win themes are recurring statements throughout your proposal that convince your customer that your proposal should win, help your customer remember your proposal while they might read multiple others, and even lend them the language to justify to others why they want to award this proposal to you.

We are normally taught to define the strategy first, then the tactics. So, intuitively, many think that you have to start with defining the win strategy first, and then you would develop action items (the tactics) to enact it. Finally, you would write the win themes (often not even related to win strategies) right before the RFP hits the street, or while you are preparing a proposal. This has become the traditional approach, and the results are often not only pitiful, but take twice as long to produce. Many of those who write proposals for a living do it this way, and suffer unnecessarily.

■ **Note**   The secret of developing a powerful win strategy is counterintuitive: Start with win themes, not win strategies; win strategies will fall out of the action items that your win themes will drive.

You see, proposal win themes actually have a direct relationship with the win strategies. When your win themes pack a punch, they are actually the well-written encapsulation of your win strategies. When you wait until the preproposal or even proposal phase to develop your win themes, you actually sabotage your ability to create great win strategies. Just like in any good strategy, you start with the end in mind, persuading your customer to select you. Your win themes are the main tool of customer persuasion.

How to Develop Powerful Proposal-Level and Section-Level Win Themes That Provide a Conclusive Set of Reasons Why the Customer Should Select You and Not Your Competitors

Win themes are a conclusive and comprehensive set of reasons why the customer should select you versus your competition.

In the capture phase, win themes are a first step in defining win strategy (and not the other way around). They help create customer messages to position your company, identify competitive advantages, and document the real reasons the company will win.

During the proposal, the win themes focus proposal writers on the benefits to the customer. In your proposal document, they distinguish you from the rest, making your proposal persuasive, and providing an even bigger advantage if your competition has not taken the time to spell out their own win themes.

During evaluation, inserting your win themes in different forms throughout the proposal helps the customer remember the key benefits of your solution, and answers the evaluators' question: Why should we select your company? Most people are not certain what a great win theme should look like. Hence most proposals read like technical papers. This is because a win theme can be many different things, including the following:

- A recurring thought, a slogan, a tag line, or a punch line—for example, a way to identify your team with two attributes that your customer wants more: "Team Acme: Vigilance and Reliability."

- A strength or a feature of the proposed solution, service, or product, with the stated benefit: "Our proprietary media monitoring database will enable us to meet the reporting schedule using only six analysts instead of eight, cutting the total project cost by 25 percent."

- A value-added proposition or a "freebie" to the government: "We will perform transition and contract start-up at no additional cost to the government."

- A major disclosure or a platform: "We approach network security proactively instead of reactively."

- A discriminator or a differentiator: "We are the only company able to bring the XYZ Technology to this project."

The best win themes for proposals are pithy statements between one and three sentences long. They include all three critical elements of the win theme: feature, benefit, and proof. The more numbers and specific names are packed into the theme, the more convincing and authoritative it will be.

This type of a win theme is the hardest to create. It takes companies days of brainstorming to develop—yet, after all the effort, the emerging win themes often remain weak.

You can turn all of this around by teaching your team to use the right process for win themes, and consequent win strategy development.

First and foremost, you have to brainstorm correctly. Instead of day-long sessions where you lock your team up in a conference room, use a series of multiple shorter sessions no more than one to three hours each, to prevent inefficiency due to wandering focus and fatigue. Shorter meetings will get maximum productivity from the attendees. It's best to use a web conferencing tool so that no one has to spend time traveling for a short meeting. You can share the screen and work over the phone to hear each other better. Don't make the mistake of having half the team work in a conference room, and other individuals join over the phone; get everyone (including the local players) on a level playing field remotely to make communications clearer. Break for homework assignments for a couple of days to get the next version of the win themes developed, and then gather again to continue your exercise.

To develop your win strategy, you need cross-functional inputs that might include people in your organization who know the customer well, subject matter experts in the statement of work, contracts, pricing, and account executives or business developers who communicate with the customer.

Start the first team meeting with a presentation on the opportunity background, and then discuss what to expect during the meeting. Then, teach people what win themes are, and how you are going to go about developing them. Here are the three categories of win themes for your team to draw on:

1. The first category of win themes are discriminators and differentiators. A discriminator is an advantage that is unique to you, which nobody else has in the world or in the market where your customer operates—and that's actually important to the customer either today or in the future. A differentiator is a strength that most of your competitors don't have when you're going after a multiple award contract. A differentiator distinguishes you from most of the competition, but is not 100 percent unique. One or two others might have this differentiator as well. Because there will be more awards than those who have this differentiator, it will differentiate you from the rest who don't. Again, remember, your discriminator or differentiator has to matter to the customer, or it is no more than an interesting fact.

2. The second category of win themes are your nonunique strengths.
This is something that is usually referred to as a "me too" in the proposal field because most of your competitors can make exactly the same claim: "I can do this too." But if your customer needs that strength, then why not give it to them?

For example, if your customer cares about small businesses and likes lots of personal contact, you could say: "We are a small business with the infrastructure of a large business, but the customer focus of a small company that considers each and every client vital." But, nothing about this statement is unique. Many small businesses can say the same thing.

So, instead of having a win theme that's very general, you can neutralize your competitors' similar win theme by making the same point, but better—by adding substantiated proof to your claim. You could add specifics describing your infrastructure, and anything that might testify how focused you are on your customer: number of visits your CEO pays to the customer monthly, specific personnel by name who interface with the customer, and so on. Quantifying, qualifying, and proving it makes a "me too" strength unique and powerful.

3. The third category of win themes are the negatives that could serve you well: the opportunities for turnaround and ghosts.
Opportunities for turnarounds refer to such situations as your company failing to deliver on a project, or getting a poor past performance reference. You can make your blunders serve you instead of detracting from you, when you represent them as valuable *lessons learned*. You can show the significant changes you have made thanks to the bad experience. Once bitten, twice shy. This puts you in an advantageous position over the competition.

You can also employ a technique called *ghosting*, pointing out to the customer your competitors' unique disadvantages. The reason it is called ghosting and not outright slandering is that you are implicating your competitor indirectly and subtly. You don't name your competitor, but point out a problem they have. You can also point out your strengths in the exact area where your competitors might be failing.

For example, if you know your competitor is getting ready to be sold, you may say: "Unlike other companies of similar size, we are not going to be divested within a year, causing turmoil and employee turnover." You could then contrast it with your stability, customer focus, and proof of delivering similar programs well.

The only warning is to be very careful, as ghosting can be a double-edged sword. You might, for example, get your facts wrong (for example, a competitor might have already corrected the problem), be too blunt and turn the customer off, confuse the customer because your ghosting is too obscure, or even offend the customer in case they didn't do a good job themselves managing the nonperforming incumbent.

■ **Note**   Once you have explained the three categories of win themes to your proposal team, introduce them to the three elements of effective win themes.

There are three mandatory elements in a win theme: *feature, benefit,* and *proof.* Figure 7-1 shows three elements of an effective win theme with their necessary attributes.

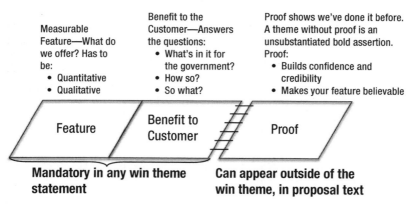

Figure 7-1. Three elements of a win theme. The most powerful proposal win theme has to include feature, benefit, and proof, to make your offer both impactful and trustworthy.

A *feature* has to be factual—the more specific, the better. It has to be quantified and qualified. It answers the question, "What do you offer?"

A *benefit* shows how the feature is useful to the customer, and then answers the skeptical question—"So what?"—by telling the customer how you are better, faster, cheaper, or less risky, and what specifically the customer will get out of the feature.

A *proof* is the evidence that makes your promises believable, and it has to be specific and preferably quantifiable or qualifiable in one or several of the following parameters:

- On what previous contract did you deliver this feature successfully?
- For what customer?
- For how many years?
- With or for how many people?
- What size systems?
- With what savings in man-hours or dollars?
- On how complex of a project?
- With what statistics or metrics?
- With how many days or months in accelerated schedule?
- With what quantifiable improvement in quality?
- With what risk reduction?
- Having overcome what specific challenges?

Tell your team that you are going to enforce the discipline of including all three elements by building your win themes using colors. It is one of the easiest ways to identify what is missing. For example, I like making all my features blue, benefits red, and proofs green as the team develops them. This provides visual clues to where you need to add or brainstorm on additional material. Examples of win themes are shown in Table 7-1.

Table 7-1. Examples of win themes that do not work and those that do. When developing win themes, you need to make sure that at least a feature and a benefit are present, and you make your statements as specific as possible.

Examples of a feature without benefit or proof	Examples of full win themes that provide a more compelling argument for selecting the company
Our Program Manager has 23 years of experience in Counter-Improvised Explosive Devices (C-IED). *(feature)*	Our Program Manager John Smith draws on more than 23 years of experience in C-IED *(feature)* to quickly make the right trade-off decisions to deliver effective solutions protecting our troops from roadside bombs (benefit), as evidenced by his performance on the ABC and XYZ projects. *(proof)*
We bring an innovative intrusion detection system. *(feature)*	Our innovative intrusion detection system monitors traffic to and from all devices on the network *(feature)*, and its impact on the speed of the network is near zero, enabling uninterrupted agency operations. *(benefit) (Proof can appear in the text, with all the technical detail.)*

After you explain the concept of win themes to your team, it's time to roll up your sleeves and develop them for your pursuit.

How to Turn Win Themes into Action Items to Outdo Your Competitors

The process I advocate for developing your win themes is unusual in that instead of starting with the features of your approach or your capabilities, I recommend that you should start with the customer's hot buttons. The reason you do this is that your offer is not about you, it's about the customer.

In other words, no matter how tempted you might be to think of your capabilities and what you have (or don't have) to provide, you should instead think of what the customer wants to have. Period. There should be no "you" in determining what the customer needs.

You must define every aspect of what the customer would ultimately desire, *regardless of whether you have it or not at the moment,* and visualize and document the desired outcome as if it were an ideal world. This will result in a list of hot buttons or key needs from your customer's vantage point.

After you are done coming up with this list based on your knowledge of the "unwritten" requirements, you should also examine all the written requirements in the draft or old RFP—every evaluation criterion and every area of scope—to make sure that you have considered every customer need.

Then, you can restate the needs you came up with as *benefits* for your win themes. After all, aren't benefits what the customer wants and needs? Then, for each benefit, you should find a *feature*—what you have to offer. This will inevitably lead you to a *gap analysis:* Do you actually have a capability (a feature) to provide the desired benefit? If so, make sure you quantify the feature and prove it. If not, you have to come up with a win strategy to obtain that capability, and figure out what actions will get you there. This is the inverted relationship between the win themes and win strategies. In other words, if you cannot come up with a complete win theme, you should create a win strategy.

■ **Note** If you cannot develop a win theme that has a feature or proof, and the customer wants a specific benefit, you should develop a win strategy to obtain that feature or proof.

Win themes drive win strategies, and not the other way around. Your overall process looks like Figure 7-2.

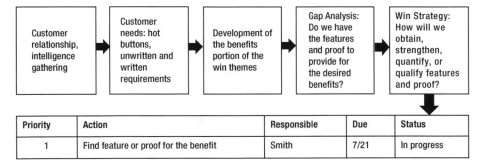

Priority	Action	Responsible	Due	Status
1	Find feature or proof for the benefit	Smith	7/21	In progress

Figure 7-2. Actionable win strategy development process. Customer needs drive the win themes development, which drives strategies and actions.

Let's look at an example of what a hot button might be for a customer looking for a team of certified ethical hackers who go around the country to test government networks and detect vulnerabilities for intrusions:

Customer's Hot Button: *Having a team that's flexible in responding to customers' needs.*

You would presume that this hot button is the benefit that the customer wants, and would provide a solution and the proof wrapped around this benefit:

Benefit: *We are always there when you need us, being available to travel on a short notice—showing* **flexibility and responsiveness to customer needs.**

Your action item might be to develop an approach that would let your customer believe that you can be flexible and responsive, and find facts in your past performance history that would show that you have shown flexibility and responsiveness.

Here is what the proof might look like:

Proof: *We have ensured that 100 percent of all personnel have passports to meet potential global mission requirements, and assigned a travel administrator to the program at no additional cost, to make on-demand travel arrangements.*

We have proven flexibility on multiple occasions. For example, during the Largo test event, a team member used his personal cell phone on site to research a Cisco password cracking technique. The research led to the successful compromise of the network password and further entry into the network. In a separate situation in DC, a team member used previous experience with the Windows registry to enable registry access on a remote machine and gain a remote desktop connection, leading to full compromise of the internal machine.

As you can see, a win theme is pithy and long—and it becomes the foundation for your technical and management approaches.

During capture, these win themes will become part of your Customer Contact Plan—for you to feed them to the customer as your marketing messages. You will progressively refine them—making them more substantive and powerful based on the customer reaction and feedback—into the form in which you will communicate them in your proposal when the RFP comes out.

During the proposal, you can dive into your win themes write-up and make sure that you have used every golden nugget you have come up with in your proposal narrative. If your writers happened to forget some of the great facts and themes, you can work them into your narrative.

As you get into competitive analysis, teaming, and solution development, you will have a chance to further develop and refine your win themes and win strategy. Remember, your win themes repository is a living document.

Identify Top-Level Actions That Create a Winning Offer

You need to sort your win themes by how important the benefit contained in the theme is to the customer. You should preferably do it at the customer needs determination stage, or you might choose to do it later, when you know which win themes are your strongest.

From this exercise, you can prioritize your actions. Your biggest and most important actions will be strategic in nature, because they will likely influence the outcome of the entire pursuit. Decide where should you be spending your time and energy to get the biggest bang for the buck—how can you cover the most ground by investing into each action.

Here are some examples of strategic actions:

- Meeting with customer and user stakeholders and communicating the strategic message and win themes.

- Creating a specific image in the eyes of the customer and the necessary customer sentiment.

- Developing and refining the technical and management solution, and recruiting "superstar" staff.

- Gathering trade-off data and preparing alternative proposals.

- Aligning potential teammates to cover the identified capability and past performance gaps.

- Implementing a strategy to find ways to lower costs, and elaborating the detail of the cost and schedule models.

Good and Bad Win Strategies

If you use the technique just described correctly, you should have all the ingredients to succeed in developing sound strategies. The biggest flaw in strategy development is focusing on your own capabilities and not the customer's needs. Putting your customer's needs first and seeking to fulfill their desires to the maximum extent possible will naturally result in good win strategies.

The next biggest flaw in strategy development that leads to poor win strategies is ignoring the competition. Your competitors are a measuring stick for your strategy, because this is a competition and not a one-company show. Make sure that as you develop your action items to find features for the customer-desired benefits, you take into consideration the results of competitive analysis. You have to compare yourself against what your competition is able to offer and then decide how you should go about outdoing them. You have to outplay your competitors at *every* step.

If you happen to be the incumbent already performing on a contract that you would like to win again, remember that business-as-usual is not a good win strategy. You have to do something innovative and bold to make good services even better.

For example, your strategy is weak if it is based on the following all too common platitudes:

- "Leverage the company and team's capabilities…"

- "Closely partner with the customer…"

- "Develop a best-value solution…"

- "Leverage our incumbent knowledge of the customer, service continuity, and zero transition cost…"

You should test whether your win strategies are any good. Because of the inherent relationship between win themes and win strategies, your win themes have to reflect your win strategies. Check the quality of your win strategies by the quality of your win themes.

Here are seven common problems companies typically encounter with their win themes, together with the ways to fix them:

Problem 1. Your win themes are lacking outright, or what you think are win themes are ineffective.

> **Solution:** To overcome this problem, make sure that you implement the process described in this book, and come up with the win themes that the customer cares about now or will care about in the future. This process makes win strategy development spot-on.

Problem 2. Your win themes come out ho-hum because most technical people who are supposed to develop win themes are not trained in win themes development, selling, or marketing.

> **Solution:** To overcome this problem, make sure that your win themes have a feature, benefit, and proof, and train your technical personnel to tell the difference between features and benefits. Organize brainstorming sessions to have them come up with the right statements and resulting strategies.

Problem 3. Your win themes are taking too long to work out, and your proposal team typically gives up at a few good ones.

> **Solution:** To overcome this problem, teach your team to use the correct win theme development process described in this book, which will save you countless hours and make your company more likely to be a winner.

Problem 4. Your win themes don't pass the "substitution test": If you put some other company's name in your win theme instead of yours, would it still sound true? "We are the low-risk, best-value provider" is not a win theme; it is an overused generality. The same goes for "We understand the customer," "We have great past performance," and "We are ISO and CMMI Level whatever...." You get the idea.

> **Solution:** To overcome this problem, make sure that you are extremely specific defining what the customer is looking for. "Low-risk, best value provider" is a generality. You have to clarify what it actually means specifically for this customer.

Problem 5. Your win themes are lacking punch because someone didn't have time to look up or verify the facts. Win themes have to have numbers in them to make them stronger. If you cannot quantify the facts, saying something arm-waving like "hundreds of thousands in savings" is weak.

> **Solution:** To overcome this problem, as you brainstorm, put placeholders such as Xs wherever you can quantify or qualify something, and then issue an action item to specific person, with a deadline, and hold them to

getting you the information. Then, make sure that you edit your win theme by adding the provided data into the statement.

Problem 6. Your win themes are self-centered and self-serving: they are about you, and not the customer. Your customer could care less about your CMMI Level 5 certification unless you tell them what it can do for them while not costing them extra, if possible.

> **Solution:** To overcome this problem, guide your team through the correct win theme development process that starts with the customer's hot buttons, instead of your capabilities. Any time anyone mentions your company's capability or solution, interrupt the person and remind him or her that it's not about you, it's about the customer. Make sure that you dig deeper with the benefits and state exactly how they would make customer's life better.

Problem 7. Your win themes are trivialized to the point that the company believes they can be recycled from other proposals. But most customers, RFPs, and timing are unique, so how could the focus of your offer be the same no matter what the customer or the current circumstances are?

> **Solution:** To overcome this problem, make sure that you focus on the uniqueness of the situation rather than its similarity to past proposals. What is different about this set of requirements and circumstances, and this customer? Then, determine customer's needs. Check if these are still the same in the win themes you were trying to recycle. If not, develop new win themes and corresponding win strategies.

Remember, most companies—despite their best intentions and even when they understand what a win theme and a solid win strategy are supposed to look like—fail to sell during capture, and subsequently in their proposals. If you don't take the time to develop and test your win strategies, your entire capture and proposal effort will unravel. But if you spend time and work hard on focusing on customer needs in your win strategy development, your win probability will go up exponentially.

In the next chapter, we discuss the intricacies of competitive analysis, which will play an important part in enhancing your win strategies.

Identify and Analyze Your Competition

Competitive analysis is your measuring stick against the rest of the world. To use a boxing analogy, your form might look impressive when you are boxing a punching bag, but it cannot hit you back. There are also no surprises and no unknowns. Ultimately, to see what you are made of, you have to be pitted against an opponent. You and your capabilities in and of themselves might be impressive, but would they stand up to your leaner and meaner opponents? In this chapter, we cover the reasons you should mind your competitors and predict their possible actions; what you need to know about your competition; how to find this information; and how to put all the pieces of the competitive analysis puzzle together to exploit your competitors' shortfalls to your advantage and outdo them through strategic actions.

Why You Should Worry about What Your Competitors Do

When I consult for companies, I often hear their business development professionals say, "Why should I worry about my competition? We have what we have to offer, and as long as we can give the government the best price we can honestly give them, we should be just fine. If they don't select us, well, so be it. We wouldn't want to perform this work at a loss anyway."

Other companies don't worry about the competition because they simply don't have time to do competitive analysis. Some haven't seen much benefit of the competitive analysis they have done before, and others simply don't know how to do it.

What would you do differently if you knew that with good competitive analysis and actions your win rate would double? Competitive analysis affects every single aspect of your capture, and can make a tremendous difference in the outcome of your pursuit.

- You have to identify competitive positioning with the customer, and ghost your competition to the customer. Knowing your customer's hot buttons will also help you determine where you stand versus your competition.

- Through your intelligence gathering efforts, you will identify your competition and research competitor information.

- Through your win strategy analysis, you will make changes to your win strategy to outdo your competition. You will be able to leverage your strengths, mitigate your weaknesses, neutralize competitors' strengths, and exploit your competitors' weaknesses—all based on the customer's hot buttons. You will be able to develop discriminators and differentiators, ghosting win themes, and preempt your competitors' attacks through turnaround win themes.

- You will be able to determine price to win (PTW) and your cost strategy based on this information.

- You will make teaming decisions based on competitive strategy, because picking a teammate prior to figuring out the competitive landscape is a bad idea.

- Finally, you will be able to determine a better solution that distinguishes you from the competition.

If you omit competitive analysis, you weaken the other five aspects of capture.

How Cursory Competitive Analysis Will Always Hurt You

Ironically, many people go through the motions because they don't understand competitive analysis, and they miss the whole point of it. They identify the competition, and they even figure out what the competition might be doing, but then they continue with business as usual.

The most important outcome of competitive analysis is not just knowing what the competition is doing; it is helping you determine how to act in accordance with this knowledge. What makes it more challenging is that your competition is not static—it keeps moving forward and adapting every day. Your job is to stay ahead of the competition and anticipate and counter their actions. It is like a game of chess.

Many companies limit their competitive analysis to superficial research on the Internet or a black hat session (a type of brainstorming session that simulates your competition's behavior and pits it against your behavior), and then focus on other things without revisiting competition on a regular basis. This could lead to serious mistakes that might cost them the procurement.

Your only recourse is to invest in competitive analysis and maintain awareness of your competition at all times.

What You Need to Know about Your Competition, and Techniques for Finding This Information

To start a competitive analysis, you first have to identify your competitors. It's important to note that when you are a large or even midsized business, it is much easier to identify your competition. When you are a small business, your competition might be harder to spot, but you should not give up. There are many ways of identifying your competitors.

Know Your Industry

You have to determine which companies offer services and solutions similar to your own. For example, if you are a midtier transportation and logistics company, you should know what other similar transportation and logistics companies operate in the same general geographical area. To sort through your competition further and narrow down the field, you have to figure out which of these companies are similar to you in the following ways:

- **Customers,** which could be focused on such areas as defense, intelligence, or civilian agencies, for example.
- **Resources,** including revenue, number and type of employees, facilities, equipment, and products.

- **Business acquisition strategies.** For example, are these companies growing through:
  - Federal sales by bidding on smaller deals and selling through GSA schedules?
  - Mainly partnering with others and subcontracting versus priming?
  - Buying their way into the contracts by low-balling or otherwise deflating their price and making their money back later as the company takes a firm foothold in the agency?
  - Teaming with the same set of businesses on most opportunities they bid?
  - Bidding on mega deals and large MACs?
  - Leveraging mergers and acquisitions (M&As)?
  - Any other methods?

The easiest way to find this information is by identifying which competitors specialize with a specific customer. You can find this information from BGov, USAspending.gov, the Federal Procurement Data System (FPDS), or GovWin IQ. You should also look up in the search engine the key words that you use to identify yourself and look through your competitors' web sites. The market analysis that you conducted early on should provide you with some of this information as well. This type of research will give you a good starting point for eventually narrowing down your field.

Business acquisition strategies are probably the hardest to pinpoint; you might want to do a much more in-depth analysis. Tune in to the rumor mill to find out about the company's reputation, ask everyone you know about the companies in question, and watch some competitors over time (perhaps even team with them on some deals) to pick up this kind of information. As you spend more time in the government contracting industry and your personal network and knowledge of different players grows, you will hear rumblings. There are also other methods of analysis we discuss later that might shed some light on your competitors' business strategies.

Research Which Other Companies Focus on the Same Customer

If you are interested in a specific office in the Department of Veterans Affairs and the need is construction, check what companies bid with this customer in the area of construction: What are the leading construction primes and subs in the agency and the department?

You can find information about your competitors that focus on a specific customer from the following sources:

- Agency web site registered vendors list.

- Listings of participants in mentor protégé program members for various agencies including SBA, DOD, DHS, NASA, Treasury, and so on.

- USAspending.gov, FPDS, BGov, and GovWin IQ analysis.

- Your customer: the agency's small business advocate in OSDBU or even the actual buyer or user at the agency.

- Your champion at the agency.

- The FedBizOpps web site, which lists interested vendors, and interested vendors in GovWin IQ and Centurion

Identify Competitors by Opportunity

You have to research your target opportunity to know the history of direct and indirect involvement from other companies. You have to check the following:

- What companies are the incumbents who did this work or are still doing the work under the current contract?

- Are there some companies that are executing some pieces of the work that now are going to be rolled under a larger umbrella in a consolidated contract?

- What companies have similar past performance with this customer to be able to win this opportunity, perhaps by teaming with others to augment their capabilities?

- Are there companies that an agency lists as their top contractors?

- What companies have registered as interested vendors for this opportunity on GovWin IQ or FedBizOpps?

- What companies are listed as potential competitors by the competitive research services such as GovWin IQ or Centurion?

- Which of your competitors showed up to the Industry Day or site visit?

- What companies have contacted you for teaming?

Again, you can find such information from USAspending.gov or FPDS and by talking to the customer. You can also find this information on BGov, GovWin IQ, or Centurion by checking opportunity history. FedBizOpps might also have archived information on this opportunity and any procurement actions, and you can search the Web for press releases and news articles. The goal of the current administration is to have maximum transparency, so soon all contracts might be posted on the Web and you won't even have to explicitly request them from the government through the FOIA process.

Check If Other Companies Do Nearly Identical Work for Other Customers Similar to Those You Are Targeting

For example, if you are targeting an Army networks contract with the specific organizations, you might want to see what other companies are operating within the similar organizations in the Army doing similar work, and perhaps other companies in other branches of the military doing similar work. For example, a company might qualify if they did networks for the Air Force if they can show large similarities in scope, size, and complexity between their other work and the new job.

Keep Your Ear Close to the Ground

You might want to find out who is bidding by asking your customer. You could also learn about it from your team on the customer site, or any of your network contacts who might be also going after this opportunity. It is always good to ask around, and to have your people check to see who is lurking near the customer, trying to woo him or her. This method works very well in conjunction with the other methods already mentioned.

Call a Competitor Directly to Say You Want to Get on Their Team

You could also ask if they would get on *your* team. They might tell you directly that they are going to prime or they might consider subbing.

The possible circle of your competitors, so identified, in some cases might include dozens of companies. You have to narrow down the field. Make decisions based on your initial research about which competitors could be a real threat to you, and which might not be that dangerous.

Don't forget: Your competitors might not be a threat on their own, but paired with powerful teammates they could be a real menace. Don't think of your competitors as companies; think of them as *teams*.

■ **Note**   Do not underestimate your competitors' strength because they could always form a formidable team with someone very powerful. Think of your competitors as teams, not individual companies.

You have to give yourself a reasonable scope for your initial search, so that you are not stuck doing research and fact-finding on several dozen companies. After all, you won't be competing with all of them. You are going to be competing with the top handful, and ultimately have to beat the most powerful one. The trick here is to get enough information to determine which top ten companies you are going to really focus on, and then narrow down the list to the top three or five.

When you don't know your competition and don't have time to find out more (which often happens with small businesses or situations when you don't have much time to do capture), you might want to create an Ideal Competitor Threat profile, in which you would paint the most realistic, yet threatening picture (where you are not "drinking your own bathwater") of what you would be going up against.

In the situations where there are dozens or hundreds of contenders on a MAC, you might want to analyze your competition in groups. You can group companies by size, incumbency, relevant past performance, socioeconomic factors such as SDVOSB or 8(a), or any other characteristics important to your customer in this specific competition.

After you come up with the shorter list, you can prioritize the companies. You only have to defeat the biggest threats, and come up with a list of competitors and potential teammates.

Kinds of Information You Need for Competitive Analysis

Prior to conducting competitive analysis, you need to collect information to make your analysis meaningful. It is not advisable to operate purely from a gut feel: You should collect as many facts as possible.

The simple answer to the question on what kind and how much information you might need about your competitors is this: Enough to get a good idea about their win strategy to outfox them at every step.

It usually boils down to your competitor's following data:

- Company profile and how it is similar to yours. (In other words, why did you single them out as a competitor?)

- Business objectives; how they are growing. This should include their strategic direction, including technology, product, and service offerings, independent research and development (IR&D) investments, and any contract winnings that are similar to this deal, all of which could be leveraged to help them win.

- Technical and management capabilities and headcount distribution that match this opportunity's scope, size, and complexity (and their ability to meaningfully mitigate any shortcomings through teaming; sometimes the shortcomings are too many for the company to be able to prime a very complex job).

- Financial health and well-being (usually determined by their product lines, the types of programs that they are executing, and traditional financial parameters), which would enable them to execute a project of this size and complexity and run a good capture and proposal effort.

- Your competitor's government customers:

  - Who are they?

  - How do they perceive your competitor and what do they expect from your competitor?

  - What pressures have these expectations placed on your customer's business?

  - How equipped is your competitor to meet these expectations?

- A recent merger or acquisition that might have placed new challenges on your competitor.

- Partnerships, teaming, subcontracting, and vendor relationships that would enable them to strengthen their chances of winning.

- Past and current performance and credibility with the customer: are they doing well or are they running into problems?

- Does the customer have a close trusting relationship with them and generally favor them as a contractor?

- Any weaknesses like high turnover or movement of senior management personnel – and any reactions on Wall Street if the company is publicly traded?

- Personnel involved in the pursuit and potentially bid on the job, such as the PM and other key figures.

- Your "hit list," or personnel you might want to hire away from your competitor or sign contingency hire letters with to hire right after the contract is awarded to you (be careful so that you don't tick off the customer because this move might seriously disrupt their operations by hiring away a key person too early). Contingency hire letters can be touted in your proposal even if they are not required.

- Probable technical, management, past performance, staffing, and pricing approaches.

- Proposal strategies.

Where to Find Information about Competitors Ethically

It is important to note that you have to be careful in gathering competitive intelligence. Stick with public sources, and avoid anything labeled "proprietary" or "competition sensitive" from that company. You are not in the business of corporate espionage: You are doing *above-the-board* competitive intelligence gathering. One win, no matter how strategic, is not worth the risk of losing your government practice. There are a number of companies that have been debarred, or forced to divest entire divisions at bargain prices, as a consequence of their unethical ways.

Finding Company Information

Once you have identified your most likely competitors, it is time to roll up your sleeves and do some research. You should create a file on your competitors, and you should study them very closely so that you can outplay them every chance you get. Generally speaking, you will have the easiest time finding information on larger companies, especially if they are publicly traded. In the world of small business, the competition is becoming tougher—and there are many "dark horses"—but it doesn't mean you should give up and skip this portion. The more mature the company is, the more public is its presence and the brighter is its "trail" in the business world, the Internet, and the news.

Eventually you will find that your competition will become more and more predictable as you do competitive research over the years, run head-to-head competitions, and develop close teaming and joint venture relationships that will give you more insight into your teammates today, which might be your competitors tomorrow.

The following are some resources and guidance that will help you get more information about your competitors.

1. Check the company's web site and see what you can find out from it. Information might include the following:

- Profile and focus.

- Executive leadership.

- Contracts and projects.

- Business size and status information.

- Whether the company has multiple departments, and if so, which department specifically you would be competing against.

- Potential partnerships and vendor alliances.

- Awards and other bragging rights.

- Annual report.

- Recent corporate press releases to see:

  - How is the company doing?

  - Has anything changed such as major reorganizations and M&As?

  - Is the company on target to meet its profit goals? If not, what are some barriers you could identify?

  - How is the company doing in achieving initiatives and goals from the annual report?

- Quarterly executive webcasts and teleconferences that show company progress in achieving the stated goals and strategies, and new initiatives (which stay posted only for a few days, so monitor your competitor closely and sign up for e-mail notifications).

- Quarterly financial results under the investor relations section and statements made by the CEO to analysts and stakeholders.

- Take a look at the year-on-year trends, and relationship between revenue and cost, changes in total revenue, and what's behind these changes. Compare current year results to the current plan:

  - Are they missing cost projections and revenue targets?

  - Has anything crept up to prevent them – and what should it be?

Remember that revenue can come from a variety of sources—not just sales. Check also direct and indirect changes in costs, which could give you clues as to where the company is focusing its growth. Note that if the revenue and expenses are growing equally, your competitors are not making a profit. Compare trends over time: Are they up, down, or flat?

Sales, business development, and proposal management are all overhead functions. When times are tough, less experienced executives will look to reduce overhead costs first by laying off business development folks. If your competitor is making money hand over fist, growing revenue might not be their highest priority, so this pursuit could be either "business as usual" and they will do it just as well as they do anything else (whereas you might decide to go out of your way to beat them), or they might grow complacent and you still should dedicate more resources than they would ever expect from you and outbid them.

Many times a company's financial condition will provide a hint as to whether they can afford and are willing to throw money at the pursuit to hire expensive resources that are more likely to lead them to a win.

If a company is publicly traded, check the analyst ratings. If you didn't find analyst reports on your competitor's web site, you can still access their ratings and what analysts think of the company via the Internet. A good place to look is the MSN Money web site at http://money.msn.com/.

A publicly traded company's annual report is the most credible resource of company information, including past performance and future objectives. Read the report to identify the driving force of the company, its critical success factors, key performance indicators (achieving percentage-growth in revenue), and what clients and projects this company targets. Read the report carefully and look for both overt and subtle subtexts that apply to company strategy.

The annual report will also tell you about the competitor's lines of business or divisions (as might the web site). Many companies or divisions within a company operate in silos. You shouldn't regard them as one company because they act like many companies under one umbrella. It is important to make the distinction between business units because you might be looking at either a much narrower competitor or a whole set of competitors. Business units have even been known to compete against each other.

Look at the financial statements from publicly held companies, as well as the 10K quarterly reports. You might skip the consolidated statements and look for the statements published for the various operating units or subsidiaries. Specifically, focus on the income statement (statement of financial condition), and look for trends such as declining sales (the top line) or earnings (the bottom line), increases in inventory (cost of goods sold), or costs.

Examine your competitor's industry trends. They might be similar to yours, and could include anything from cybersecurity, to budget cuts, to productivity improvements, to rapid changes in technology, to new challenges and innovations. These are your competitors' external influences that affect strategy. You could glean this information from the following sources, all of which cost money:

- **Standards and Poor's (S&P) 500 report** (www.standardandpoors.com) includes industry profiles and trends, current industry environment, how the industry operates, key industry ratios and statistics, and comparative financial analysis.

- **Gartner Analyst reports** (www.gartner.com) forecast IT spending with competitive landscape and recommendations for strategic positioning.

- **Datamonitor reports** (www.datamonitor.com) cover business issues—where your competitors are focusing, and how they will be spending technology budgets—analysis and forecasts in the areas of health, technology, automotive, energy, consumer markets, and financial services.

You can also search your competitors' and their key executives' names via a business periodicals search that includes several services that might be worth your investment, depending on your industry:

- **BGov** (www.BGov.com) includes news clippings from more than 30,000 media sources and analyst reports.

- **EBSCO Host** includes the Military & Government Collection offering current news pertaining to all branches of the military and government, with full text from nearly 300 journals and periodicals, with indexing and abstracts for more than 400 journals. See www.ebscohost.com/government/military-government-collection.

- EBSCO Host also has **Business Source Corporate**, the world's largest, English-language, full-text periodical business database, providing more than 2,700 quality magazines and journals that offer invaluable information on virtually every aspect of business. It also offers more than 1,400 country economic reports from EIU, Global Insight, ICON Group International, CountryWatch, and more; 10,150 substantial company profiles; and more than 5,200 full-text industry reports. See www.ebscohost.com/corporate-research/business-source-corporate.

- Another EBSCO Host resource is **Regional Business News database** (www.ebscohost.com/public/regional-business-news). It provides comprehensive full-text coverage for regional business publications. Regional Business News incorporates coverage of nearly 100 regional U.S. and Canadian business publications.

- **InSite 2** (www.insite2.gale.com/is2/enduser_index.cgi) provides a single point of access to authoritative business information; 430,000 company profiles and industry reports; executive biographies; business articles from more than 5,000 premier publications, and much more. This is an important resource in gathering global business intelligence for monitoring company activities, the products and technologies they develop, and the markets in which they compete.

- **Mergent Online** (www.mergentonline.com) is a professional-strength research tool that tracks more companies in more countries than any other database, Mergent Online includes comprehensive information on company financials, descriptions, history, property, subsidiaries, officers, and directors. Its database includes business and financial information using financial variables and company name or ticker symbol.

- **EDGAR**, the Electronic Data Gathering, Analysis, and Retrieval system (www.sec.gov/edgar.shtml), performs automated collection, validation, indexing, acceptance, and forwarding of submissions by companies and others who are required by law to file forms with the U.S. Securities and Exchange Commission (SEC). All companies, foreign and domestic, are required to file registration statements, periodic reports, and other forms electronically through EDGAR. Anyone can access and download this information for free.

Additional interesting sources you might want to use in competitive analysis are **LexisNexis, Marquis Who's Who**, and **GlobalSpec**.

Although you might not want to invest in expensive data sources (especially if you are just starting out in government contracting), you should always focus on important information gathering sources that are specific to the customer and to the contract you are chasing:

- Competitor's win–loss record for similar programs.

- Review of the old copies of the RFPs in which the competitor was the winner, which might be similar or related to this opportunity.

- Specific program web pages that competitors create to target their customers and MAC vehicle users.

- Published lessons learned on programs.

- Customer debriefs.

- Asking your customer what they think about your competitor's performance.

- Asking your customer's customers how they are experiencing your competitor's services if your competitor is an incumbent.

- Interviews with former employees, without discussing proprietary information, of course.

- D&B report that will show important information such as risk rating and Paydex score—again—very "ghostable" especially if your rating and scores are high and your competitors' are lower, and if they have used up most of their line of credit

- Conference presentations by your competitors and your customers that cover your competitors' work.

- White papers on certain technologies and approaches.

- Former teaming partners and vendors disclosing information that is not proprietary and doesn't fall under their nondisclosure agreements (NDAs).

- Consultants hired for black hat (competitive analysis brainstorming) exercises.

- People in your company who have worked with the competitor before.

- Past performance information in FPDS or other sources that get data from FPDS (for example, BGov cleans up FPDS data and makes it easier to analyze).

- Competitor's rates from FOIA requests or research databases, and your supply chain management if they have worked with this contractor before (and they have not submitted a sealed bid).

- Labor rates of your competitors' personnel when they fill out your job application.

- Competitors' hiring initiatives, such as ads in the newspapers and online job boards.

- Hiring competitive intelligence professionals, who are usually a wealth of information on different companies.

- A database of open source information you should build on your competitors to consult again and again in the future.

Filing Freedom of Information Act Requests

Another great source of competitive intelligence is FOIA requests. This is the process of officially requesting competitors' information from the executive branch of the government (the legislative and judiciary branches and state and local governments do not abide by the FOIA but have similar types of provisions that might enable you to get even more information than you could obtain from the Feds). By law, any person has the right to request in writing access to federal agency records or information, and your competitors' information becomes part of the public record once they win a contract.

You might not see all the data (because it is sanitized, and there are some exemptions and exclusions from the FOIA), but you will still be able to glean useful information. The key to FOIA requests is to start early (as in months or even a whole year ahead), because it takes a long time to get the information requested.

Here is a sampling of what you can get on your competitors via the FOIA process:

- A copy of their contract with the scope of work.

- Old RFPs.

- A copy of the proposal (yes, proposal; if it won, the government retains a copy and will provide it to you).

There is no central office in the government that processes FOIA requests for all federal agencies; each agency responds on its own. To request FOIA documents, you need to do the following:

1. Identify which agency (and especially which part of that agency) has the records you are seeking.

2. Check that agency's guide on how to file a FOIA request; these are usually posted on the Web.

3. Get in touch with the FOIA contact at that agency in the Freedom of Information Act Office. Always verify that this is the right place to send your request; if you don't, your request could take too long. You can learn more about FOIA contacts at the www.foia.gov web site.

4. Most federal agencies now accept FOIA requests electronically, including by web form, e-mail, or fax. Submitting a FOIA request to a federal agency is not difficult, but a well-written request might help you avoid delays and further questions from the government agency. Normally there is no specific standard language you have to use, but you should check to see if a specific agency does require something that's unique to them.

5. Send the request. Don't address it to a specific person (or give the name of the main contact and state "To Whom it May Concern" next to the name). If you are mailing the request, include a note that this is a FOIA request in the letter and on the envelope.

6. Wait for your tracking number. The agency is required to confirm your request has been received; it then has 20 days to make a

decision on whether it will release the records to you. Sometimes, when you request many documents, the agency might "suggest" a delay.

7. Wait for your records. The agency will eventually send you these records "within the reasonable time." This time depends on how busy the agency is and how much data you have requested. They often have to read the whole thing line by line, and get back to your competitor to ask them to "censor" or redact the text. In your best case scenario, both the agency and your competitor will be sloppy and you get more information than you had hoped. People have been known to receive completely uncensored proposal documents or sloppily censored documents. This is when you strike gold.

8. Follow up and stay on top of your FOIA request or it will take even longer. Services such as Centurion and GovWin IQ are adept at requesting FOIA documents and are highly effective at getting them within a month or two because they have someone who keeps following up and stays on top of the process.

Here are a few more things you need to know about FOIA requests:

FOIA requests can be very annoying to your customer, so if you are in the process of building a relationship and it is somewhat touch-and-go, you should be careful. Some organizations decide to avoid FOIA altogether as a matter of policy for this very reason—they call it "staying under the radar."

FOIA indeed puts you on the radar not only by letting your customer know you have teeth, but also with your competitors. Your competitors have to approve what gets released to you—they get to sanitize their materials before you receive them—so they will know right away that you are bidding. If you are not the incumbent, you might want to think twice, as now you will become the target of their ghosting and strategic action plans. Although the customer might not inform them officially *who* is requesting the information, they are likely to find out anyway.

The incumbent contractor should always execute a FOIA request to see what has been given to the competition.

Some companies prefer to "hide" and use a third party to file a FOIA request: They ask their subcontractor or a consulting company to do it for them. Another third party option, such as GovWin IQ, files FOIA requests in droves and sells them for a fee, so you definitely should check that route. There is only one downside to using such services if no one has already requested a document. Asking for a document through GovWin means that you will make your competitors better off in case they have neglected to execute FOIA on their own. These services will post the document and sell it to others if they get it for you, but the speed of getting the document might be worth it.

Putting the Puzzle Together

A competitive analysis process might seem complex, but it is rather straightforward when you get the hang of it. Just like with strategies, it starts with customer's requirements, their profile, and hot buttons. Then it leads into all the research we have covered to identify and understand your competitors. The core of competitor analysis, however, comes in steps 5 through 8 in Figure 8-1: This is where you transform all your knowledge into action.

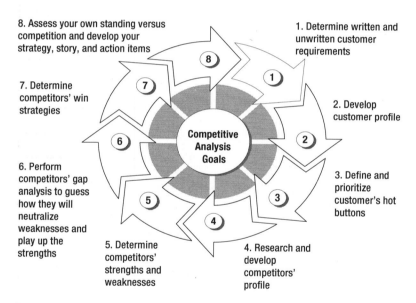

8. Assess your own standing versus competition and develop your strategy, story, and action items

7. Determine competitors' win strategies

6. Perform competitors' gap analysis to guess how they will neutralize weaknesses and play up the strengths

5. Determine competitors' strengths and weaknesses

Competitive Analysis Goals

1. Determine written and unwritten customer requirements

2. Develop customer profile

3. Define and prioritize customer's hot buttons

4. Research and develop competitors' profile

Figure 8-1. Competitive analysis goals. Competitive analysis includes eight goals that culminate in developing your own strategy, story, and action items based on the competition's stance.

After you determine all the key details about your competitors and select a few against whom you will have to compete the hardest, you will have to perform analysis of their strengths and weaknesses.

The most common framework used for this analysis is *SWOT:* strengths, weaknesses, opportunities, and threats. You can easily find information on how to perform this analysis on the Web.

After you perform this analysis for each of the competitors, you might want to rank each of the competitors against the evaluation criteria and customer's hot buttons, as shown in Table 8-1.

Table 8-1. Competitor ranking. This format is useful to see how each competitor stacks up against the written requirements and customer's hot buttons.

Potential Customer Evaluation Criteria	Ranking (+ (strength), 0 (neutral), - (weakness))	Rationale for the Ranking
Written Requirements:		
Technical Approach		
Management Approach		
Past Performance		
Corporate Experience		
Staffing and Key Personnel		
Cost		
Hot Buttons:		

After you have done this analysis, you might want to figure out, for each competitor, how they will maximize their strengths, minimize their weaknesses, attempt to neutralize your team's strengths and exploit your team's weaknesses, and finally, what kind of innovative deal they might try to propose.

After you are done examining your competitors, you need to look at yourself through the same goggles and perform a similar analysis for the "home" team.

You can then aggregate the rankings in a single table (Table 8-2), including your own score.

Table 8-2. Aggregate rankings. It is useful to look at all the rankings side by side to determine who the biggest threat is, and devise actions to defuse it.

Customer's Evaluation Criteria	Your Team	Comp 1	Comp 2	Comp 3	Comp 4	Comp 5
Written Requirements:						
Technical Approach	+, -, 0					
Management Approach						
Past Performance						
Corporate Experience						
Staffing and Key Personnel						
Cost						
Hot Buttons:						
Total Score:						

Finally, based on this insight, you want to see how to adjust your win strategy based on the competitive analysis, and figure out how you can maximize your strengths, shore up the weaknesses, neutralize competitors' strengths, and emphasize their weaknesses.

An outcome of your competitive analysis should be action items added to your win strategy.

It is important to understand that your competitor will be doing the same things as you: They will be courting your customer and implementing their win strategies. Your competition's strengths and weaknesses are also not set in stone. You have to continue assessing and reassessing the situation and adjusting your documentation and actions accordingly.

In the following chapter, we discuss the next logical step in capturing a pursuit: teaming.

Create a Team That Compels the Customer to Select You

Most government contracts are accomplished through teaming. The government tends to bundle smaller contracts into larger vehicles and multiple award contracts that require integrated multifaceted solutions. Rarely does an entity in the world of services and solutions do the entire job on its own, without any help on a contract that includes a diverse scope of work. Even if they could perform on their own, it would be hard for them to win the contract, because it would mean that they have to have past performance references relevant to every single aspect of work.

The government likes teaming, because teaming enables them to tap into the expertise of multiple companies with only one company (the prime) responsible. It is "one throat to choke"—one party that assumes the responsibility and the risk for completing the contract, making it easier for the government to manage the contract. Additionally, any time a company is new to the market or customer, teaming is the way to break in. Teaming helps agencies meet their small business contracting goals, so they require that large companies team with small ones, and small companies often need the resources of large ones to help them excel in a contract. This chapter covers how to choose and engage the right partner companies, select an appropriate teaming strategy, avoid potential teaming pitfalls that could create problems or even disqualify you from bidding, and take into consideration other nuances important to teaming.

Choose and Engage the Right Partner Companies

Very few companies in the services and solutions arena go it alone because teams offer beneficial combinations of capabilities, cost, and performance for each job, and help companies win bids they normally couldn't. Teaming is when a potential prime contractor agrees with one or more other companies to serve as its subcontractors under a specific government bid, or when two or more companies form a partnership or joint venture to act as a potential prime contractor. Teaming typically happens before submission of a proposal, but might also happen after contract award.

Teaming is a natural segue from your customer relationship building, intelligence gathering, win strategy development, and competitive analysis efforts. It is also a natural component of the sixth aspect of capture: solution development. The preceding aspects help you select the right teammates, and solution development helps you refine your selection and fill any gaps.

It seems counterintuitive for companies to want to team. Why would you want to dilute your profits, and give valuable scope to somebody else?

As you write proposals to win work with different companies, you don't really want to share your proprietary information with others and teach them how to win other similar contracts. These same companies might be your teammates right now, but could compete with you on future pursuits. You don't want to have less control and, if you are a subcontractor, more limited contact with the government and less credit for your past performance on this contract when you go after other pursuits.

If you form a separate entity called a *joint venture* (JV), your company might have extra liabilities and some of the decisions will be outside your control. Even worse, you might not comply with the small business size limitations if it is a small business set-aside procurement.

When you are a subcontractor, there are many ways a prime contractor could take advantage of you and not deliver on their promises during the proposal stages. They might pay you late or try not to pay you at all, limit your access to the customer, or absorb your best people into their workforce and leave you high and dry.

If there are so many reasons not to team, why do companies do it anyway? The reasons to form a team are many, despite all the risks. Through teaming, your company is able to do the following:

- Pursue the contracts you otherwise would not have the ability to win and execute because you can draw on another company's resources to increase:

  - Overall technical and management capabilities to execute the scope.

  - The depth and breadth of coverage in different areas of scope for better past performance relevancy.

  - Your ability to write and produce a better quality proposal, if your teammates have more experience developing proposals for this type of pursuit or overall.

  - Your ability to provide solutions based on specific know-how, technology, software, or equipment available through your teammate.

  - Bench strength for surge support.

  - Your relationship with the customer.

  - Financial resources or bonding.

- Access new markets and agencies where you do not yet have past performance, experience, and relationships.

- Access critical information, services, and capabilities early in the bidding process if you team with an incumbent contractor or one that has inroads with the customer.

- Access specific MAC vehicles if you are teaming postaward.

- Lower costs by finding a less expensive provider for certain aspects of the work.

- Pool resources to further the state of the technical art or research.

- Benefit from a teammate's presence in other geographical locations.

- Get security clearances for your personnel and facilities through companies that can hold these clearances and can sponsor you for your own facility clearance.

- Negotiate a potential quid-pro-quo to get work share on another contract that your teammate has (or is going after), in exchange for a place on the team.

- As a large company, gain an opportunity to take advantage of the small business set-aside opportunities.

- Distribute the financial risk of performing the contract among the teammates.

- Increase revenue and working capital through the contracts you could win by subbing (that you wouldn't have won otherwise).

- Expand experience and business networks.

- Expand and diversify your portfolio of offerings to advance your company's skills.

- Shrink competitors list: If you are on the same team exclusively with each other, you are not competing with one another for a specific bid.

If any of these reasons resonate with you as applicable to the contract you are pursuing, you should team.

Your next path of action is to find the right teaming partner. You can find teammates in multiple places, using a combination of the methods described here to confirm your findings:

- Ask your customer what companies they think might be the best ones to team with, or listen closely for any hints they drop.

- Ask other teammates and your own seasoned staff who might know different companies.

- Look up top subcontractors by agency and research them further:

  - Look up spending by contractor for each agency at USAspending.gov or BGov.com.

  - See what types of areas they specialize in on their web sites.

- Check what kinds of contracts they have as their past performance back at USAspending, BGov.com, or www.FPDS.gov. If you cannot figure out what type of contract it is, you might want to look it up on the Internet or in capture research databases such as BGov, GovWin IQ, or Centurion Research.

- Sift through the agency's web site, which might route you to their MAC contracting vehicle web sites or state which companies are their top contractors, and check the mentor–protégé participant list for that agency.

- Ask your friendly small business advocate at the OSDBU.

- Check the interested vendors lists at FedBizOps.gov and GovWin IQ.

- Use the teaming module on GovWin (a free version of GovWin IQ) and The Federal Contractor Network (TFCN) at www.tfcn.us.

- Check SBA SUB-Net, a free tool for small businesses looking for opportunities, including teaming with primes that post solicitations on SUB-Net (http://web.sba.gov/subnet), and SBA's Dynamic Small Business Search is a good place to find small business teammates (http://web.sba.gov/pro-net).

- Consult the Department of Defense Subcontracting Directory from the Office of Small Business Programs (OSBP) that includes prime contractors with contact information and includes a guide to marketing to DOD: www.acq.osd.mil/osbp/sb/dod.shtml.

- Read such online publications as Government Executive (www.govexec.com) and Washington Technology (www.washingtontechnology.com) listing top government contractors.

- Check whether the company has a GSA schedule at GSA E-Library (www.gsaelibrary.gsa.gov/ElibMain/ElibHome).

- Search the Internet by keyword in the desired area of expertise.

How Good Teaming Partners Are Like Parking Spaces

Now that you have identified a few candidates for teaming, you should investigate them further to learn more about their capabilities and intention for this pursuit.

Good teaming partners are like parking spaces in an office building's parking lot. The closest ones to the building get taken by those diligent souls who arrive to work before 7 AM and have half their day's work done before their colleagues roll in at 9 AM. If you are one of those people who come in after 9 AM but before the lunch break has started or morning meetings have ended, you might have to circle around the lot to find the spot that's furthest away from the door, the one that no one wanted.

The key to success is to start the teammate identification process early, so that you don't find yourself teaming in the 11th hour with companies that will bring you no closer to winning than bidding by yourself.

Your path of action is then to start a dialogue early with the most competitive companies to get them on your team. You can find contact information on their web site and ask who is in charge of teaming for government contracts; use the number provided on FedBizOps in the interested vendors section, or look up their contact information on BGov, GovWin IQ, or Hoovers.com. You will need to make a good case to them for why they should work with you as opposed to going after it on their own or with someone else, select a teaming strategy, and then negotiate their place on your team (or your place on theirs). You can then repeat the process with a few others if your first choice elects to be a competitor instead of a teammate. All of this takes time, and there are others lurking in your tracks, so these tasks are time-sensitive.

Companies often start this process a year or more prior to the RFP issuance. They seek to lock up the potential teammates that they are absolutely certain will help them win, so that they cannot go with others.

There are few reasons to wait on committing to a company. The main one is an uncertain government procurement strategy (not knowing, for example, if the government makes it an 8(a) set aside versus just a small business set aside or full and open competition). In that case, you might want to maintain a dialogue and work as if you were teammates toward the win, but have an out clause in case the government switches gears on you.

It is important to note that on many procurements, you can join a team after the contract is awarded, but don't count on that as a major growth strategy, as it is harder to arrange.

Teaming Strategies: Types, Timing, and Pros and Cons

As you are in discussion with your potential teammates, you need to decide how you are going to form your team. The various forms of teaming, with their pros and cons, are described in Table 9-1.

Table 9-1. Types of teaming. Each teaming type has its advantages and disadvantages, so you need to carefully select the appropriate relationship for your specific pursuit.

Type of Teaming	Attributes	Pros	Cons
Prime	Holds the contract with the government. Manages its subs, if any.	Has direct relationship with the customer. Gets the most valuable past performance reference. Has greater control over price and scope.	Answers for the entire contract, no matter whether the subcontractors perform or don't perform. Needs to have the cash flow to pay the subcontractors and make purchases before being paid by the government.
Subcontractor	Has a contract with the company that holds the government contract. Might have subs of its own under it.	Gains access to the contract it otherwise wouldn't be able to obtain. Has ability to work in new markets with new customers and requirements. Earns past performance with the new customer.	Often has limited contact with the customer. Gets lesser credit for past performance on this contract. Is subject to prime trying to reduce price or scope after the award, or be relegated to low-value work. Has little control over price, so the team might not win.

Type of Teaming	Attributes	Pros	Cons
Joint venture (JV)	A separate legal entity with joint ownership and management. Might have its own personnel, facilities, or equipment (populated JV), or subcontract work to parent companies (unpopulated JV). Combines strengths and expedites decisions. Usually exists to bid on a specific contract.	All JV members are prime contractors. JV members without past performance get to leverage other members' past performance as if it were their own. Can protect from liability and lead to tax savings. Might help avoid the high cost structure of individual companies.	Could run up against occasional government bias against JVs based on negative experiences. Might be hard to administer and manage. Might require parent companies' financial and performance guarantees despite limited liability. 8(a) JVs could take time to be approved by SBA prior to proposal submission. Can be tricky because of size considerations and rules.
SBA Mentor–Protégé joint venture	A JV made of two companies: an 8(a) and a large business. Approved by SBA to be a mentor and protégé under 13 CFR 124.520. Can bid as a small business for any federal contract, if the protégé qualifies as small business for the size standard corresponding to the NAICS code in the RFP.	Gives huge advantage to companies that mentor 8(a)s to take advantage of the small business set-aside opportunities. Enables 8(a)s to grow aggressively. Can help 8(a)s raise capital.	Favors 8(a)–large firm arrangements the most, although there is a talk about creating a similar program for SDVOSBs and HUBZone companies. Because it is not just for a few deals but for many, it requires quite a bit of commitment on the part of both companies—with all the strings attached. You can learn more about the program at www.sba.gov/content/mentor-protege-program.

Type of Teaming	Attributes	Pros	Cons
Contractor team arrangement (CTA)	A teaming arrangement between two or more contractors that hold GSA Schedules to work together to meet agency requirements for a large and complex solution. Any team member can be designated the team leader. Each member is a prime. Those without a GSA schedule can be subs to primes with the schedule.	Helps each teammate compete for larger and more complex GSA orders, for which these teammates might not qualify individually. Each team member holds a government contract. The team leader is only responsible for their own and not their teammate's performance. Everyone gets direct past performance credit. Everyone bills at their prices.	Only works for GSA Federal Supply Schedule orders and doesn't transfer to other government contracts. All members of CTA have to be small to qualify for a small business set aside. It is unclear what happens when one member is nonperforming, and it is unclear how to handle other team members, leading to group irresponsibility.

Understanding Size Rules and Teaming Pitfalls That Could Disqualify You from Bidding

The majority of teaming arrangements usually take place between large and small businesses, where either one could be the prime depending on the procurement type. A full and open procurement where anyone can compete will usually have large businesses as the primes with small business subcontractors, whereas in small business set asides, you might see small–large arrangements, and even teams of multiple small businesses.

Because the size rules are complex, small business size is the largest cause for protests. Teaming could be one of the contributors to the problem. Therefore, you must understand the rules that have to do with the small business type and size, and how the government views your size.

The RFP will state a couple of things you have to pay attention to when teaming. It will include a NAICS code that will tell you what is considered the small business size for that procurement, and the associated dollar value that you cannot exceed as your average gross annual receipts for the past three years to qualify (for most businesses in the services industry), or the maximum number of employees (applicable to such businesses as manufacturing, telecommunications, and transportation companies). It will also state whether the contract is a set aside or full and open. On full and open contracts, the NAICS is there to show a threshold at which a large business will get credit for subcontracting with small businesses.

For example, if the RFP is released under NAICS 541512, Computer Systems Design Services, then the small business under that NAICS should have made no more than $25.5 million in average gross receipts for the past three years by the time of proposal submission.

As already mentioned in Chapter 2, you can find the full list of NAICS and their associated dollar and employee size standards at www.naics.com/naicsfiles/Size_Standards_Table.pdf.

It would be too simple if it ended there. In government contracting, there is a concept called *affiliation*, which essentially means that the government can add up the size of all the companies teaming together instead of looking at the size of just the small business prime, and treat the team as one bidder. If the government considers companies affiliated for size purposes, it will add teammates' gross receipts numbers (or employee numbers) together; if they do that, the sum might exceed the size standard of the NAICS for that RFP, rendering the team's proposal invalid. Behaviors that can leave you vulnerable to an assessment of affiliation include going after the same bids with the same team over and over again, using each other's offices on a regular basis, or repeatedly sharing resources such as a proposal team. Even if you do not advertise these facts, a protest by a bitter competitor who is privy to these details could lead to a decision that you have been acting as one company.

Generally speaking, you don't have to fear this in your regular teaming arrangements, even if you tend to go with the same teammates, because teaming agreements don't automatically create an affiliation. Just make sure that you have a formal teaming agreement in place.

JVs that are not of the SBA mentor–protégé kind, however, can create an affiliation. You have to follow many rules if you want to bid on small business set-aside solicitations as a JV. JVs should be formed for a specific "bundled" pursuit (where the government has combined multiple different requirements to form a larger project), before you submit the proposal. JVs have to be formed for a particular purpose, such as winning a specific contract.

To avoid affiliation, a small business JV can be awarded no more than three contracts in two years (with some exceptions). If the JV is ongoing, and is pursuing multiple contracts, it is considered a partnership, not a JV, and the companies will be affiliated for size purposes.

For a procurement having a revenue-based size standard, the dollar value of the procurement, including options, has to exceed half the size standard corresponding to the NAICS code assigned to the contract. When the employee-based size standard applies, the dollar value of the procurement has to exceed $10 million.

For example, if you are going after a $5 million contract, and the NAICS code for the procurement is $7 million, it is perfectly okay because $5 million is more than $3.5 million (which is half of $7 million).

You also need to follow the rules shown in Table 9-2 that are specific to each type of small business JV. If these rules don't make sense and you are doing it for the first time, get a government contracts lawyer or contact a consultant to guide you through the rules. There are even more nuances and considerations in forming a JV, so use Table 9-2 to check if you qualify in general, and then work through the details with professional help.

Table 9-2. Small business joint venture rules. It is important that you understand the rules and any exceptions that apply to your team, to avoid repercussions.

Type of JV	Rules
8(a)	One firm is 8(a) certified.
	All partners in the JV are small businesses (unless it is a mentor–protégé JV) under the procurement NAICS code.
	The 8(a) firm must own 51 percent or more of the JV and receive 51 percent or more of the JV's net profits. It should control the JV, including furnishing a project manager.
	The JV has to get SBA District Office approval before proposal submission.
HUBZone	All partners must be HUBZone certified.
SDVOSB	Managing partner must be SDVOSB, and SDVOSB must furnish the project manager.
	All partners must be small.
	51 percent or more of net profits must go to SDVOSB.

Type of JV	Rules
WOSB or EDWOSB	One member must be an EDWOSB or WOSB.
	JV agreement must designate an EDWOSB or WOSB as the managing venturer of the JV, and an employee of the managing venturer as the project manager.
	The WOSB or EDWOSB must provide a copy of the JV agreement to the contracting officer and can do so through the SBA's WOSB Program Repository.
Small business	All partners must be small businesses.
	Each partner must be smaller than the NAICS code size, provided the procurement is bundled.

Another set of rules you need to be mindful of applies to how much work share a prime can subcontract and how much they must perform on their own. Generally the government doesn't like pass-throughs. Here is what a government requires small businesses to perform in a teaming arrangement:

- In the services arena (but not construction), the small business prime has to perform 50 percent of the cost of the contract incurred for personnel with its own employees.

- In the supplies or products arena, the prime has to provide 50 percent of the cost of manufacturing the supplies or products, not including the cost of materials.

- In general construction, the prime has to execute at least 15 percent of the cost of the contract with its own employees (not including the cost of materials).

- In special trade construction, the prime has to be responsible for 25 percent of the cost of the contract with its own employees, again, not including materials.

Traditionally, the government has not enforced these rules very strictly, but in the past couple of years the SBA has been cracking down on companies that violate them egregiously. SBA even went as far as slapping down a top-50 government contractor, GTSI, for small business contracting rules violations. As a result, their business suffered so badly that they were eventually sold.

The government is contemplating a rule change whereby it would create a mentor–protégé program for SDVOSBs and HUBZone companies that has similar benefits to the 8(a) mentor–protégé program, such as an ability to form a JV with a large business without being affiliated for size purposes. It will be exciting if and when it happens.

How to Qualify a Teammate to Help You Win and Avoid Problems Down the Road

When you are selecting teammates, you have to adopt a certain mindset. You want to make sure that you are seeking not just any company with complementary capabilities, but an all-star team member. You have to make sure that your teammates have the right capabilities for this customer; they have superb past performance; and they are bringing the knowledge, passion, and even possibly a relationship with the customer. Try to avoid adding members to the team who are less than a perfect fit just because you have a great relationship with them. Remember, you have to win the proposal by convincing the government that your team is superior, and you cannot do so if you cut companies in just "because." Everyone has to be a superstar and make a major contribution—this is how you win.

Make sure that you analyze your solution for every area of the work scope, and determine the gaps each teammate has to fill, rather than approximating and guessing. This is how you avoid problems down the road; you don't want to find that you are missing a key capability during the proposal.

As you get ready to finalize your teaming decisions, you need to perform careful due diligence on your candidate teammates to decide whether you want to partner with these companies, and what issues should be addressed in your teaming agreement.

You have to thoroughly examine the company by answering questions such as these:

- What is this company's reputation with the customer?

- What is the company's reputation in the industry?

- What is the company's past performance with this customer and other customers?

- Specifically, does this contractor have a reputation of completing quality work on schedule and within budget?

- Do they have any "black eyes" such as cure letters or terminations for default?

- Have you teamed with this company before, and how successful was your teaming arrangement?

- Does the company have any known organizational conflicts of interest (OCI) or appearance of OCI for this procurement?

- Can you get good information on the company's financial state, assets, and liabilities that would assure you that this is a solvent and responsible partner? What does the D&B show, and what's in the company's annual reports?

- Does the company have solid accounting and administrative mechanisms to be part of this contract?

  - In other words, some companies might not be DCAA-approved. If the procurement requires it, you might have bet on the wrong horse.

  - Conversely, some contracts may require you and even your subcontractors to do earned value management (EVM) reporting, and you have to make sure that your subcontractors have the ability to track and deliver the right data.

- Does the company have any past or pending lawsuits against them?

- Do any of the company's executives have individual legal claims against them? Have any of them been "debarred" or prohibited from doing business with the government?

- Is the company on the list of contractors excluded from federal procurement programs (you can check in the EPLS in Sam.gov)?

- What kind of press is there about the company per your Internet search?

- Are all the required licenses, bonding and insurance documentation, clearances, and necessary certifications in order?

- Would they be a competitor who would use the knowledge gained on this pursuit with you or against you in the future?

- What resources is this company willing to dedicate to positioning for and preparing the proposal?

Carefully weigh all the answers. The more work you do up front, the better off you will be during the proposal, and the more chances you will have to win. The earlier you start this process, the better. If you do it early enough, you might even be able to run your teammate choice by the customer, vetting the companies, and making changes if necessary.

Negotiating a Binding Teaming Agreement

Once you start teaming discussions with a company, you will have to sign a mutual nondisclosure agreement (NDA). It will protect your proprietary information and confidentiality. This way, you can work out all the details on teaming for a specific pursuit. After the NDA, some companies might use a letter of intent to sign a teaming agreement as an interim step, but normally the path is straight from an NDA to a teaming agreement.

The first facet of your teaming negotiations usually involves who is going to be the prime and who will be the sub. It might be obvious and the decision is easily made. In some cases, though, it is not always a straightforward decision like in the case of a small business set-aside opportunity, and you don't have to accept the status quo.

Many times a smaller and less experienced company can lead the team if it plays the game right. For example, a small business might have identified a great opportunity, structured the early capture effort correctly, and built relationships with the customer that now prefers this small business to win and do the work. Perhaps there is no other small business to implement the rule of two, and the procurement ends up in a full and open competition. This small business could then reach out to an established large company in that agency to augment its past performance and experience, but insist that it would prime for the customer relationship and preparation reasons.

Normally prime is a more beneficial position, but there can be many reasons why companies wouldn't prime. For example, their past performance as a prime might not be strong enough to win, or they might simply not have the resources to write the bulk of the proposal. For these reasons, many companies live on subcontracting dollars for years as a matter of preference before they venture into priming.

The next step is to sign a binding teaming agreement. A small business will have to negotiate hard to protect its interests. Usually the prime or the larger company will send their teaming agreement form to a smaller firm, and it will have to hash out the details and address any problematic clauses.

You have to understand how the game is played to succeed in the teaming agreement negotiations process. Prime contractors and subcontractors have different goals for teaming and their interests naturally conflict. Primes are looking for exclusive commitment and proposal support but want to reserve the right to award to a cheaper source after they win, especially if they underbid other portions of the cost proposal and now are trying to get well.

The subcontractor will want to lock in the subcontract after award, after all that they have done to bring it about, and it is usually in their best interests to go nonexclusive. You have to strike the right balance of obligations and privileges, and make sure that you have clarity on what you sign.

As you can tell from the agreement, you have to address many areas proactively and discuss them up front. Once you have decided whether you are going to prime, sub, create a CTA, form a JV, form a mentor–protégé relationship to form a JV, or gain benefits from agency evaluation, here is what you need to discuss:

- **Exclusivity:** Ideally, you want the teammate to be exclusive to you, meaning that they are teaming only with you for this pursuit, and no one else. If the contract is awarded to someone else, your teammate might later team with the winning prime because your teaming agreement terminates. Sometimes your teammate might not be exclusive, so you want to specify how they are going to support your proposal effort.

- **Obligation to team:** Now that the subcontractor has spent all its resources in supporting the proposal effort, does the teaming agreement obligate the prime to award the subcontract to the company? Or would it mean that the subcontractor is going to negotiate in good faith, meaning that the real negotiations might not begin until the contract award, and the subcontractor could lose the subcontract to someone else after having done all the proposal work?

  Should the prime agree in advance to pay the subcontractor for proposal expenses if the government somehow cancels the subcontractor's part of the work or disapproves the subcontract? How will the prime handle a sudden increase in the subcontractor's prices? How will the subcontractor handle the prime's wanting to self-perform the scope, give the subcontractor less qualified positions, or award the subcontract to another, cheaper provider? How will the dispute be resolved?

- **Capture, proposal, and negotiations preaward:** How is everyone going to do capture and proposal work together? What specific personnel will they provide? How will they share costs of the capture and proposal effort? Who will represent the team in negotiations with the government and how will others support these negotiations? In what capacity? Ideally, you want people to support your proposal if they are getting work share. Sometimes it becomes problematic with some contractors not holding up their end, so you have to have penalties in place scope-wise to "incentivize" them to comply. It is harder to pull off with a smaller company as a prime, and the large company not performing. You might want to put a provision for them to compensate you for the use of outside proposal consultants in case they fail to deliver proposal resources.

- **Special quid-pro-quo clauses:** Are there any special stipulations with regard to the work share? For example, would sharing work on this project by the prime with the teammate take place in exchange for the work share on another project that the teammate primes? Do you need to make other stipulations, such as conditions on whether you win this work, and whether they win the work? Is there equitable amount of work share that you are discussing? How will you determine equitability?

- **Management controls:** Who is going to manage the project on a daily basis (usually a PM from the prime)? Will there be team representatives required as part of the program management office (PMO) or special team leads to reach for resources? Will there be ways to reach compromise in daily decisions? To whom would conflicts be escalated? What is the proper hierarchy when addressing performance issues with a teammate's employee, for example?

- **Roles and responsibilities during project execution:** Who is responsible for performing what part when the contract is awarded? How much expertise, capital, people, facilities, equipment, and other contributions does each teammate need to make for project execution? What specific personnel is each team member required to provide, especially key personnel? Are these personnel dedicated 100 percent of the time, or some other set amount of time to the project? What are the performance responsibilities where it comes to performance quality, cost, and schedule? Are there incentives and disincentives?

- **Ability to subcontract to the next tier:** Can a teammate subcontract some portion of the work to the next tier of subcontractors?

- **Insurance, bonding, and indemnification:** Will the parties' existing bonding and insurance cover this new pursuit, or will the parties have to purchase separate coverage? Who will have to get this coverage, and who will pay? Will teammates share the costs? Can one party indemnify the other party, and what acts and claims can it cover?

After the contract gets awarded, the subcontracting agreement replaces the teaming agreement, as shown in Figure 9-1.

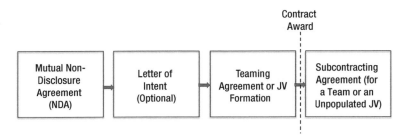

Figure 9-1. Legal documents progression. Your teaming arrangement requires proper documentation to ensure you are protected and don't violate any rules.

Teaming agreements are good to include with your proposal as part of the cost volume, even if they are not required, and it is also useful to have state that you have prenegotiated subcontracting terms. This way you can claim you could hit the ground running immediately after the award, rather than being mired in lengthy negotiations.

Do note that teaming agreements are hard to enforce because they are too nonspecific. You have to solicit help of a good lawyer to put together a bulletproof agreement text for you. Don't rely solely on a lawyer or a contracts person to negotiate the terms of the agreement on your behalf, however. You have to understand every single clause that goes into the agreement yourself, so read the documents you sign carefully.

To be enforceable, it is important that the teaming agreement spells out the exact scope by tasks, with a description of your effort that is as precise as possible. Alternatively, it could indicate the percentage of work to be guaranteed to you (in either labor hours or dollars). You could also identify the exact positions you are going to get by labor categories. The more clarity you have, the better.

Once you have your teaming agreements signed, you will have to integrate your exclusive teammates into your capture and proposal effort. This way, you will use the combined talent of your team to figure out how to beat the competition. It will be especially useful to get them to participate in your solution development brainstorming, discussed in the following chapter.

Prepare a Solution Before the Request for Proposal

Now that you have the team lined up, you are in the final stretch—the countdown to the RFP issuance might have already started. There is a lot to do because you have to put together the solution that you will showcase in your proposal. Solution development is where all the aspects of capture finally come together and culminate in succinct work products that summarize all the work you have done during capture. While fighting the natural tendency to skip solution development, you will have to run brainstorming sessions to figure out exactly what you are going to propose. You will need to structure your brainstorming correctly to avoid wasted time, as it is the easiest thing in the world to spend hours discussing your approach and getting nowhere useful. One prerequisite to running efficient sessions is to postulate the requirements before the government issues the RFP. Then you have to use a formulaic structure and checklists to guide your experts in figuring out solutions. This chapter takes you through the sticky wickets of solution development and explains what you can figure out in advance of the RFP issuance, and how to do it without wasting precious resources.

Fight the Natural Tendency to Skip Solution Development

I wish I could tell you that once you write a great proposal, you can recycle it over and over again. That might work for product-based companies, although even then you have to continuously update your boilerplate documents to keep them fresh, and customize them carefully for each customer. It doesn't work at all in the services and solutions arena. Government customers see boilerplate a mile away, and they consider it disrespectful. You actually have to bite the bullet and develop a solution: what you are going to propose this time, in response to the specific requirements of a particular customer.

Solution development normally consists of a number of workshops or brainstorming sessions in the latter part of capture designed to prepare you for the proposal. Your task is to put your proposal in a whole different league by wowing your customer with the details of the solution and persuasive presentation. Needless to say, it takes time and effort.

Solution development involves multiple SMEs getting together and figuring out the approach you are going to propose. The nature of this process will cause you to inevitably wonder: Why do you have to do all this work in advance, spending money and valuable resources on an RFP you haven't seen yet? It's not like you actually have an excess of free time or money; I don't know anyone who does.

But you have to face the truth: Once the RFP drops on you, the typical 30 days you get will be barely enough to prepare a winning proposal even if you have done capture and run solution development sessions. We discuss in the next chapter why this is the case.

Without your solution developed ahead of time, 30 days is enough time to write a proposal only if you are the incumbent and know the job inside out— or if the subject matter of your proposal is within your writers' core expertise and this is exactly the kind of work you do all the time.

If you are in a situation where your proposal duration is even shorter than 30 days (as is predominantly the case in government contracting these days), you absolutely have to mobilize yourself and commit the resources to solution development as early as you are able to do so.

With solutions development, you have a couple of options. One is to do classical brainstorming where people sit around the conference room table, and jump to whiteboards to discuss something that never makes it to the proposal, and at best gets the participants to start thinking about the offer. This option consumes a lot of time, is inefficient, and could be exactly why government contractors often justify avoiding or greatly curtailing solution development in their pursuits.

Another option is to run formulaic facilitated workshops with a specific set of outcomes in mind, with clear agendas, and with the right people. This is the preferred path of action.

Instead of skipping solution development, like many companies do, consider an alternative where you will use your SMEs' time efficiently and effectively to produce real results.

Structure Your Brainstorming Correctly to Avoid Wasted Time

The first step in running successful solution development workshops is to invite the right people to your sessions. You have to look at the customer requirements and check whether you have identified all the critical technical and management staff skills and check if any skills are lacking. You can bring in these SMEs by reaching into your organization, or even reaching out to your teammates or subcontractors. This is also your first real test to determine whether your team is capable of responding to this RFP and writing a winning proposal. At this stage, though, you are able to add another teammate if a critical skill is missing. It is a lot harder to course-correct if you wait until the RFP is issued.

Similarly, you need to identify or recruit the right SMEs for project execution; these are the people whose resumes you will include in the proposal. You might also need them for the demos of your technical capability as part of acquisition process, or for the orals if your customer requires them.

The second step is to prioritize what kind of brainstorming sessions you will run first. For most proposals, you will have to organize a number of sessions that are dedicated to figuring out the following:

- **Technical solution:** The exact step-by-step how-to of what you will have to do on a daily basis to execute this project, including process flowcharts, schedule, tools, people responsible for getting the work done, and so on.

- **Management solution:** How you will organize your team to manage the job, and what tools and techniques you will use to make sure the project is completed well, on time, and within budget.

- **Risks and their mitigations:** Showing to your customer that you have thought through possible areas where your project could fail, and added failsafe measures throughout.

- **Staffing approach:** How you will allocate personnel resources to the project, which is usually intimately tied to your technical and management solutions.

- **Pricing strategy:** How you will go ahead and make sure that your solution is cost-competitive.

You will also prepare as many pieces of your proposal in advance as you can, such as your past performance references, resumes of the staff you are going to bid, and written plans such as your subcontracting approach, to give yourself a leg up on your competition.

The third step is to ensure that your requirements are clear, and you come to every meeting with an agenda and a set of checklists to methodically guide everyone through the process, which we cover next.

How to Guess at the Requirements Before the Government Issues the Proposal

Now that you are preparing to brainstorm, you might wonder this: How are you going to figure out what the customer is going to ask for in the RFP?

Your first order of business during the intelligence-gathering stage is to check whether an old RFP is available for this contract if it is a recompete. In fact, there are relatively few new requirements, other than in the fields of R&D.

The government has to periodically (usually every five years) recompete opportunities, and you might be able to get your hands on an old RFP from sources such as Centurion and GovWin IQ that keep these documents on file. You then have to look at the scope of work and figure out whether you need to make any "adjustments" because your intel may show that this go-round some things could be different.

Note that sometimes the government bundles multiple past contracts together into what they call a new requirement. Do your research and check if they happened to compose this "new" requirement from several existing contracts.

You could luck out if the government issues a draft RFP (DRFP). It doesn't happen on every procurement, but is recommended on the government side to get better feedback from the industry. On occasion, instead of a DRFP, a customer might issue just the statement of work (SOW) for the industry to comment on, shedding some light as to what the RFP might look like.

If you cannot get your hands on customer-issued technical requirements, you have to "postulate" the requirements, which takes some research and analytical work. Generally speaking, your task is to piece together as much information as possible from this customer and create your own SOW. Look for similar SOWs available from the government for other projects that resemble this one. Even if it is a different customer, they might buy the exact same type of services or products, and therefore will have already created a SOW for them. If a problem is known, but there are no requirements available, you have to develop the requirements as if you were the government creating an RFP. You might not be as detailed as you would like to be, but at least you will have a list of requirements along the macro parameters.

Also search for any RFPs and RFQs from the same contracting office that's going to issue your solicitation to see how they tend to structure their proposal instructions and evaluation criteria. Then go ahead and "Frankenstein" your own RFP out of all the pieces of intel that you have gathered.

Now that you have the set of requirements, you need to prioritize what area is the most important for you to explore first. If the RFP issuance is imminent, you could start with the hardest topic, and sequence all the other topics to come after.

Having a specific topic in mind will enable you to initiate a brainstorming session, fuel the discussion, get precise feedback from the SMEs, and identify areas that require additional fact finding, refinement, and other action items.

Go ahead and invite all the right SMEs to partake in the session. You can do it either in person or virtually, using a combination of a web meeting tool (such as GoToMeeting) and tablets (such as Wacom tablet, www.wacom.com) to create a virtual whiteboard. Schedule an interval of at least two hours, and no longer than four hours, to prevent inefficiency due to exhaustion. Facilitate the discussion and be ruthless to prevent people from going on tangents.

Use Checklists to Guide Your Experts in Figuring Out Solutions

Even with all the facilitation, your discussion is bound to wander if you don't impose a better structure. To prevent an aimless discussion, it is important to use a set of checklists for your brainstorming sessions. We have a set that we provide to our students as a handout in our Advanced Capture Management course, so you don't have to develop your own. These checklists will help you design an approach unique to your specific project, time and time again.

A checklist essentially spells out what you need to discuss, and provides a set of solution options you could use, so you don't have to keep reinventing the wheel. It is better than boilerplate, however, because it doesn't create an illusion that a solution is already developed (and it is not). It is a decision-making framework for how you need to think through a solution.

An example follows of the mix of steps, tips, and reminders of the available options that go into a management approach development checklist. (This is one of the tasks that go into developing a comprehensive management approach.)

Design an Organization Chart

☐ Create an initial organization. Make decisions regarding the candidacy and functions for the people you bid: PM, their deputy, transition manager, quality manager, your SMEs, and any other key personnel either required or great to have shown by name for the project.

☐ Show the project is important. Skip a level of management if necessary for built-in escalation and executive sponsorship.

☐ Pick a format for your org chart:

- Classical org chart with resources and reporting chain of command. Make a decision whether you are going to make it into a photo organization chart, with photos of your key personnel. This format is especially beneficial if the customer knows and likes your team.

- Functional chart, especially useful when you don't know the names of all the people who will be holding positions, or don't have enough room for the level of detail to show all the people. Call out the functions: Security Management instead of Evan Jones, Security Manager, for example. A functional chart can be put together as well by showing Integrated Project Teams (IPTs) if your customer favors the idea.

- Cross between classical org chart and functional chart: Show names, positions, relationships, roles, and responsibilities/functions.

- Graphic org chart or functional chart that explicitly states the benefits of each feature right on the chart. Show benefits of why you are organized a certain way, explaining every element on the org chart, such as:

- Program management office (PMO)

- Integrated product or project teams

- Flat structure

- Organization by function

- Organization by location

- Organization by resource allocation

- Split by levels of responsibility

- Organization by teammate

☐ Spell out great authority granted to the PM, up to what amount can they make their own decisions without further approvals, and what are their mandates.

☐ Are you going to add any unusual functions as a "value added," like a board of advisors ("gray beards"), customer advocate position, or any other innovative position or governing body to make your work more efficient?

☐ Where is your customer on the org chart? It is important to show the customer in your graphics, and your org chart is the perfect place for showing who is going to be the interface with the customer, or the single point of contact. Will there be multiple interfaces?

☐ Should you show all the stakeholders and interfaces with these stakeholders here, or will you save them for a communications chart?

My recommended approach is to type your answers straight into the checklist and to photograph everything on the whiteboard to ensure that you capture the material from the brainstorming session. If you are running a virtual session, use "print screen" function on your PC to record all the whiteboarding exercises.

As you walk through the checklist during your brainstorming session, you might find that some questions get answered swiftly, but others could take much thought and time to explore. Often your discussions might lead to more specific questions and breakout sessions. In the end, using a checklist to work through every solution facet is a comprehensive and well-rounded approach, because it will help explore every aspect of the solution, rather than have you zoom into some parts and ignore others.

Note that for technical people, technical sections are often easier to brainstorm on than management sections. Here is an excerpt of the couple of dozen topics that go into developing a technical solution, with each topic having similar level of detail that was shown in the preceding organization chart example.

1. Reach an agreement on the customer and system's context and environment. Answering this question will help you write the bigger "Why" (why is this project important to the customer?) and "What" (What is it that we are delivering? What problem are we solving? What are the benefits?) for the technical approach overview.

2. Before proceeding to developing the solution, reach common understanding of system requirements and specifications. Remember not to take any exceptions from the RFP because this will make you noncompliant, get you a deficiency, and make you lose points during the evaluation.

3. Elaborate on the material from the win theme development session and review the competitive posture.

4. Investigate the opportunities to leverage your team's larger organizations' technical capabilities and not one department or sector: IR&D, organization-wide resources, thought leaders, vendor alliances, and so on.

5. Identify key trade-offs as part of your decision-making process that led you to offer the superior solution to the customer. This is another "Why" for your sections in addition to the powerful introductory paragraphs that answer "Why" the customer should carefully read the sections in the first place. This "Why" gives the rationale for why you have selected this solution, why you have made these decisions, and how your decisions serve the customer's best interests. These trade-offs also provide an award justification "cut-and-paste" language for the evaluator—showing why to select your solution—and why not to select your competitors' solutions.

6. Develop a top-level technical approach. This is the material that goes in the introductory (summary) section upfront that integrates all the elements of the technical approach that fall into

a coherent picture, or, in other words, "a thousand-foot view." This way the customer can know right away what you are offering, rather than having to read through the rest of your proposal to find out.

7. Take each system component or subsystem and expand on the details and elements of your solution. Based on these solution details, you can develop not only text, but flowcharts and graphics that explain the advantages of your solution.

Determine who are the stakeholders and users of your solution, and how this insight affects your solution design. Understanding of the stakeholders shows your customer that you would not make them look bad in front of their customers and other agencies, and you can showcase this comprehension in your proposal.

Most technical people fall into a trap when they spell out in detail what will be done, but are sorely remiss in figuring out the detailed how. Make sure that you focus your session on how you can do the following:

- Show the customer that you truly understand the stated and unstated requirements and the environment.

- Show your step-by-step approach, including people, processes, and tools you will use.

- Demonstrate low technical risk.

- Prove your technical solution's superiority while ghosting the competition.

- Offer overwhelming proof that you can deliver exactly what you promise to deliver.

Your technical approach must resonate with the customer's goals, issues, and hot button issues; it should support improved performance, reduced cost and have a reasonable implementation schedule; it must be low-risk; and it has to ghost competitors and support justification for change to improve mission performance.

Your price strategy will warrant a similar brainstorming session, usually after the initial management and technical approach brainstorming sessions are complete.

Price is a huge part of your solution. There are many variables you must consider in developing your price strategy. Most important, you must gather intelligence on the evaluation factors that your customer will choose. *Best value* evaluation means that the customer will not necessarily choose the lowest bidder, and in some cases you might be safe as long as you bid within 10 percent of the key competitors, fall within the government's budget, and have the best technical approach that brings tremendous value to the customer. If you know that your approach is on par with your competition and won't be significantly better, however, you need to be cheaper than them. An industry statistic states that as many as 90 percent of all best value awards go to the lowest bidder.

If the evaluation is *lowest price technically acceptable (LPTA)*, then you have to be cheaper than the competition as long as your technical approach is compliant. The government decides if you pass or fail your technical and management approach. The lowest bidder will win automatically among those who get a pass.

Do understand that customer's budget is a major factor. Price must be within the customer's funding stream, so you have to make a significant effort to figure out what the customer's budget might be. Proposal pricing deserves a book of its own, and we also teach a course, Developing a Winning Cost Volume, that can be immensely helpful. To give you some quick guidance and get you started, however, you should consider asking the customer directly about the budget. Some of the more sophisticated government personnel will be willing to at least give you a ballpark, if not the exact number. They know that it will only cause you to come in under that number to be competitive.

You should also check the President's Budget, study Exhibits 53 and 300 for IT procurements, check Program Objective Memorandum (POM) DOD agencies use for budget formulation, and then back out as much as 15 percent for government personnel costs to manage the program.

You also need to develop price to win (PTW) to guide the solution. PTW is a number based on your calculations of what your competitors might bid—and what your price should be as a result to beat your competition. PTW must be within the customer's budget, and must seem realistic to the customer—able to meet RFP requirements. It must be within the range of key competitors (and if the procurement is best value, not necessarily lower). It should be executable and profitable for your company. Developing a PTW is both an art and craft, so get the professionals involved. Consulting companies can help get you the right expert to guide you through the process.

Your *pricing strategy* is a way to sharpen your pencil to cut your price and arrive at the PTW. You can use a variety of techniques, which will be part of your brainstorming. Here are but a few examples of a thought process you might go through in determining your price strategy:

- **Determine your options for facility:** Where are personnel going to work (customer site, your office, etc.)? Do you need warehouses, labs, and so on? Potentially examine use of alternative facility. Vary rates (on the customer's site vs. fully burdened) and adjust burdens and facilities (for large contracts). Recalculate and use new wrap rates based on your latest utilization percentages.

- **What are customer needs vs. wants where it comes to staffing?** Give them the absolute minimum, only what they need.

- **Don't add out-year escalation:** Promote personnel and keep all the rates the same instead of increasing the price every year by a certain percentage to account for raises and inflation; decrease the level of effort of your most expensive staff positions, and "green" your personnel in the out years. If you hold your labor rates constant over the optional contract periods, it is the same as giving your customer a discount.

- **Determine if you need to lower your fee (profit) to be more competitive:** Right now government contractors make an average of 5 percent, and this number keeps going down.

- **See if some tasks could be accomplished less expensively:** Perhaps subcontracting terms could be changed. Instead of time and materials (T&M), try firm fixed price or cost plus award fee; or allocate work to those subcontractors that have cheaper pricing for specific labor categories.

Your contract type will dictate your cost strategies, as they will vary depending on how the government plans to contract the work from you.

Figure 10-1 shows a classical representation of quadrants for pricing and value. As far as your price strategy goes, you need to be in the lower right quadrant right below your competition. This way you can almost assure your win.

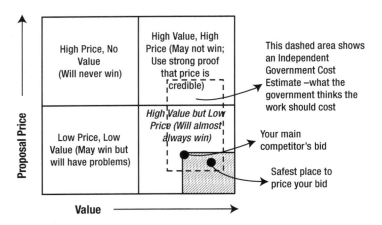

Figure 10-1. Price and value quadrants. The safest place to price your proposal is lower than your competition, with greater value, but within the Independent Government Cost Estimate.

What Can You Figure Out in Advance, and How to Do It Without Wasting Time or Money

Your advance preparation should include flowcharts, notes, graphics, and bullet points that describe every aspect of your solution, proposal section by proposal section. Ideally, this information will enable you to go straight to drafting your proposal, without much additional brainstorming, once the RFP is issued.

Your goal is to stage as many materials as possible in advance for your proposal, so that you experience less stress at the proposal stage, and use all the time allotted on more important tasks. You will be able to develop more drafts of the same section so that it evolves into more mature and polished writing. You will also be able to hone your cost solution through several iterations, because it is heavily dependent on your technical, management, and staffing approaches. In the end, it might make a difference between winning and losing your proposal.

The types of materials you want to set up in advance are many. You need to make decisions on your key personnel and obtain their resumes. You will then need to format all their resumes in a consistent template that follows your customer's exact requirements. Select which references you and your teammates will use for past performance and put all of them in a consistent format as well.

Issue all the data calls requesting information from your subcontractors in advance, giving everyone ample time to prepare thoughtful responses and provide the necessary information that you already know will go into your proposal. You can also take care of the mechanics such as getting all your teammates' logos in the right format.

You should set up the template for your proposal and design an attractive cover that reflects your customer's color scheme (usually "borrowed" from their logo colors) and the proposal theme. You will also want to prepare your executive summary draft, cost proposal draft, any plans such as quality assurance plans or subcontracting plans, and collect in one place any other information that you already know you will need.

Finally, you need to develop a proposal plan. This plan essentially boils down to where you are going to run your proposal, who will participate from you and your teammates in proposal writing, and what roles they will play. You should also create a provisional proposal schedule you can then change based on the actual release date and deadlines.

Figure 10-2 shows the benefits of preparing your solution, all the prestaged materials, and proposal plan in advance.

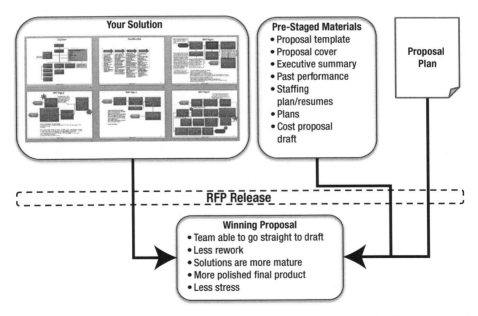

Figure 10-2. Solution development components. Your brainstormed solution flowcharts and graphics, pre-staged materials, and proposal plan enable you to prepare for the proposal in style.

With all the materials ready, you will be able to position yourself for a winning bid. The next two chapters take you through the steps necessary to develop your proposal and submit it to the government.

The Race Is On: Get Ready to Write a Winning Proposal

It's on. The RFP is out, probably released on an inconvenient date and after a few delays, right before the holidays. You could get 30 days or even a bit longer, up to 45 days—but if your RFP is anything like the ones a majority of government contractors get these days, you will have two weeks or less to respond. On occasion a proposal might get extended, but you cannot count on it until it happens.

Those who are new to the process or don't know what a winning proposal looks like might think that they have plenty of time to put together a winning response, but those in the know realize you don't have a minute to waste even if you have an almost unheard-of luxury of 45 days. Your job is to analyze the RFP, confirm that you still want to bid on this opportunity, and then outline the proposal, schedule your writing task as if it were a project, and get the document ready and delivered by the deadline. The deadline is firm: If you miss it, you will be disqualified.

It's important to remember that your job is to win a proposal, not just to complete it by the deadline. With that in mind, you need to learn the proper process for developing winning documents. In this chapter, we'll cover why proposals win (and why many don't), how to make an educated decision to bid or not bid on a proposal, how to read government RFPs correctly to understand exactly what the government is looking for, and finally the reasons why you need a proposal process, and how it should work to get you maximum results.

Why Proposals Win (and Why Many Don't)

Before you dive headlong into writing a proposal, your **first** task is to get a proper mindset about this whole competitive proposal business. You have to have the right appreciation of this undertaking.

Writing government proposals can be rewarding but is tough. It is a full-blown profession. When you venture into proposals, you need training in writing persuasive proposals, professional help, or both. Fortunately, they are easily obtainable. You might find it useful to watch free instructional webinars on various aspects of proposal development at www.ostglobalsolutions.com/training/webinars, or consider OST Global Solutions courses and consulting support.

Second, winning proposals have to be compliant with and responsive to every requirement that the government has included in the RFP. Compliance is the first order of business of government proposals. Before your proposal can be compelling, it has to be compliant.

Compliance means paying attention to every item that the government has requested, down to every word. For example, when you read the following requirement: "Offeror shall demonstrate the experience and ability to perform tasks required for Management Support (PWS 1.5.1. and subparagraphs)," you will know that when you write about how you will accomplish each task under Management Support, you will have to highlight two things separately: "experience" and "ability to perform." You will also need to read the Performance Work Statement (PWS) paragraph 1.5.1 and its subparagraphs, and address every single requirement in the exact order in which it appears in the PWS. If you are noncompliant with one or more requirements, your proposal will be either downgraded or found nonresponsive and thrown out of the competition.

Third, winning proposals is a team effort. It is easy to miss or misinterpret requirements because they are so numerous within a proposal. Someone has to review your work. Even if you are the only writer in your company, someone else should check your writing for you.

Once you grow your business and start responding to larger proposals, you will see that it takes numerous parties to shape your proposal into a winner. Your and your teammates' SMEs have to participate and lend their technical know-how and ingenuity to find innovative solutions to customer problems. Your business development and capture personnel have to contribute customer insight. Your writers have to translate all the work into persuasive text and graphics. Your pricing experts will price the entire offer competitively and in line with the technical proposal. Your desktop publishers and graphic artists will have to make the proposal attractive, and your editors will polish it. Your contracts manager will make sure you are compliant with all the regulatory requirements and clauses. Your reviewers will ensure that your proposal "answers the mail"—in other words, that it speaks to every requirement; will score high during the evaluation where it comes to approaches, offers, and facts; and is winnable.

Fourth, proposals are expensive to develop because they take so much effort. I have seen an estimate that suggested that a proposal can cost up to $2,000 per page. The good news is that you don't "graduate" to those costs for a while—and, when you do, you will have the money to pay for them. You will probably be relying on your prime as a subcontractor to shoulder the majority of the proposal writing, while you are participating, watching, and learning. Smaller proposals are usually (but not always) simpler and require less effort to win than large proposals with steep competition.

The government even reimburses you for your business development and proposal expenses by paying for your overhead and general and administrative (G&A) expenses that are billed to the government in addition to your hourly rate and fee (profit). Proposals are a necessary investment, though: If you don't bid, you won't win. And if you try to scrimp and save on proposals instead of pulling out all the stops to win, your win rate will likely suffer.

Fifth, your content has to be sharp. You need to make sure that you don't fall into common traps such as skipping solution development, or going with the same tired boilerplate text from proposal to proposal. As I already mentioned, customers can see through that, and get extremely annoyed—which results in losses. Remember that every proposal is different, even to the same customer for the same service. Circumstances are always different and these can lead to shifting customer priorities. You have to emphasize the current priorities and explain "how" you will do what you will do for the customer, and not just "what." "How" goes back to taking the time to think through the solution, and then describing step by step how you will implement it.

Sixth, you have to realize that your proposals are not technical papers, despite dry technical requirements. They are sales documents and therefore have to be highly persuasive but devoid of sleazy salesmanship and marketing lingo. Your proposals will require customer focus, win themes that we discussed earlier in this book, graphics on every other page, and professional presentation. Your writing has to be grammatically correct, personal, and highly readable. Your proposals have to impact your evaluators emotionally to sway them into trusting your abilities to do a good job if you get the award.

Seventh, writing winning proposals requires a process: Proposals are complex planning and writing projects with short deadlines that you have to undertake in a specific way to succeed. We discuss this process later in this chapter.

In a nutshell, many proposals lose for common reasons, which include failure to successfully manage the seven areas just discussed. Their loss usually has nothing to do with being less deserving as a company. They are just poor proposals, making it easy for the competitors to win. Don't let your proposals fall into the same traps.

Remember, in the short period of time that you have to produce your proposal, you will struggle to fit in all the activities required to do a thorough job of convincing the evaluators they should select you. This is why you want to start as early as possible, during capture, staging your materials for the proposal. Prepare to make a significant investment of your resources—time and money—to win a proposal.

Making an Educated Decision to Bid or Not Bid on a Proposal

So, you are looking at the RFP. Even though it might seem like a no-brainer to go after, you still need to be absolutely sure this is where you want to spend your time, energy, and money.

Bid–no-bid decisions can be tough to make because it can be difficult to say "no" to an opportunity when it looks oh so attractive to you. In fact, even large and established companies have a broken bid–no-bid decision process, where they say "yes" to far too many bids that they do not have the slightest chance of winning.

Hopefully you will have gone through capture and had a number of chances to learn the ins and outs of the opportunity. Therefore, short of red flags in an RFP that would prevent you from winning, you will have already made the determination to go ahead with the proposal.

But what if you didn't go through capture and you come across a highly attractive RFP? How would you decide whether it's worthwhile to spend your limited resources on this opportunity?

Your first question should be this: Do you know this customer and do they know you? If you have a relationship with the customer, know what they are looking for, and have great capabilities and past performance (between you and your teammates) to respond to RFP requirements, then you can probably bid.

If you don't know the customer, and the only thing you know about this opportunity is what's in the RFP, and your capabilities and past performance are a bit of a stretch, then bidding would be a poor business decision.

Generally, this simple rule-of-thumb formula for determining whether or not you should bid will suffice, but we use a more sophisticated approach for making your decisions based on calculating win probability. You can download it on our web site for free at www.ostglobalsolutions.com/bid-no-bid.

How to Read the Government RFP Correctly to Understand Exactly What the Government Is Looking For

RFPs can be daunting if you are not familiar with them. They are thick documents with intimidating-looking forms in them, and contract clauses that won't fail to put you to sleep even after ten cups of coffee. To make it even more complicated, each one is organized differently, so even experienced proposal people have to dig to make heads or tails out of it.

Most typical federal RFPs are organized in an alphabetical order:

- They have sections A through M, and often come with a number of attachments.
- These sections serve standard purposes for nearly all RFPs.
- The RFP instructions are called "requirements."

Section A is a Standard Form, SF-33 or SF-1449 (for commercial items), or another form with similar content. It is the title page of the RFP that looks like a table with information and signature blocks:

- It summarizes basic information about the opportunity, such as the due date, contracting office information, and Table of Contents to help navigate the RFP.

- Sometimes the form accompanying the RFP might contain other information, such as the number of copies of the proposal you need to submit. Read the form carefully.
- The form requires your signature when you submit a proposal. If the government issued amendments, you might need to acknowledge receipt of these amendments in the form, and submit the amendments signed to acknowledge their receipt.
- Once the government awards the contract to you and countersigns this form, it becomes the cover page of your contract.

Figure 11-1 shows part of an RFP cover page that includes the due date and time, solicitation number, place where the proposal has to be delivered, contracting specialist's contact information, the table of contents for the RFP, and other information.

SOLICITATION, OFFER AND AWARD	1. THIS CONTRACT IS A RATED ORDER UNDER DPAS (15 CFR 700)	RATING	PAGE 1 OF PAGES 113

2. CONTRACT NO.	3. SOLICITATION NO.	4. TYPE OF SOLICITATION	5. DATE ISSUED	6. REQUISITION/PURCHASE NO.
	N00189-09-R-0002	[ ] SEALED BID (IFB) [X] NEGOTIATED (RFP)	07 May 2009	N6861009RC31002

7. ISSUED BY CODE N00189	8. ADDRESS OFFER TO (If other than Item 7) CODE
FLEET INDUSTRIAL SUPPLY CENTER 1968 GILBERT ST SUITE 600 NORFOLK VA 23511-3392 TEL: FAX:	See Item 7 TEL: FAX:

NOTE: In sealed bid solicitations "offer" and "offeror" mean "bid" and "bidder".

SOLICITATION

9. Sealed offers in original and ______ copies for furnishing the supplies or services in the Schedule will be received at the place specified in Item 8, or if handcarried, in the depository located in ______________________ until 12:00 PM (Hour) local time 12 Jun 2009 (Date)

CAUTION - LATE Submissions, Modifications, and Withdrawals: See Section L, Provision No. 52.214-7 or 52.215-1. All offers are subject to all terms and conditions contained in this solicitation.

10. FOR INFORMATION CALL:	A. NAME	B. TELEPHONE (Include area code) (NO COLLECT CALLS)	C. E-MAIL ADDRESS
	JENNIFER L. ANDREWS	(757) 443-1319	[illegible]

11. TABLE OF CONTENTS

(X)	SEC.	DESCRIPTION	PAGE(S)	(X)	SEC.	DESCRIPTION	PAGE(S)
		PART I - THE SCHEDULE				PART II - CONTRACT CLAUSES	
X	A	SOLICITATION/CONTRACT FORM	1	X	I	CONTRACT CLAUSES	82 - 91
X	B	SUPPLIES OR SERVICES AND PRICES/ COSTS	2 - 19			PART III - LIST OF DOCUMENTS, EXHIBITS AND OTHER ATTACHMENTS	
X	C	DESCRIPTION/ SPECS./ WORK STATEMENT	20 - 72	X	J	LIST OF ATTACHMENTS	92
	D	PACKAGING AND MARKING				PART IV - REPRESENTATIONS AND INSTRUCTIONS	
X	E	INSPECTION AND ACCEPTANCE	73	X	K	REPRESENTATIONS, CERTIFICATIONS AND OTHER STATEMENTS OF OFFERORS	93 - 99
X	F	DELIVERIES OR PERFORMANCE	74 - 76				
X	G	CONTRACT ADMINISTRATION DATA	77 - 81	X	L	INSTRS., CONDS., AND NOTICES TO OFFERORS	100 - 106
	H	SPECIAL CONTRACT REQUIREMENTS		X	M	EVALUATION FACTORS FOR AWARD	107 - 113

OFFER (Must be fully completed by offeror)

NOTE: Item 12 does not apply if the solicitation includes the provisions at 52.214-16, Minimum Bid Acceptance Period.

12. In compliance with the above, the undersigned agrees, if this offer is accepted within ________ calendar days (60 calendar days unless a different period is inserted by the offeror) from the date for receipt of offers specified above, to furnish any or all items upon which prices are offered at the price set opposite

Figure 11-1. Section A: Solicitation/contract form. You have to carefully study the RFP cover page to identify useful information regarding the proposal.

Other RFP sections include the following:

- **Section B—Supplies or Services and Prices:** Helps the government receive pricing in a consistent manner, so that they can compare apples to apples where it comes to your and your competitors' prices. It is the form you will likely have to fill out for your cost volume and submit with your proposal.

- **Section C—Descriptions, Specifications, Work Statement:** Contains the scope of work, or what you are going to do on the project. The scope of work can appear in different forms, including product specifications, Performance Work Statement (PWS), Statement of Objectives (SOO), Statement of Work (SOW), or even performance objectives or tasks.

- **Section D—Packaging and Marking:** Shows how you are supposed to package your products for delivery.

- **Section E—Inspection and Acceptance:** Explains how the government will inspect and accept your products.

- **Section F—Deliveries or Performance:** Refers to government performance standards or how they will accept deliveries.

- **Section G—Contract Administration Data:** Has information on how the contract will be administered.

- **Section H—Special Contract Requirements:** Contains many pieces of information crucial for your proposal response, with the most important ones, perhaps, being key personnel requirements.

- **Section I—Contract Clauses:** This is where you will have a number of references and full-text clauses from the Federal Acquisition Regulations and the agency's own regulations.

- **Section J—Attachments:** Serves as a "flexible" section designation. This is sometimes where the scope of work will go if it doesn't stay in section C, and where you might get lots of different attachments, such as the templates the government will want you to use.

- **Section K—Representations, Certifications, and Other Statements of Offerors:** Provides a form where the government will ask you to spell out to them every detail about your company. Sometimes they don't require you to do so when you have filled out your forms online at SAM.gov

(ORCA), but at other times they will want both online forms and the solicitation-specific Section K.

- **Section L—Instructions, Conditions, and Notices to Offerors:** Tells you all about how you have to submit your proposal (and even protest an award decision if you don't like it).

- **Section M—Evaluation Criteria for Award:** Provides an insight into how the government will go about evaluating your proposal.

My first rule for analyzing RFPs is that you shouldn't read them like a book, from the beginning to end. You have to go in a specific order. The most important sections that you should read first (after you look at Section A) are L, M, and C (and sometimes key attachments such as J), asking questions such as these:

- **Section L:** What does the government want in the proposal? How many volumes and pages, how many copies do you have to submit, where, and how—in print, electronically, or via email? What do they want to see as far as the content is concerned? Are there specifications as to the font, margins, paper quality, page size, and any other proposal instructions?

- **Section M:** How will the government evaluate the bid, and decide which proposal wins?

- **Section C:** What is the work the government is asking contractors to bid on?

Then, and only then, do you want to read through the rest of the RFP.

Again, many RFPs are organized differently. They might be numbered, or they might be set up alphabetically with sections that mean totally different things. They could have different parts to them and not come in a single document. It can be awfully confusing, especially in the beginning. No matter what you are faced with, the trick is to look for similar elements:

- **Instructions for submitting a proposal:** They could be scattered or in one place. You will have to know at the very least the deadline, what the government wants to see in your proposal, and whether your submission is page-limited.

- **Evaluation criteria:** There should be some, if rudimentary, mention on how your customer is going to evaluate and possibly score your proposal, and how they are going to select a winner.

- **Scope of work**: The work you are required to do after contract award.

Then, you want to look for other parts that typically belong in an RFP, similar to the alphabetical sections discussed earlier.

Sometimes you might find the instructions to the offerors in the cover letter, and then the rest of the requirements in the RFP. This often happens with task order RFPs.

Remember, it might be daunting to read an RFP for the first time, but, after a few dozen of them, you will have mastered it.

Here are some things you need to get from the RFP:

- What are the due dates for your proposal, award, start of work, orals, industry days, and so on?

- How should it be delivered (physical, electronic, or both)? Do you have to ship it, or is it a local delivery?

- How large is the deliverable in the number of volumes, pages, copies, and so on?

- Can you fulfill all the requirements, such as having the right past performance references and key personnel and being able to execute the scope of work (either on your own or by bringing in teammates and subcontractors)?

- Is there anything in the RFP that creates changes in your overall win strategy (including pricing strategy); your teaming; your technical, management, past performance, and staffing approaches; or your price?

- Do you have any questions that came out of examining the RFP requirements? Does everything make sense? Does the RFP provide enough information so that you can bid?

- Has anything changed since the draft RFP or the previous (incumbent) contract's RFP, if there was a draft RFP or an incumbent?

- Did the customer act on your recommendations and ways of shaping the RFP?

- Is there anything in the RFP that's a "red flag" that might lead you not to bid?

- Does the RFP appear to be wired for the incumbent or another competitor?

Once you have analyzed it, it's time for you to buckle down and think through how you are going to tackle the proposal.

Why You Need a Proposal Process, and How It Works

A robust proposal process is part and parcel of writing winning proposals. Being able to translate all the great information collected during capture into a compelling, concise, and compliant proposal by the due date (and without undue stress) is what a good proposal process is all about. Process eliminates chaos and helps coordinate everyone's efforts.

Unfortunately, many people think that the proposal process boils down to reviewing the RFP, writing the proposal section by section, and turning it in by the deadline. It's not that simple. The proposal process is a set of milestones, steps, interim deadlines, and reviews that have to be adhered to, so that the document is ready in the best possible state for improved win probability. Many people don't want to follow the discipline of these interim process steps, believing that the "real" proposal deadline (when it's due to the customer) is the only one they have to respect.

Having a process will help you manage expectations for yourself and the team: You will know what to do, by when, how, and by whom. People who are writing the proposal with you will also be more accountable to you, knowing what you will expect of them. You will be able to know when and where you need specific resources. For example, you will know when you will need your technical SMEs the most, when you will need your reviewers, and when you will need editors.

In the process of developing a proposal, you will also have an opportunity to positively impact the quality of the document if you are not the only one writing it. You will continuously read the sections others produce to make sure that you can course correct if they have drifted from the requirements. You can measure progress against the specific milestones, knowing exactly where you need to be by a certain point. You will also know that you need to reassign or add resources if certain sections are not ready and you fall behind. You will also maintain better momentum with the process, rather than when you don't have a process.

You will also have a clear workflow established for those situations when you don't have much time to waste, like getting your SMEs to write the volumes and sections, getting the drafts to the proposal writer to be polished, getting them back to SMEs to review, getting them to management for formal review, getting them back to writers to address comments, and then editing these volumes and sections, producing them, printing, binding, checking, and packing.

When you analyze the lessons learned at the end of your proposal, you will be able to pinpoint what could be done better and therefore improve the process. This would be nearly impossible to do if you proceeded in an ad-hoc manner.

So, with all these arguments for the proposal process, how does a proposal process work? Table 11-1 shows the six-phase proposal process that OST Global Solutions has developed based on proposal best practices. It starts with the integration phase, which is important for making sure that the proposal is orchestrated the right way. It is the backbone of the proposal document. The process culminates in the postsubmittal phase, in which most companies miss an opportunity to make a difference, but which could be instrumental in winning.

Note a set of the final milestones (reviews) at the end of the planning, writing, and polishing phases that are assigned colors. These are proposal reviews to check your proposal progress and quality against what's "normal" by that stage in the proposal process and what the customer is looking for, and to ensure that you are on track for delivering a winning proposal. I discuss reviews later in this chapter.

Table 11-1. Proposal Process. This proposal process has six phases with key milestones, to ensure iterative document delivery with quality checks throughout, and chances to increase win probably even after proposal delivery.

Milestones	Activities	Deliverables
Phase I: Integration		
RFP release	Read the RFP	Compliance checklist
Bid–no-bid decision	Plan for the proposal	Annotated proposal outline
Final milestone: Kickoff meeting	Prepare the compliance checklist, outline, assignments list, and other materials	Writing assignments to authors
		Style guide
		Kickoff briefing
	Prepare for the proposal kickoff	Various handouts to the authors helpful in developing section material
Phase II: Planning		
Brainstorming meetings	Develop solution details through brainstorming meetings	Responses to the data calls
Just-in-time training		Questions to the government regarding unclear areas of the RFP
In-process reviews	Perform in-process reviews of authors' sections	Compliant proposal draft with bullets, plans for how to address each element, and graphic concepts, ready for in-process reviews and Pink team review
Questions to the government deadline, and other interim deadlines (might fall here or later)	Conduct just-in-time training for the authors on how to do a better job preparing text and graphics	
	Issue data calls to teammates	Cost proposal draft ready for in-process reviews and the Pink team review
Final milestone: Pink team review for the technical and cost proposals	Collect from the team, review, and submit questions to the government	Pink team review brief instructing the reviewers on how to review the proposal
	Prepare proposal for the Pink team review	Reviewers' debrief to the authors on the proposal review results and recommended improvements
	Prepare assignments for reviewers, and the Pink team brief	

Milestones	Activities	Deliverables
Phase III: Writing		
Just-in-time training In-process reviews **Final milestone: Red team review for the technical and cost proposals**	Integrate all the reviewer comments Develop and mature proposal section drafts and graphics Perform in-process reviews of authors' sections Conduct just-in-time training for the authors on how to edit and polish their own sections Prepare proposal for the Red team review Prepare assignments for reviewers, and the Red team brief	Compliant and compelling proposal draft with text and graphics, ready for in-process reviews and Red team review Cost proposal draft with price strategy implemented, ready for in-process reviews and the Red team review Red team review brief instructing the reviewers on how to review the proposal Reviewers' debrief to the authors on the proposal review results and recommended improvements
Phase IV: Polishing		
Pens down for the completed final draft (full draft, or staggered submission section by section) Read-out-loud review **Final milestone: Gold team review for the technical and cost proposals**	Integrate all the reviewer comments Prepare the final proposal draft Edit and lay out the final draft Finalize the graphics Triple-check compliance Finalize the cost volume and other proposal volumes Read the entire proposal out loud in a group to ensure there are no errors Prepare proposal for the Gold team review and sign-off	Proposal draft ready for editing and desktop publishing Edited and polished proposal ready for a read-out-loud review Final proposal ready for Gold team review and management sign-off Proposal ready for production

Milestones	Activities	Deliverables
Phase V: Production		
Printing of a hard copy proposal or electronic copy production CD, DVD, thumb drive, or in rare cases, iPad preparation for physical delivery Proposal assembly White glove review or book check (reviewing each page of the proposal) **Final milestone: Shipping and delivery of the hard copy proposal or uploading/ emailing of the electronic copy**	Provide detailed information about printing and delivery requirements to those who will print the proposal for you Agree on the production timeline Provide list of tabs that will go into the binders and separate sections Print proof copy and review Upon corrections and approval of the final-final copy, print the whole proposal and "build" (assemble) the volume binders Check the proposal page by page Create CDs and check on three different computers to ensure they open For electronic submission, arrange for the responsible person to email or upload the proposal after checking the document Confirm delivery	Production requirements: types of paper, number of volumes, number of pages in each volume, number of copies and sets, type of delivery, and other specifications from the RFP List of tabs Copy-edited proposal that went through Read-Out-Loud and Gold Team reviews, now ready for production Printed proposal and CDs for hard copy delivery Electronic proposal in the final form for electronic delivery Proposal delivery confirmation via shipper or hand delivery receipt Email read receipt showing electronic delivery confirmation or a time-stamped upload to a portal Call to the customer confirming that the proposal has been received, if no read receipt has been sent

Milestones	Activities	Deliverables
Phase VI: Postproposal		
Lessons learned session I (soon after proposal submission) Orals, if required by the RFP Milestones imposed by the discussions process (if it is initiated by the customer) Customer debrief Lessons learned session II Win party **Final milestone: Archiving of your materials for future use**	Organize and conduct lessons learned sessions I and II Present orals if required by the RFP Continue monitoring competitive landscape and implementing postsubmission win strategies Participate in the postsubmission activities such as discussions and Best and Final Offer (BAFO) as required by the customer Request the winning or losing debrief within three calendar days from the award announcement Plan the win party Archive the proposal and RFP Parse the proposal into reusable sections and file in the proposal library File lessons learned and debrief results in your proposal library	Lessons learned sessions I and II results, documented and filed Orals briefing, if applicable (and if it was not submitted together with the proposal), and orals presenters presenting your offer Responses to customer's evaluation notices (EN) and clarification requests (CR), if they enter discussions Your BAFO submission, if applicable Request for the debrief and debrief attendance Win party in case of a win Proposal, RFP, proposal summary form, debrief results, and parsed proposal filed in the library

Let's go over the process in greater detail.

Integration Phase

In the integration phase, your task is to organize all the materials and the proposal team to be on the same page. This is assuming that you have more people than just yourself writing the proposal.

The integration phase culminates in the proposal kickoff meeting, which is the most critical part of the proposal process when it involves a team. You have to achieve nine goals when holding your kickoff that will forestall numerous problems down the road.

The *nine goals of the kickoff meeting* are covered in detail in the following sections.

1. Building a Team

Putting faces to names and helping people get to know each other helps your proposal. Every proposal requires a little—or, more often, a lot of—extra effort from each person: extra creativity, extra dedication, extra hours, extra resourcefulness, and the list goes on. Anything that goes beyond the call of duty requires people to exhibit good will, and the fact that we do more for the real people we know and like is programmed into our psyche. Especially when there are no other incentives—such as rewards to winning proposal teams or promotions to new positions on the program that was awarded—generating good will through team building is essential.

2. Setting Your Tone from the Start

The kickoff is usually the first time you meet some of your team members and the first time you get to present your plan for the whole proposal in front of your colleagues and management. Your goal as someone responsible for delivering a winning proposal is not only to tell the team what the plan is, but to ensure that it will be followed. Thus, you need to deliver a clear message that you are to be taken seriously so that your team follows your directions. You need to convince everyone that you are the person in charge. You will also need to exude confidence to inspire your writers to do the following:

- Persevere through working long hours, often sacrificing their personal time.

- Meet aggressive deadlines.

- Find scarce information and resources.

- Tap into and apply their creativity.

- Overcome writer's block.

You will also need to instill in your and your teammates' management the confidence that you are the right person for the job. This will gain their buy-in to support your decisions throughout the proposal on everything from how you choose to run the pursuit to how you plan the program's execution.

3. Manage Expectations

Because everyone has a different idea of how to go about writing proposals, you need to manage their expectations on how you are going to go about putting yours together. There are numerous different approaches and personal preferences, as well as opinions on how things should be done. On your proposal team, there will be some people who have no idea what a proposal entails, but will apply what they know about writing projects to proposal development. Even if you work with the same people every time, every proposal is different, which will require customizing some approaches and techniques in an unfamiliar way. Your task is to explain every bit of your approach to writing proposals, including your proposal process, your management style, and techniques for tracking progress. You will also need to cover your expectations for meeting deadlines, communication with you and others, teamwork, weekend work, and especially for asking for help ahead of time (and not after the section is due for a review).

4. Communicate Proposal Roadmap and Plan

Your plan for getting the proposal done is related to managing expectations so that your proposal team members can plan their work and lives accordingly. To accomplish this, you first need to come up with a plan. You need to share dates and times for brainstorming, "pens down" for proposal sections, reviews, and other important milestones.

The most important aspect of communicating your plan to the team is to explain that there is a real reason for having a process in place with strict guidelines for when certain drafts and sections need to be completed to keep the entire proposal development process manageable and on track. Many people who are not used to the proposal process feel as if you are imposing artificial deadlines before the "real" due date of the proposal. You have to explain that proposal process is iterative, and one cannot just write a proposal the night before it's due and have a high win probability.

5. Obtain Management Buy-In

It does not matter how well you've planned the effort; if your and your teammates' management does not understand what you are doing, it is likely that they won't support you with resources and decisions. Therefore, you should invite them to the kickoff session. They especially need to know everything about the opportunity background, your plan, your team, your anticipated risks, and your decisions. This way if you hit a snag down the road, they won't be blindsided by your request for assistance.

6. Integrate and Issue Proposal Assignments

To avoid losing momentum and having your proposal team succumb to entropy, you should have your outline and assignments ready in time for the kickoff. Proposal assignments must consist of a detailed proposal outline with instructions to authors, and names of those responsible and those who will be helping them.

7. Educate Your Team About the Opportunity

You have to ensure that your entire team is on the same page about the opportunity and actually remembers its key facts. The lowest common denominator will drag the entire team down. Even if there are one or two people who don't have the same information, your writing progress could slow down or even go astray. Do not assume that people have read the RFP or remember what you have already shared with them. To educate your team about the opportunity, you will need to summarize all the opportunity facts, background, and RFP requirements. You also want to tell your proposal team about the customer and customer's hot button issues, competition, win themes, and even key elements of your approach.

8. Train Your Team

Unless you are incredibly lucky and everyone assigned to the proposal is an experienced writer, you will need to do some just-in-time training to get everyone on the same page. Do not assume that your team knows how to write compliant sections or come up with great ideas for proposal graphics. You will need to honestly assess your entire team's proposal expertise to see if they know how to read the RFP, structure compliant proposal sections, write compelling proposal text, use proposal collaboration tools such as Microsoft SharePoint, and develop great graphics.

9. Get the Ball Rolling

At the end of your kickoff meeting, you need to tell people what to do immediately after the meeting. You want recap the assignments, recap your expectations, and remind everyone about schedule for the next few days and the next milestone.

If you nail your kickoff meeting, your entire proposal experience will change for the better because it will be inherently more organized and orderly. This will help you work fewer hours on your proposal, win more pursuits, and even enjoy the bidding process.

Planning Phase

With the kickoff meeting out of the way, you will enter the planning phase. You will need to organize a number of brainstorming sessions to figure out every element of your solution. You will also have to make sure that your writing progresses every day, which is usually done through in-process reviews. These working reviews allow the person in charge of the proposal to read other writers' work to check if they are on track. You also need to conduct status meetings on a daily basis to keep your team on the same page. These usually take only 15 minutes, but go a long way toward maintaining momentum.

Your in-process reviews will have to continue into the writing phase to ensure that you maintain tight control over your proposal. After all, in proposals, "trust" is a dirty word. Your motto about proposal sections and graphics should be this: "If I haven't seen it, it does not exist."

As mentioned earlier, at the end of each major proposal phase, you will have to hold major reviews that are more formal than your in-process reviews. They are commonly referred to as "color teams." Formal reviews, such as Pink, Red, and Gold Teams, are a proposal best practice. Never submit a proposal without at least one formal review, even if your schedule is short.

Usually, there are two to five reviews (depending on the proposal duration) in the course of a proposal, where you invite up to a dozen people to act as if they were the government evaluating your proposal, and provide their comments to you. The reviewers might include your and your teammates' management, SMEs, consultants specialized in reviewing proposals, and others whose opinions you respect and who have experience conducting constructive and productive reviews of government proposals. If you are just starting out in the government contracting arena, reach out to OST and we can review your work.

The number and type of reviews depends on your process and proposal duration. You need to plan for enough reviews to keep the pressure on proposal writers and have enough checkpoints to ensure great proposal quality. At the same time, you need to avoid creating a counterproductive environment called "death by reviews," where the team spends more time preparing for the reviews and reviewing of the proposal than it does in actually writing the document.

Most government RFPs will require you to separate the cost offer from the technical offer, so you will need to submit at least two volumes. It is easy to focus on the technical volume review and forget all about the cost volume. Many companies get their cost proposal developed at the last minute, and as a result, it has mistakes, and often doesn't match the technical proposal.

To prevent this from happening, you need to run your price volume reviews so that they take place in parallel with or immediately following the technical volume reviews. Some trusted reviewers have to read both volumes to make sure that these volumes agree; and that the price volume does as good a sales job as the technical one.

Your goal is to set the desired outcomes for each review for your particular proposal pursuit, no matter what color of the rainbow you choose to call your review. Let's look in more detail at some traditional colors and associated goals in the review sequence: Pink Team, Red Team, Read Out-Loud Review, Gold Team, and White Glove.

1. Pink Team

The Pink Team is normally the review of the first proposal draft. Pink Team expectations include the following:

- The proposal is 60 percent ready for submission.
- The outline is firm and can be "frozen."
- The draft is fully compliant with the RFP.
- The resume template is compliant.
- The past performance template is compliant.
- Technical and management approaches are clearly formed. Although it might be an imperfect presentation, all the key content and graphics concepts must be there.
- The story of why you should win is there.
- There are great ideas and clear win themes that show what makes this offer better, faster, cheaper, and less risky.
- There are sufficient inputs to decide the following:
    - Is this the right corporate experience for the whole team?
    - Are the right key and supporting personnel proposed?
    - Are these the right past performance references?

Misspellings, page count problems, art numbers out of sequence, and faulty grammar are normal at a Pink Team stage and should be ignored.

You can also include specific questions to the reviewers about things you would like them to look or check for and give them the list of win themes they need to find reflected in the draft. Especially for larger volumes, ask your reviewers to review that portion of the content that coincides with their subject matter expertise.

Usually the Pink Team takes place at the 40 percent time mark relative to the overall proposal duration. If the proposal duration is more than 30 days, writers can rest on the review day, and only listen to a debriefing of the review results.

Pink Team, just like any other formal review, has to have a kickoff to make sure all the reviewers are on the same page. You need to explain all the facts about your opportunity, review schedule, goals, expectations from reviewers, and reviewer assignments to the specific sections.

At the end of the review, you will need to have the reviewers confer to come up with a unified set of comments. They will have to note strengths and weaknesses of each section and the score assigned to the section, and then provide their recommendations and consensus on actionable comments to get the section score higher.

After the reviewers are done documenting and discussing the findings, they debrief proposal writers to share their insights. The proposal manager gets the detailed comments and decides which ones the writers should act on after the review.

2. Red Team

The next proposal review is the Red Team, taking place at roughly the 70 percent time mark of the proposal. Red Team expectations are as follows:

- Proposal is 90 percent ready, with some final honing left to do to sharpen win themes, benefits, and discriminators or differentiators.
- Proposal has solid win themes and benefits to the customer throughout.
- Proposal is fully compliant.
- Executive summary is written.
- Page count is within 95 percent of target number.
- All forms and tables are filled out.

- Graphics are professionally rendered, but their numbers in text might be still out of order or not called out; there are some imperfections.

- Proposal is written in complete, grammatically correct sentences, but has not had the final edits.

- Proposal already has a cover and table of contents, but not yet a list of acronyms.

3. Read-Out-Loud Review

Although it is not part of a regular proposal process, it is highly recommended that you conduct a read-out-loud review. Reading text out loud is based on the fact that when we sound something out, we are able to catch many things that escape the eye when reading.

Read-out-loud review expectations are that the proposal is fully edited and formatted. Then, you can take turns with a few others on your proposal team and read the printed text while someone else good with grammar and spelling corrects errors in the proposal document. Your goal, instead of doing a group edit, is to find inconsistencies, bloopers, and errors that might have escaped your editor's eye. Reading out loud is a tedious process, so you have to estimate the review speed to be six to nine pages per hour and allocate time as necessary.

4. Gold Team

Gold Team is the management review of your proposal before it gets printed and finalized for delivery. Each company and organization has different criteria for the Gold Team. It varies from being "another Red Team" to the mere formality of a skim read and the final sign-off. The Gold Team is often the last opportunity for company management to read the final bid over with the goal of approving it for submission; it serves as the final blessing. Gold Team expectations are that the proposal is essentially 99.9999 percent customer ready and just needs management's blessing.

5. White Glove

After the proposal is printed and all the pages have been inserted into binders, you need to do a White Glove review (as in use the white gloves to avoid smudging the crispy white pages of your customer-ready proposal). This review is also called a *book check*. Book checks are important because in any large print job, there are always misprints and defects: Some pages don't print at all, and others might get blemishes on them, for example. You don't have to worry about white gloves with 28-pound paper recommended for printing proposals, but you might want to use grease-free finger moisturizer for turning pages to avoid having to moisten your fingers using, well, the conventional means.

When book checking, it is important to note that it is easiest to accurately perform this task when someone else is there looking at the proposal with you. Here is how you should go about it: Each person should have a copy of the same volume. Book-checking is a type of call-and-response process. For example, the first step is to call out the name of the proposal: "Cover page, Professional Monitoring Services. Volume III, Certifications." The other person's response (if they have the same information) should be simply "Yes" or no response if there are no errors they can see on the page. The next page would subsequently be called out as "Foreword, three-i (III-i)," and so on.

Continue these steps until you and the other person have completely gone through the entire proposal. In the event a page is missing or compiled improperly, place a sticky note on the page, continue the book-checking process, and subsequently return to the problem pages. After you've corrected and reprinted those pages, you are ready to ship the proposals to the client.

When a customer asks for CDs, you will need to make sure that after burning them, you always test them on three different computers that don't have the same CD burning software. Software has been known to fail to "close" the CD so that it can be read on any computer, and you may deliver an unusable CD to the government. Needless to say, it would render you non-compliant.

The last stage of your proposal process is to deliver your proposal. If the delivery is electronic, give yourself enough time to upload or email your proposal, with many hours or even a day to spare. For a physical delivery, you want to print at least two full proposal sets—and if you are submitting sealed packages from subcontractors for your price volume, request that they furnish to you two sealed packages instead of one. You will return to them the extra one (naturally, unopened) once you confirm the delivery.

You want to have the main way of delivering your proposal, and an alternative "dead man" way. This way, if something goes wrong with delivering one set, such as a delayed FedEx truck, a late flight, or a traffic jam, you will be able to deliver the second set and avoid losing all your hard work.

Now that you understand the proposal process, the next chapter will discuss how to structure and how to go about writing your proposal.

Wrangle the Nitty-Gritty of Proposal Details

Writing winning government proposals is as tedious a job as jobs get. You have to provide everything that's requested in the exact form dictated in the RFP, and if you miss even one requirement, it will reflect poorly on your proposal or could even get it thrown out of the evaluation. You don't have creative license to come up with your own structure; instead, you have to be inventive and persuasive within the strict confines of the format and page count imposed on you. Sometimes the task might seem impossible, like a rather typical requirement to summarize your technical and management approach and provide a performance work statement in 10 pages for a complex $90 million project. Compound the challenge with a schedule that is 30 days on the long side, and more like 5 to 10 days on the short side, and you get the picture. To master proposal preparation, you will have to acquire several key skills, especially planning your work, paying attention to every detail, outlining your proposal correctly, and making your proposal more persuasive within the bounds of what's allowed. In this chapter, I cover how to develop a schedule for your proposal to avoid the last-minute scramble and produce an error-free, professional set of bid documents. Then I discuss the importance of attention to detail, and take you through the process of outlining a compliant proposal to get the highest score from evaluators. Finally, I show you how to make your proposal sections more compelling through executive summary, win themes, persuasive language, and graphics.

How to Develop a Schedule to Avoid the Last-Minute Scramble and Produce an Error-Free Professional Set of Bid Documents

Given the tough job you have ahead of you, and given your understanding of the proposal process, you have to develop a detailed schedule as you would for any complex project. To get started, download this month's calendar from www.timeanddate.com/calendar; if you are more engineering-minded and are trained in Microsoft Project, set up a real project schedule with a critical path.

Here are the guidelines for building a good proposal schedule:

- **Plan backwards: Start with the proposal deadline.** Allow for proper delivery time, making sure that you account for Murphy's law. Give yourself triple the time you think is necessary, just to be safe.

- **Be sure to plan ample time for editing, formatting (desktop publishing),** and printing your proposal. Determine key dates for Gold Team, Read-Out-Loud, Red Team, Pink Team, and kickoff, in that order. For short-duration proposals seven days and under, allow for at least one review. A good rule of thumb for scheduling Red Team is to build it into your schedule at about 70 percent of your entire schedule time frame.

- **Allow for the proposal manager to spend some time with the document prior to each review.** Don't forget to include "pens-down" time for all the writers.

- **Schedule reviews tentatively.** Leave a day or so of wiggle room to accommodate the schedules of important attendees. Allow time for recovery between the reviews: Don't schedule a Pink Team and then a Red Team two days later.

- **Don't omit deadlines that are specific to this customer and this proposal.** Don't forget such milestones as the deadline for your questions to the customer, the deadline for submission of past performance questionnaires to your references, and your price-volume preparation milestones and reviews.

You can download a free sample of a proposal schedule after which you can model your own proposal schedules at www.ostglobalsolutions.com/proposal-schedule, and you can learn more about planning your proposals at our Foundations of Proposal Management class.

It's All about Attention to Detail

As you are planning your proposal, you have to make sure you go through every single detail in the RFP. You have to pay attention to little sentences that are easy to overlook. One of the things you have to watch out for is early deadlines. For example, the government might ask you to submit a statement that you don't have an OCI 15 days before the proposal due date. Or you might be required to submit your intent to bid by a certain deadline. Your past performance references might be due one or two weeks before the proposal is due. One proposal I saw had a 60-day deadline; I suspect a deadline that far off might have gotten people to relax and focus on other priorities for a few days, instead of reading the RFP right away, as soon as it was issued. Perversely, there was one line hidden in that 145-page RFP that said that bidders had to submit to the contracting officer the list of those government references who will respond to past performance questionnaires seven days after the issuance of the RFP!

There will also be pesky little requirements and specifications hiding in the most obscure places in the RFP. RFPs are pieced together by multiple people, and could have requirements stuck in them in a variety of places. These requirements might even conflict, which could require that you ask the government a question prior to the deadline.

The secret to getting on top of all these requirements is not just reading the RFP. You will have to "shred" the RFP. *Shredding the RFP* is necessary because compliance is king in government proposals.

If your RFP is not overly complex, your shredding is limited to cutting and pasting the requirements into your annotated outline, and keeping track of all the submission requirements through a simple checklist. You can create this checklist by going through the RFP line by line.

In more complex RFPs, it is entirely too easy to miss a requirement, so you will need to go through a more rigorous process.

Your first task is to identify every requirement in the RFP. You will have to highlight all the requirement words. Examples include *shall, will, require, must, should, comply, request, not,* and *ASAP.* You can use the Find and Replace function in Microsoft Word to do this. Press Ctrl+f to open the dialog box, click the Replace tab, type *shall* in both the Find and Replace boxes, and select Format → Font to highlight all occurrences of *shall* in the document.

You can then go ahead and search and replace all plain *shalls* with different color or italicized, underlined, or bold *shalls.* You can then repeat your searches for the other requirement words using a similar method. Then, you can either build a Word macro or manually cut and paste those requirement sentences as you come across them in the table format, as shown in Table 12-1. The RFP numbers and requirements are in the first two columns from the left, then you have two columns (Compliant – Yes or No) for a reviewer to check to make sure each requirement is addressed; the last column is the correlation of the requirement to the proposal section where it is addressed.

Table 12-1. RFP shredding format. This table will help ensure that you have addressed every requirement during proposal reviews, as you assign someone to go through your proposal and check each section for compliance.

RFP Section	RFP Language	Compliant?		Outline Section
		Yes	No	
C.4.1.1	The Contractor *shall* conduct phase-in procedures beginning 60 calendar days prior to the performance date specified in Section F of the contract.			2.4.1
	The Contractor *shall* submit a phase-in plan for evaluation with its proposal.			2.4.1
	The phase-in *requires* coordination with the incumbent Contractors.			2.4.1

RFP Section	RFP Language	Compliant?		Outline Section
C.4.1.2	At least 60 calendar days prior to contract completion, the Contracting Officer (KO) and Contracting Officer's Representative (COR) *will* notify the Contractor of all outstanding requirements that *shall* be completed prior to contract termination.			2.4.2
	The Contractor *shall* provide personnel with a level of knowledge, skills, abilities, and aptitude in services to support the deliverables of this contract.			2.4.2
	Contractor employees working under this contract *shall* be able to fluently speak, read, and write English.			2.4.2

You also need to build a compliance checklist that covers everything that has to do with the instructions to the Offerors. It should begin to illustrate what your proposal should look like when it is printed and delivered. It should include elements like the due date, delivery method, and quantity of the proposal volumes; any requirements for the proposal title page and headings; volume titles; font requirements; and page counts.

It is also very useful to see how your requirements cross over, to ensure you have addressed every single section of the proposal. Table 12-2 shows an example of a cross-reference matrix that tracks compliance, progress, and assignment distribution. In the status column, it is nice to use colors to track completion of the sections and to create peer pressure on the authors, so that they honor your deadlines.

The scheme I like to use to track section status has four colors: Red shading of the status cell means that the proposal section is not started or behind schedule; yellow means work has started but the section needs significant work; green means that part is in good shape; and blue means the section is completed and is customer-ready.

Table 12-2. Cross-reference matrix. This multipurpose matrix is useful for tracking compliance, issuing assignments, and tracking section completion status.

Proposal Outline		RFP Compliance				Proposal Management		
Prop. Sect. #	Proposal Section Title	L	M	C	Other	Author	# of Pages	Status
2.0	Technical Approach	L.3.a	M.5	C.5.1	H.8	John Smith	1	
2.1	Conceptual Design	L.4	M.5	C.5.2	J.2	Nora Jones	4	

Really large RFPs could take hours or days to shred, so you might want to invest in software. There are a variety of software packages out there, with the leading ones being Meridian by XRSolutions: www.xrsolutions.com, and Visible Thread, www.visiblethread.com. Consulting services can also parse your RFP on demand using software, and then congruently build your outline or work packages (storyboards) with proper directions for your authors on what exactly they should address in their sections.

How to Outline a Compliant Proposal to Get the Highest Score from the Evaluators

Every proposal must have an outline. There are two types of proposal outlines: the one that comes in the form of a *cross-reference matrix* just discussed, and the other in the form of an *annotated outline* in a Microsoft Word document that contains all the requirements that apply to each section, along with the detailed instructions to the authors. You might want first to put together a cross-reference matrix outline, and then build an annotated outline.

An annotated outline is a method that allows you to integrate your proposal upfront. It helps your writers visualize the future proposal and what your response should look like.

The best way to develop a proposal outline is to start with the instructions describing how the proposal should be put together. Then incorporate the evaluation criteria. Finally, add in the statement of work and other requirements. Appendix B shows a step-by-step example of how you should go about developing an outline.

As you develop your outline, you need to mimic your customer's order, numbering system, and the language they use. Your section names should closely parallel what the RFP says. Don't introduce another order so that you can tell the story better. You will only confuse the customer, who will have a hard time finding the sections and figuring out your logic.

Note that multilevel bid requests are tough to outline; some requirements will be the same, some will be unique, and some will conflict. Rarely is there one and only one correct way to structure your proposal. In this case, you need to clearly indicate your methodology for structuring the proposal the way you did, and providing road signs for the customer throughout your writing.

After developing an initial outline structure, you need to shake things out such as adjustments of content between sections, reconciling, and removing duplications without sacrificing compliance. Keep the requirements language in your draft until you have worked through all the key words in the text.

How to Make Your Proposal Sections More Compelling Through Executive Summary, Graphics, and Persuasive Language

Now that you have taken care of making sure your proposal is compliant, and addressed every single aspect of the requirements, you need to take your proposal to the next level and make it highly persuasive. In the world of proposals, ways to persuade an evaluator range from writing a great executive summary to win themes we discussed in Chapter 7 to highly readable language to graphics and presentation to make your proposal more attractive and easily digestible. Mastering these tools will help you significantly raise your win probability. Let's discuss each tool in turn.

Proposal Persuasion Tool 1: Executive Summary

Your first tool of proposal persuasion is a well-written *executive summary*. This part of proposal is incredibly important, but is subject to people making three types of mistakes.

The first type of mistake is either under- or overestimating the importance of the executive summary. Many people don't bother writing an executive summary, questioning why they should because often it is not required by the RFP. They might believe that it's a waste of pages in a limited page-count proposal, and because they haven't seen a decent executive summary in the course of their careers, they skip it altogether. Others argue that it's the most important part of your document and you should always write one. They point out that the source-selection authority is going to read it, and so is the customer's executive team.

Unfortunately, because it is deemed so important, it inevitably gains more attention from the color team reviewers than the rest of the proposal. This results in well-written executive summaries but poorly written proposals. Everyone ends up obsessing over the executive summary more than the rest of the proposal at reviews and, by proposal submission date, you might end up with 35 versions with way too many fingers in the pot. The right answer is this: The executive summary is important—just as much as the rest of your proposal.

The second type of mistake is faulty process. You should start to write your executive summary during capture and then allow it to evolve as you learn about your customer and what your customer's hot button issues are. The executive summary should evolve as the proposal evolves. Many make the mistake of starting the executive summary too late in the process. They rationalize that the executive summary is a summary and, therefore, can be best written after everything else is written. Often people write an executive summary right before or after the Red Team or they throw it in right before the proposal is submitted. Waiting to start the executive summary until a late stage doesn't permit the necessary amount of time for it to be fleshed out adequately, and will usually result in a poorer product.

Another process error is to assign the wrong person to write the executive summary (provided that you are not the only person writing the proposal). When a busy executive gets involved into writing instead of someone who has time to do a good job, it often results in cutting and pasting or a last-minute rush. The best person to write the executive summary is the person who knows the customer and the opportunity best and is available to write your executive summary early.

The third type of mistake is poor content. The first content mistake is to make the executive summary about *you*—your company and your team. It should never be focused on your company, but rather on *your customer*, and how you will be serving their needs. It's only about you in the context of the customer.

The second content mistake is rambling without any clear structure—giving your company's history and background, philosophy, a summary of the document, and so on—all the while boring the evaluator to tears. Executive summaries actually should present their arguments in a specific formula that produces an intended impact on the evaluator.

So what is the executive summary supposed to cover and do? First and foremost, it is supposed to get the evaluator interested in reading your proposal. The evaluators are human, and if they instantly become turned off or bored starting with the executive summary, you are in trouble. He or she will mentally check out, and all the sweat, blood, and tears that might have gone into developing your proposal could be in vain. By the time an evaluator makes it through the executive summary, he or she will be yawning or—the opposite—excited to read your proposal. It is mostly up to you and the quality of your executive summary.

Second, it must present a very clear and concise picture of why you should win, telling your *story*.

It is true that an executive summary could be the only part of your proposal document the ultimate decision maker might read. But the reviewers might get a copy of the executive summary as well, especially when your proposal is split into pieces for evaluation purposes. So the reviewers will get your executive summary and just the one section he or she is evaluating, which can be completely torn out of context. Even though these evaluators are scoring your section against the localized requirements, they really don't know the big picture unless they read that executive summary. They don't know who the team is, for example, and what your claim to fame is—or why they should care—without your explaining it well in a clear and concise manner in one spot.

Even if the reviewers are reading the entire proposal, they might drown in the details without a document that tells them what to focus on. As you know, customer-provided outlines rarely let you tell a good story, so the evaluators could become quite lost. Having a good executive summary will help you to clearly explain to the reviewers why you should win the proposal.

Although executive summaries are often not scored, having a good executive summary to put the right kind of big picture in front of an evaluator really helps you get the higher score for each of the scored sections.

There is an internal purpose for the executive summary as well. If the executive summary is drafted early, it can focus your team, your solution, and your proposal.

The easiest way to start an executive summary is with a formulaic outline, rather than a blank sheet. I developed my formula for high-impact executive summaries based on direct-response marketing techniques and have test-driven it on hundreds of proposals. I have also put together a self-study course, Executive Summary Secrets, that takes the mystery out of writing effective executive summaries. It has been highly acclaimed by professional proposal managers worldwide. Here is a short version of the proven six-part formula for successful executive summaries from this course:

- **Part 1: The hook.** This briefly spells out the customer's problem: What's keeping your customers up at night? There are at least eight different ways to create a strong hook that will cause the customer to be interested enough to want to read on, instead of putting the customer to sleep by starting the proposal with the pathetic introduction, "We are pleased to submit..."

- **Part 2: The overall win theme.** This indicates why your solution answers the biggest problem that this customer might have, as you laid out in the hook.

- **Part 3: The introduction.** This covers who you and the team are and how you are qualified to solve the customer's problems.

- **Part 4: The body.** The body includes highlights of the features of your solution and benefits that cover what's in it for the customer. There are five different types of body you could have to make it a high-impact executive summary.

- **Part 5: The top-level roadmap.** This is an optional part: Sometimes the RFP is so prescriptive that the customer does not need a roadmap to navigate your proposal, but sometimes it's necessary.

- **Part 6: A Summary.** This covers why the customer needs to select you, with a *call to action*, a hard-hitting sentence that says, "Here's why you should pick us." This is the only part of the proposal where it is appropriate to overtly appeal to the evaluator.

This formula is completely scalable to any length of the executive summary, from a couple of paragraphs to the full-length executive summaries.

Proposal Persuasion Tool 2: Win Themes

The second element of proposal persuasion is win themes. We discussed win themes development at the capture stages in Chapter 7. By the proposal start, you should have evolved your win themes and filled them with all kinds of quantified and qualified facts. Now in the proposal, you will need to integrate them into your text and graphics. You can do it in a variety of ways:

- Under section headings, to summarize the gist of the section's benefits.

- In text boxes to showcase facts, past performance, and benefits of the approach.

- Woven into the text and graphics to convince the customer that this is the right and credible solution.

Figure 12-1 shows a few ways win themes could appear in a proposal.

2.0 MANAGEMENT APPROACH

Bringing to FDA a modern application environment to make its life-saving mission even more efficient and effective

The FDA Adverse Event Reporting System (FAERS)/MedWatch^Plus Portal Systems Redesign/Development project is a high-profile FDA program that has an ultimate goal of enhancing the FDA's capability not only to save lives, but to help avoid any serious complications, mishaps, side effects, injuries, and unnecessary pain and suffering. As an example, on January 17th, 2008, the FDA issued a public advisory warning parents and caregivers against treating children less than 2 years of age with over-the-counter cough and cold medicines because of a possibility of "serious and potentially life-threatening" side effects. This is only one of many potentially life-saving announcements that FDA issues based on its important investigative work that will rely on the new FDA Adverse Event Reporting System (FAERS) and MedWatch^Plus Portal. These new systems will improve the method of submitting mandatory and voluntary adverse event reports. Data submission will be made easier, and will thereby expand the breadth and quality of data analyzed by FDA. This improved and increased level of data flow coupled with the steady flow of data from the drug companies, will improve accumulation of adverse event (AE) information from physicians and consumers.

The Acme Team Offers:
- Rigorous processes for rapid completion of requirements review and prototyping
- Proven approach for selecting and deploying relevant pharmacovigilance COTS products
- Proven project management team with 7 outstanding key personnel members
- Knowledge of FDA systems and relevant data standards
- Experience performing large-scale adverse event data migration and cleanup
- Data warehouse expertise
- Proven track record of delivery in the FDA
- Vendor-neutral approach

The Acme Team is proposing a solution that will bring the FDA a new, modern application environment to make its life-saving mission even more efficient and effective:
- By taking an "enterprise" view of the data, FDA will be able to more readily recognize and act upon adverse events in a more timely fashion.
- By consolidating and standardizing data, FDA will realize savings in reduced support resources and manpower.
- By viewing data aggregated from various sources, FDA will reduce stovepipes and enable decisions to be made with greater statistical significance and assurance.
- By developing improved data gathering mechanisms and processes, FDA will simplify AE submission and be able to analyze more and better data.

Figure 12-1. Win themes presentation in a proposal. Win themes can appear in the proposal in a variety of ways. In this example, they are shown with dotted lines.

Remember, to make your win themes even more impactful, you need to quantify and qualify the information. For example, in the second bullet in Figure 12-1, "*By consolidating and standardizing data, FDA will realize savings in reduced support resources and manpower,*" if a company had percentage of savings figured out from past projects, it would make the win theme statement more powerful.

Proposal Persuasion Tool 3: Language

The third element of proposal persuasion is highly readable text. To be persuasive, your proposal text has to have compelling content and correct structure. It should use metaphors and stories to make it more engaging. It should also use appropriate language and be so simply written and accessible that even a high-school student could understand your solution.

Your compelling content comes from solution development and figuring out how you are going to execute the work.

Correct structure boils down to understanding that you need first to generate interest in reading your section, and only then get into the technical details that would lead you to that conclusion. You shouldn't write proposals the way you were taught to write papers in college; instead, you should write them like journalists write their articles. They either catch your interest in the first second or don't, and your task is to catch an evaluator's full attention with the first sentence instead of putting them to sleep. Therefore, you should start your proposal sections with the key challenge, a risk, or a major benefit of fulfilling the requirement. Once you make the point of your section up front, you can amplify it and build on it, taking into consideration what the evaluators have already learned. Present the big picture first, then more and more detail, addressing all the Ws, usually in this specific order: why, what, who, how, when, where, and wow.

Metaphor and story as appropriate to proposal development are two advanced methods of making your proposals stand out. Metaphor relates something that an evaluator might not appreciate enough (but should), to something that they instinctively understand and find relatable, and create a vivid association in their mind that makes them realize the true value of what you are saying.

It enables an evaluator to create a mental picture that's worth a thousand pictures (as you know, a picture itself is worth a thousand words). Metaphor is by far the most powerful tool of persuasion and should not be overlooked just because it's hard to work into such a dry medium as government proposals.

Story can take at least a dozen forms in a proposal, with the most common one being anecdotes about your experiences on past projects. It's not that you tell about these experiences, it's how you tell about them that makes your proposal come alive and captures your evaluators' attention. Every story has to have three parts—a setup, a crisis, and a resolution—and it has to illustrate the points that you are seeking to drive home. You will need to interview your technical staff to get the details of their challenges, how they overcame them, and even their feelings about them. You should sprinkle such stories throughout your proposal to make it interesting and compelling.

While you are at it, you have to make sure that you use the correct language for your proposal. What sells in proposals from the language perspective are your tone and your ability to relate to the customer by speaking their language.

Your tone has to be sincere, confident, and credible. You will achieve that by speaking in the first person ("we" instead of "Acme Corporation"), which might fly in the face of what you have learned. You should be formal enough, but not so formal that your proposal reads like a bureaucratic opus.

Sincerity comes from doing just the opposite of sleazy sales, and that means avoiding adjectives and superlatives such as *world class, seasoned, premier*, and so on. Adjectives are like perfume: You shouldn't marinate in them. It's fine to have one adjective every few pages, but it will be a major turn-off if you use them too much. By the way, didn't I just create a mental picture for you with my metaphor?

Instead of relying on adjectives, you should convey passion though hard-hitting facts. It means that you have to work harder to get the specifics. Consider this:

> **Weak:** Mr. Smith understands the conditions in the theater and is highly experienced in overseas operations.

> **Better:** Mr. Smith knows firsthand the conditions in the theater because of multiple deployments in Desert Storm, Operation Iraqi Freedom, and most recently Operation Enduring Freedom.

> **Best:** Mr. Smith knows firsthand conditions in the theater because of two tours in Iraq during the Desert Storm and Operation Iraqi Freedom, and most recently three deployments during Operation Enduring Freedom.

Your credibility also comes from listing the facts and experiences that position you well for the job. Even though you might be submitting your reference projects in another volume, your technical proposal should include information about your experience interlaced in the text. Most likely, different evaluators will read your technical volume and your past performance volume, so the technical evaluators will not be able to appreciate the degree of your credibility if you include information about your relevant experience only in a separate volume.

Keep your language simple and straightforward. Just tell the customer what you will do for them and what the benefits of your solution are. You want to capture their attention with the hard-hitting win theme statement or key hot button up front, then show your understanding of the problem, then articulate your solution, with major features and benefits, and then prove that you can do what you claim. You will need to quantify, qualify, and substantiate. Then you want to summarize the most important advantages, if you have room.

You also want to make sure your text is highly readable. *Readability* refers to the level of education an evaluator has to have to understand your proposal. The more often an evaluator has to stop to think about (or interpret) what you're really trying to say, the worse score you are likely to get.

Try to think like your audience, the government evaluators. Each evaluator is responsible for reading and scoring multiple sections of proposals submitted by you and your competitors. Each set of proposal sections consists of dozens or hundreds of pages of boring but often necessary technical content. Usually on the Source Selection Evaluation Board (SSEB), only a few people are truly interested in the proposed solutions. Those are the people who made this program a reality and who are responsible for its execution. The rest are often the "stuckees" who are doing their "jury duty" when it is their turn to serve as the evaluators. It is possible that as many as 80 percent of SSEB members might be neither technically proficient in the topic nor enthusiastic about the technical gobbledygook through which they have to navigate.

Not only are many evaluators apprehensive about serving on an SSEB, but they also might not have the PhDs or technical degrees necessary to fully understand the topic of your proposal. Unlike those who have spent a lot of time in academia, they might not be in the habit of reading and understanding long research papers written by experts for other experts. As a result, their eyes glaze over at the long, dense, and jargon-heavy technical sentences. They skip past the paragraphs that do not make immediate sense. Your score suffers and, in a close competition, you could lose.

To avoid this kind of scenario, you need to get in the habit of improving proposal readability. Your proposal, therefore, should be understandable at a 9th or 10th grade level if it is nontechnical, and at an 11th or 12th grade level if it is highly technical. This chapter is written at the 10th grade level, so you have a point of reference.

It is difficult for authors to simplify and substantively edit their own work. It is a good thing, then, that there are easy-to-use tools right at your fingertips.

The easiest tool to use is Microsoft Word. Go to the Review tab, and click Spelling and Grammar. Click Options, and then go to Proofing. A Word Options screen should open with a menu on the left side, with Proofing highlighted. This screen will also have a section called When correcting spelling and grammar in Word with a number of check marks next to different options. Put a check mark next to Show readability statistics. Then, in Writing Style, check Grammar and Style, and click Settings… to open another menu that will let you adjust the settings to your preferences. I advise that you set it up the following way:

- Comma required before last list item, select Always

- Punctuation required with quotes, select Inside

- Spaces required between sentences, select 1

- Click OK once you are done to close the menu.

Click Recheck Document and run through the whole cycle of checking your document's grammar and style. Ignore the issues that shouldn't be corrected, and correct the issues that should be fixed.

At the end of your grammar and style check, a box will pop up with readability statistics about your document, as shown in Figure 12-2.

Readability Statistics

Counts	
Words	8492
Characters	43677
Paragraphs	354
Sentences	406

Averages	
Sentences per Paragraph	2.2
Words per Sentence	18.1
Characters per Word	4.9

Readability	
Passive Sentences	6%
Flesch Reading Ease	51.0
Flesch-Kincaid Grade Level	10.5

Figure 12-2. Readability statistics in Microsoft Word. These readability statistics are a valuable metric for determining how reader-friendly your proposal section is.

First, look at the Averages section of this box. If you are averaging more than four or five sentences per paragraph, you have a higher chance of an evaluator getting lost or stuck. You will want to cut down or break up your paragraphs.

If you are averaging more than 20 words per sentence, it is likely that you are attempting to address too many ideas at one time. A scorer is apt to miss important information when it is clumped together like this, so keep your sentences short.

Next, look at the Readability section of the Readability Statistics box. Passive sentences are those in which the sentence's verb is acting on its subject, rather than the subject acting on the verb. It is best to avoid passive sentences wherever possible. For example, "Section 1.3 outlines our management approach" is a much stronger sentence than "Our management approach is outlined in Section 1.3." Passive sentences are sometimes unavoidable, but your writing is much more vivid and concise when you limit passive voice to well below 10 percent of your sentences.

When it comes to the Flesch Reading Ease statistic, you want to stay in the 40 to 50 range or higher. This statistic rates your document on a 121-point scale depending on the average syllable count of your words and the average number of words per sentence. If your score is under 20, make a real effort to eliminate four- and five-syllable words. Very few such words are essential.

The Flesch-Kincaid Grade Level statistic is the aggregate measurement of your document's readability. It translates the Flesch measurement into a U.S. grade level between 1 and 12 (with higher grades representing college education) to give you a sense of the number of years of school experience that an average person would need to understand your writing. For instance, if your draft gets an 11.2, you can assume that an average 11th grade student could follow it, which also means that it will not put your evaluators to sleep.

Remember, your goal should be for your section to measure somewhere between the 9th and the 12th grade levels. This ensures that you handle complex subject matter in a direct and evaluator-friendly way.

After you make the changes, rerun the scan again to see if your readability has improved. Remember, caring about readability translates into caring about your evaluators, and caring about your evaluators leads to winning.

To learn more about making your proposal writing more persuasive, you can find many free articles on proposal language and writing at www. ostglobalsolutions.com/resources/articles.

Proposal Persuasion Tool 4: Graphics

Another tool of proposal persuasion is graphics. Graphics will always prevail over text. Quite simply, they are infinitely more effective at presenting the marketing and sales message. You wouldn't even fathom not using graphics when you put together a marketing or sales brochure. Yet, people routinely underuse graphics in proposals.

It is important to define that for proposal purposes, *graphics* or *visuals* are not just pretty graphs and flowcharts or photos. Instead, they are all the visual elements that break up the monotony of the text. A visual could be a figure, a text or a focus box, or a nicely rendered table.

You need to remember seven cardinal rules about proposal graphics.

1. Place a visual on at least every other page, but a graphic on every page is even better. If someone were to leaf through your proposal, he or she should be able to get your story just from the visuals.

2. Keep your graphics simple and uncluttered. Busy graphics lack the intended impact. Ruthlessly edit the extra text out after you are done designing the graphic.

3. Maintain vertical (portrait) orientation of the graphic. If you have a busy chart and are inclined to present it in a landscape mode, think about the evaluators who have many proposals to read, and will have to crank their neck attempting to read the graphic. Most likely, they won't bother, and will keep leafing through the proposal while missing important messages. Try and see first if your artist can lay out the graphic in portrait format. You might be surprised how much a graphic artist can do.

4. Design your graphic so it can stand alone, independent of text. "Stand alone" means not just the graphic by itself, but the graphic and its action caption. You should not require a page of text to explain each graphic, nor should you provide a lengthy explanation. An evaluator should be able to analyze the graphic and get even more information and data from it than from the text. A great proposal graphic replaces text.

5. Provide action captions that answer four key questions:

    •   What is on the graphic?

    •   What is it doing?

- What is it doing better than the competition?

- What is the benefit to the customer?

If you simply answer these questions, and edit your statements down to a single sentence, you will be able to write a powerful action caption.

6. Make your graphic understandable in less than 10 seconds. It might take longer than 10 seconds to digest all the rich data and layers of messaging in the graphic, but your primary message should be clear to the reviewer at a single glance. Evaluators often scan a proposal before delving into it and reading it in detail. You need to have them get your message quickly so they put your proposal in a "must read more closely" pile of proposals that are undergoing evaluation.

7. Follow traditional logic of the flow and direction to avoid confusing the evaluator.

- Left to right

- Top to bottom

- Clockwise

Figure 12-3 shows an example of a transition-out plan shown in a graphic form, instead of as text or a table. This plan shows what activities will take place when someone else has won a contract and a company now has to hand off all the work to them without any negative impact to the government. What works about this graphic is that it replaces a lot of text that would describe the same process; it clearly spells out activities through a timeline depiction, and is easy for an evaluator to understand. It also is organized left to right and top to bottom, and has an action caption.

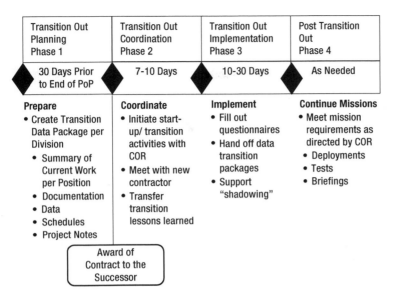

Figure 12-3. Example of a transition out graphic for a proposal. This graphic, usually rendered in color, works well because it is clear, concise, and stands on its own, without any text necessary to explain it.

To develop great graphics for your proposals, you have a couple of options: Conceptualize and develop your own graphics from scratch, or tap into a wonderful resource, www.GetMyGraphic.com. Here, you can purchase graphics that you can modify in Microsoft PowerPoint and insert into your proposals, or simply derive inspiration and create your own.

Proposal Persuasion Tool 5: Presentation

Your last but not least tool of proposal persuasion is presentation: your proposal's overall professional look and feel.

The first rule for proposals is to eliminate grammatical and spelling errors. This means editing your proposal multiple times, in every possible way: electronically, in hard copy, on the screen using a projector, and by reading it out loud. Errors will undermine your credibility even if you have a perfectly competitive solution. Scrub, scrub, scrub—and when you are absolutely done scrubbing, scrub some more. This is why it is a best practice to hold a read-out-loud session at the end of your proposal.

You also want to be consistent in the appearance of your graphics: All your proposal visuals have to have the same palette, shapes, and fonts. Consistency breeds trust, and you want your evaluators to trust you implicitly.

You also should spend some effort on a proposal cover to make it attractive so that your customer wants to read your proposal. The images on the cover should be reflective of your customer, rather than your brand. When you are just starting out, it is fine to have generic covers and not spend much money on developing a custom cover for each proposal. When you grow, however, you should invest in having a graphic artist develop a nice cover for each large and highly contested pursuit—just as your competitors, no doubt, will do.

Take the time to lay out your proposal properly. Research shows that double-column and single-column layouts are equally readable if there are graphics, so if your customer hasn't indicated a preference, it will make your life easier to use a single-column format. If you have a complex layout with multiple sections and double-sided pages, you might want to get a professional desktop publisher to help you with production. Government contractors rely on consultants or even have in-house desktop publishers to make documents attractive.

Last, but not least, you need to learn the ins and outs of pricing government proposals. No matter how persuasive you are in the technical proposal, you are unlikely to win if your price is high. You have to have a clear idea about the customer's budget, your competitors' prices, and the threshold at which you can execute the job and still make a profit.

Remember: The competition for government contracts is steep. Winning requires pulling out all the stops and doing everything within your power to make your technical and price offers more compelling.

The next chapter discusses how to optimize your proposal development process and grow your company aggressively in the federal market, so that you can flourish into a major government contractor.

You Have Won a Few Proposals— Now What?

Your company has now won a few proposals and has begun to see some real growth in revenue. Your task is now to gear up for aggressive growth. You have to execute superbly the work you have already won, to generate stellar performance ratings that you can leverage in the past performance sections of your subsequent bids. You have to keep aggressively bidding, raise the number of contracts you win, increase your capabilities, and grow into a major government contractor. You also want to optimize expenses, eliminate waste, and even acquire growth capital or purchase other businesses that will expand your capabilities. In this chapter, we discuss what comes next, after you have gotten past mere survival. We cover the techniques for building and aggressively growing your government contracting business, using internal and external resources effectively, and building a bid engine that will catapult your business revenue to hundreds of millions of dollars and beyond.

What's Next: Techniques for Building and Aggressively Growing Your Government Contracting Business

Business growth in the federal market doesn't happen by accident. Many companies grow up to a certain point through hard but rather chaotic efforts. Many get stuck, however, at a certain size, and then begin shrinking. You should implement six strategies to grow aggressively in the federal market:

1. Employ a strategic business development planning process.

2. Develop a robust pipeline.

3. Establish practical and repeatable processes.

4. Train your entire workforce to morph into a sales force.

5. Use internal and external resources effectively.

6. Build a bid engine.

Together, these strategies will catapult your business to hundreds of millions of dollars and beyond. Let's discuss each of the strategies in turn.

1. Employ a Strategic Business Development Planning Process

The first strategy is to employ a strategic business development planning process. There are a few techniques to run this process but essentially, all the key decision makers in your company have to get together and answer the following questions:

*   Are you in the right market?

*   What is the market currently doing? What are the trends?

*   What is going on with your current customers, and what other customers should you pursue?

*   What competencies should you develop in addition to what you already do?

*   What growth strategies should you employ?

*   What are your financial goals for the year in sales and bookings?

*   How much should you bid on to achieve the goals you set?

- If you are of a certain socioeconomic status, such as an 8(a) program, how will you avoid size triggers that will get you out of the program prematurely, and cause you to lose all the great benefits it provides?

- What are some of the key pursuits in your pipeline you have to win to achieve your goals?

- What is the budget to achieve your goals? Will this budget be enough?

Speaking of budgets, you need to determine how much you should bid on government contracts annually and each month. Your first step is to determine a reasonable goal for your bookings by the end of the year. Bookings are money from your wins that are expected to be received from your customers based on signed contracts. Then, you need to determine how many bids you are going to submit to reach that goal. This is easily done: Simply take your year-end bookings goal and divide it by your win rate.

If you have not calculated your win rate, you might want to use an industry average of 33 percent. Let us say you hope to make $20 million in bookings. Using a 33 percent win rate, you will find out that you will likely need to bid on roughly $60 million worth of projects. This way, when you only win a third of them, you will still hit your $20 million mark.

Your next step is to determine how many proposals you have to write to reach $60 million. For example, would you rather bid on three RFPs worth $20 million, hoping to win one, or would you rather bid on six RFPs worth around $10 million each, hoping to win two.

Note that your past performance will also be a factor in your planning, because the government is unlikely to award you a contract with a dollar amount drastically higher than what you have performed on in the past. If you haven't managed a prime contract for more than $5 million, it is unlikely that you will get an award for a prime contract of $20 million or more, unless you have done significant preparation to build a compelling case to a specific government customer, and your competition's past performance record turned out to be no better than yours.

Once you come up with an answer, you might want to look at your pipeline of opportunities and see if you can identify the bids that will make up your $60 million in the time frame that you have identified, or assign an action item to aggressively hunt for these opportunities and identify them within weeks of your strategic planning session (otherwise it will be too late).

In all your planning, you will have to take into consideration that there is a lag time for government awards. Some of them can be made within one to three months, especially as task orders on MACs. Others could take up to a year or two to award.

Depending on the specific opportunities, you might realize that you will have to bid on your $60 million worth of opportunities in the first two quarters of your fiscal year to hit the $20 million mark by year end, because you have to give the government roughly six months to award. Just to be safe, you might want to submit even more bids, knowing that the government almost never keeps to the schedules they set.

You will then figure out how many proposals you have to produce per month to get there. You will have to factor in your cost and capabilities when making your determination. How many projects can you handle at one time? How many resources can you commit to one project? How much money can you afford to commit to going ahead on multiple RFPs?

When planning your budget for pursuits, it is best to use a top-down method. Take the money you have committed to business development, or are willing to invest, and divide that by the number of pursuits you have to have. You should note that for small businesses that work their staff around the clock and where the owners will invest a lot of their sweat equity, the cost of capture and proposal pursuit varies from 0.5 percent to 0.75 percent of the total booking value.

For example, if the value of one-year base and four option years' contract is $10 million, the pursuit will run you about $50,000 to $75,000 from capture through proposal preparation. If that seems like a lot to you, you might want to translate this number into hours to understand the resources required from you. At roughly $100 per hour cost of resources—which is you and your employees with their overhead, fringe, and general and administrative (G&A) costs added on top of their hourly rates—you will spend about 500 to 750 hours per pursuit. That translates into two people working on a proposal for a month at 200 hours each, and a couple of hundred hours allocated to capture (which is a few months of part-time work). As you can see, although the amount of money seems high, it is not a lot of hours to play with to do a great job. You have to remember that you need to resource your proposals to *win*—not just to complete them.

■ **Note**   Allocate enough resources to win proposals, instead of merely completing them.

Your math will be telling during your strategic business development planning session—where you will either adjust your goals, decide to shift resources, or make additional investments. You also might want to continue to subcontract to others a little longer than you had hoped, to reduce your expenses, but don't use it as a crutch. It's almost always better to be a prime.

2. Develop a Robust Pipeline

Your second strategy for growth is developing a robust pipeline of pursuits. Without a great pipeline, your growth will be entirely dependent on luck. Unlike playing a lottery, you want to have a more solid foundation for your business.

Your pipeline can take the form of an Excel spreadsheet, or some other well-known solution such as Salesforce. At OST, we provide business development services to companies and we build pipelines for companies. In the process of doing that, we find that most businesses that use Salesforce don't know how to configure it properly, and use it to no more effect than an Excel spreadsheet.

A key to the right pipeline is to use a simple but robust tool, dedicated resources for updating the pipeline, and a process for its effective management. Your pipeline tool's most important capabilities will include an ability to sort data to get the right reports and at-a-glance views, ability to track progress, reminders, tasks, and the ability to record and aggregate information about each opportunity in one place.

Your processes should include rules of participation for all who contribute to adding opportunities to the pipeline to grow it. The participants include those who find opportunities, those who complete tasks to move your opportunities forward as they learn more information, those who attend regular meetings to review your pipeline, and even those whose role is to weed through your opportunities to select only the ones that you have a realistic chance of winning.

3. Establish Practical and Repeatable Processes

Your third growth strategy is to establish practical and repeatable processes that everyone will use consistently, and will continuously improve to make you even better at winning business. You will want your processes to be detailed enough. Too high-level processes that only spell out big steps, without delving into detail, such as establishing major proposal milestones (Kickoff, Pink Team, Red Team, etc.) are useless and even damaging. They make a company feel as if it had processes and these processes made no difference. This is when a company abandons processes altogether, and uses whatever works for any given pursuit. As a result, it never learns from its mistakes, and uses resources inefficiently.

You are better off finding a company to help you with process development, because it will save you years of headaches to do it correctly from the start. At the heart of your operations, you will create a process book that covers the full life cycle of business development. It has to describe detailed roles and responsibilities for your staff participating in business development, include a chart for proper communications, and include detailed checklists and templates for each step.

Your processes will require buy-in from the company, and culture shift through training and enforcement of these processes. If no one trains personnel or champions process implementation, the company will most likely abandon even the best of processes. Your job is to prevent that from happening.

4. Train Your Entire Workforce to Morph into a Sales Force

Your fourth strategy, discussed in Chapter 1, is to train your entire workforce to morph into a sales force. You will need to train your operations staff who work directly with the customer implementing your contracts in business development and proposal writing.

Take into consideration that most of your staff will hate selling, so you will need to help them overcome these feelings, and then teach them real techniques for identifying, targeting, and securing opportunities with existing and new customers. They will also need training to find out what keeps the customer up at night, and what hidden requirements need answering to make your proposals shine.

Your capture and proposal managers will need cross-training in capture, proposals, winning MACs and task orders, win theme development, compliant and persuasive proposal writing, executive summaries, and cost strategy. Your SMEs and operations personnel will need training in proposal writing and solution development in addition to capture and business development. Everyone will need training in the tools and processes you will use.

5. Use Internal and External Resources Effectively

The fifth strategy for growth is to use internal and external resources effectively. When you are just starting out, your business development team might consist of you—and, well, you. If you are lucky, you might get other help, such as your technical personnel pitching in. A small team size is effective for small businesses, which only handle a few government bids a year, but as your company grows, you will need to expand the number of personnel you have working or helping with business development. When you need to crank out three, four, five, or ten proposals a month, you have to figure out how to scale intelligently. Your goal is to add the right staff at the right time, be they internal resources or external.

Internal resources hiring has to be timed to make business sense. First, you have to determine your current and desired proposal volume per month, and staff your organization at 75 percent of the expected throughput. If your proposal volume is lower than one proposal per month, it's smarter to use consultants for larger bids, and write smaller bids in-house, burning the midnight oil.

When you go after proposals that you must win, hire real consulting professionals. The temptation is to go cheaper on the hourly rate, but if you are just starting to build your capability, you need experts—even if you bring them in just to outline your proposal, and review it midprocess. If you are obsessed with the hourly rate, you might save money on the wages, but could lose even more money and time if you don't win, or have to rewrite what they have done. Proposal consultants will run you on average $150 per hour—some will charge more and some a little less.

Your typical first hire will be a business developer with the capability of being a capture manager. His or her goal will be to build your pipeline and find opportunities you can bid on in the near term, midterm, and long term.

Here are the roles and responsibilities for your business development organization's positions.

Business Developer (Also Called Sales Manager, Account Manager, or Account Lead)

- Identifies customers

- Fosters and maintains trusting customer relationships

- Markets the company to the customer

- Identifies and qualifies opportunities (not one, but many)

- After the "interest" decision, hands each specific opportunity over to the capture manager

- Continues to participate in the capture process by partaking mainly in the customer interface and intelligence gathering efforts

Capture Manager

- Takes over each specific opportunity from the business developer—usually one opportunity at a time

- Fosters the relationship with the customer

- Shapes the RFP and vets the solution

- Develops and updates customer contact plan

- Gathers intelligence

- Prepares bid review presentations

- Manages the development of the win strategy

- Leads activities that include developing, updating, and maintaining the capture plan

- Leads the development of win themes

- Performs competitive analysis and facilitates black hat reviews

- Develops teaming strategy

- Oversees development of the solution that includes technical and management approaches, cost strategy (in conjunction with the PTW exercise), staffing plan, and risk management strategy

- Prepares the proposal resource plan and oversees capture and proposal budgets

- Assists with assembling a winning proposal team

- Participates in the proposal effort by making sure the capture findings are reflected in the proposal

Proposal Manager

Next, you might need to bring in an internal proposal manager, and train your technical staff in persuasive proposal writing. Check out some of our free webinars to help train your staff at www.ostglobalsolutions.com/training/webinars. A proposal manager's set of roles and responsibilities include, at a very minimum, the following tasks:

- Participating in the capture early on to help stage the capture materials for the proposal and learning in detail about the opportunity

- Working in conjunction with the capture manager to implement win strategy in the proposal
- Taking over the leadership role after the RFP release
- Planning the proposal
- Outlining the proposal
- Conducting a proposal kickoff and issuing assignments
- Training the authors
- Developing and tracking a proposal schedule
- Leading status meetings
- Overseeing and tracking daily progress on all proposal activities that include section drafting, graphics development, and cost volume preparation
- Preparing proposals for reviews and delivery
- Working in conjunction with the orals coach to prepare for orals (if they are required for your proposal)

Technical Writer and Graphic Artist

Your next set of hires will likely include a writer and an all-in-one desktop publisher, technical editor, and graphic artist. Your technical writer will write and edit proposal sections, while working closely with the SMEs. Your jack-of-all-trades person will serve three roles at once:

- Professional graphic artist to transform your graphic concepts into professional-looking, attractive graphics
- Editor to ensure your proposals are error-free and polished
- Desktop publisher to format your documents for professional appearance

You will need to involve your SMEs in the proposal process as much as possible after you train them in proposal writing. They can all take persuasive proposal writing courses to become decent writers, and even take advantage of the free webinar on how to overcome the proposal writer's block at www. ostglobalsolutions.com/training/webinars. This way, you will be able to cut down on the amount of work you have to do personally as the designated business developer and reduce your resource costs.

Other Roles

As you grow larger, you might bring in a price strategist, a pricer, a professional contracts manager to help you navigate the intricacies of the FAR and other customer requirements and lead your customer negotiations, a procurement manager to help you negotiate and manage teaming arrangements and subcontracting agreements, and even a PTW expert to make your bids more competitive from a pricing standpoint.

Successful companies are careful in adding all these overhead positions, and they don't try to do everything in house. They perform careful financial, analysis taking all costs into consideration, and use a mix of internal staff and consultants. They bring in external resources for the following:

- Surges
- Special expertise
- New ideas
- Staff mentoring

You will need to carefully track your staff's performance and efficiency. You will need to decide how efficient and effective they are in their win rates and throughput, and either develop or replace them. Develop a relationship with a trusted consulting firm and have the resources on tap when and where you need them.

6. Build a Bid Engine

Once you do your planning, establish a pipeline, develop your processes, build an organization, and train your staff, your sixth strategy is to add four success components to help you take your business development capability to the next level.

1. Customer information repository or a customer relationship management (CRM) tool
2. Metrics
3. Collateral library
4. Continuous improvement

These components, together with the foundation you have built, will form a robust bid engine. Let's discuss them in greater detail.

Customer Information Repository or a CRM Tool

You should create a repository of information on your requirements, contracts, and customers for your MACs. Usually companies use a CRM tool to do this, and in the best-organized organizations, it is integrated with the pipeline. The CRM helps you track all the key decision makers, update their profile regularly, and indicate whether they are a friend, enemy, or neutral to your company. It is also important that you keep track of their top pet peeves and hot buttons. Collecting and distilling all materials and articles about this particular customer into a succinct description is important. This summary description should also include salient points from their presentations and interviews, with all the original sources kept in the same database.

Metrics

You should carefully track your win rate (a ratio of bids won versus lost), and your capture rate (a ratio of dollars won versus dollars lost).

You also need to distinguish between types of bids won and lost, such as prime bids versus subcontracting bids, task orders versus regular requirements contracts bids, and large versus small bids. This will give you a more accurate understanding of your win and capture ratios and how they are changing.

It is also important to pay attention to what types of work you are winning, what you are losing, and how well your competitors are doing in each area. This will allow you to gain information on the environment of the industry, your strengths, your weaknesses, and how they compare to those of your competitors. You will need to revisit your performance semiannually or even quarterly to adjust course if necessary. This way, your growth won't be an accident that did or didn't happen.

Collateral Library

You should develop a capture and marketing collateral library. I have already mentioned it in Chapter 1, but to remind you, this library should include all the templates you might use in proposals to expedite and streamline your proposal development process. It should also include all your marketing materials such as white papers developed by your technical personnel that relate to the specific areas of your core expertise, and the areas that your contracts cover; and also information that you might want to reference, such as Bloomberg Government and Gartner analyst reports, case studies, brochures, and other information your business development or program staff can hand to the customer for them to get to know you better and to build trust.

Also include in your library the proposals you have won and lost, all previous RFPs, and debriefing information from your customers. It should also include a compilation of your and your teammates' past performance information, with quotes showing kudos from the customer.

There should also be a database of resumes for personnel you bid frequently; management, subcontracting, quality, and transition plan templates; and common win themes. Don't forget contact lists for everyone who could be involved in the capture and proposal processes, including consultants you could call in if you are short on resources. Gather your PTW information and competitive intelligence, carefully citing the sources of your information. Also, keep handy any golden nuggets such as your company's accomplishments and certifications.

Don't forget to set up an immensely useful graphics library, so that you can reuse all the graphics you have developed in multiple proposals.

Continuous Improvement

Finally, you need to implement a continuous improvement process in your business development. After every single pursuit, conduct a "lessons learned" session. You will need to assess what you did right, what you did wrong, and what you can change for better results in the next proposal.

You will need to make an effort to formally brainstorm on and document your lessons learned, upload these lessons in a common area dedicated to just that, and also establish a procedure to review the file prior to your next proposal.

For each pursuit, you will need to examine your actual proposal quality and the capture and proposal process that it took to produce this proposal. You will need to look at both the positive aspects and the negatives. Examine what has worked well. Also honestly inquire as to what problems came up during proposal preparation, whether they were avoidable, and ways to prevent them from reoccurring in the future.

Invite everyone who played a major role in the proposal to participate in the lessons learned session, including the production and graphics personnel. You might even want to invite major teammates who have worked together with you on developing the proposal. You might want to avoid upper management showing up to your session, as it does not elicit the best types of openness and focus on positive outcomes.

You need to conduct two lessons learned sessions—one right after the proposal, and another one right after the debriefing by your customer (which you should always request within three calendar days of the award announcement, whether you won or lost).

To keep improving your performance, you will need to do the following:

- Immediately implement the changes in your process and act on what you have learned.

- Review the lessons learned prior to each proposal and reiterate some of them to your team during the proposal kickoff.

- Over time, as the lessons learned accumulate, conduct a review with a small team to see if there have been any trends that you hadn't noticed on just a few pursuits, and then make major changes to the way you do business development, resulting in massive successes.

Armed with all this information, you will be able to achieve significant growth rates. According to our observations, benchmarks, statistics shared between management consultants specializing in business development, and the top government businesses lists, companies in the federal market that earn less than $2 million in annual revenue boast average 200 percent growth rates; companies earning up to $7 million report an average 50 percent growth rate; and companies taking in up to $100 million grow at a hefty rate of 20 percent per year. You can be wildly successful in this market if you apply the tools that professionals do. So, go ahead and win business. The sky is the limit!

Capture Plan
Generalized Outline of Slide Presentation

1. Title Slide

Title of the pursuit, capture manager, date of the latest version

2. Action Item Completion Status

Status of the action items assigned at the last opportunity review

3. Opportunity Summary

- **Program Name:** Examples: Full and Open, Small Business Set Aside, Streamlined Competition, etc.

- **Program Description:** A brief elevator speech on what this program is—the essence of it, and brief scope—no more than a short paragraph

- **Customer:** Your buying agency, and also the actual requesting agency, if applicable

- **Contract Type:** Examples: GWAC, IDIQ, CPAF, CPIF, CPFF, FFP, T&M, Fixed Labor Categories, TOs and DOs, etc.

- **Acquisition Strategy:** Examples: Full and Open, Small Business Set Aside, Streamlined Competition, etc.

- **Value:** Program budget set over the number of years. Example: $50 million over 5 years (2-year base and three options)

- **Value to the Company**: This is what you look to get out of it; this is what you will get not counting what your subs will get

- **Alignment with the Company's Goals and Objectives**: Is this a core business opportunity? Does this fit within the company's goals?

- **Incumbent(s)**: Yes/No, new requirement; Incumbents for specific scope of work that is now going to be bundled into a new program, or company name that's doing this work right now

- **Competition**: List your most important competitors

- **Company Role**: Prime or sub

- **Schedule**:
  - RFI date:
  - DRFP date:
  - RFP date:
  - Proposal due:
  - Orals:
  - Award:
  - First Task Order (if it's a MAC):
  - Any other key dates:

- **Place of Performance**: Geographical locations, your site vs. customer site, etc.

4. Opportunity Background

Summarize what's important to know about the program; for example, how did it come about, how long has it been around, are there any associated key events and issues, who were all the companies that have worked on it, and has there been any political undercurrents/Congressional scrutiny, and any technical background that's important. The purpose of this slide or set of slides is to catch up and quickly educate anyone new to this opportunity.

5. Technical Capabilities Analysis by the Area of Scope

- List all the scope areas in the RFP, and rank yourself (including your team) in the areas of capability. You could even provide your approach to address each area.

6. Technical and Management Discriminators and Strengths

- List all the unique and not-so-unique strengths that you will showcase in your technical and management approaches.

7. Customer Analysis

- Profile
- Buying problem
- Organization chart
- Source selection team's hot buttons
- Buying and evaluation processes
- Our past performance and positioning with this customer
- Customer map
- Goals
- Pain points
- Champion? Friend? Enemy? Neutral toward our company?

8. Competitive Analysis

- Insert here the results of the competitive analysis

9. Internal Analysis

- Strategic fit
- Financial analysis
- Capture budget
- Capture management plan

10. Win Strategy

- Win strategy statements for your:
  - Technical approach
  - Management approach
  - Cost/price approach
  - Past performance approach

11. Action Plans

- Customer contact plan
- Intelligence gathering
- Teaming and subcontracting
- Win strategy refinement
- Further competitive analysis
- Proposal development
- Solution design

12. Executive Summary Mockup

- Key pieces of information you will include in your executive summary, such as your hook, main win theme, why you have each teammate on your team, features and benefits of your approach, and your call to action.

How to Develop a Proposal Outline

Step-by-Step Example

When you are ready to get into the nitty-gritty of tackling your first proposal (Chapter 12), developing and annotating your outline can be daunting. The following set of typical RFP instructions (indented in italics) will serve as a working example to help familiarize you with the methods for developing your outline (in bold) and annotations (in italics immediately following the bold) for a proposal section of a fictional company, Acme.

---

1. Read the section L instructions (instructions to the offerors):

L.1.6 Program Management (Volume 2) shall be prepared in accordance with these instructions including Paragraph 2.0.1 of this section, and will be evaluated in accordance with the evaluation criteria in Section M, Evaluation Factors for Award.

L.2.0.1 VOLUME 2, Factor 1 - Program Management

L.2.0.1.1 Management Organizational Structure. The offeror shall include their proposed organizational structure with explanatory rationale. The offeror must show outlined plans for each organizational element and defined responsibilities in support of requirements in the contract level PWS. At a minimum the plan should address:

- *Clear lines of responsibility and authority for controlling, reporting, and reviewing work*

- *Process for streamlining decision-making while maintaining accountability*

---

2. Your annotated outline would start with the headings generated from the customer's requirements, and the exact language from the requirements in the RFP pasted below in italics:

1.0 Factor 1: Management Organizational Structure [L.2.0.1.1]

L.2.0.1.1 Include the proposed organizational structure with explanatory rationale.

Show outlined plans for each organizational element and defined responsibilities in support of requirements in the contract level PWS.

1.1 Clear lines of responsibility and authority for controlling, reporting, and reviewing work [L.2.0.1.1]

L.2.0.1.1 Clear lines of responsibility and authority for controlling, reporting, and reviewing work.

1.2 Process for streamlining decision making while maintaining accountability [L.2.0.1.1]

L.2.0.1.1 Process for streamlining decision making while maintaining accountability.

---

3. Your next step is to check the Evaluation Criteria (or section M in this RFP), to see what it says:

M.1.4, Factor 1: Management Organizational Structure and Ability to Create Teaming Arrangements: The Government will evaluate the offeror's outlined plans for each organizational element and defined responsibilities and business management practices, processes, and expertise to manage the contract to determine if the proposal exceeds, meets, or does not meet the requirements.

4. Now you can add the section M (or evaluation criteria) requirements to your outline:

1.0 Factor 1: Management Organizational Structure [L.2.0.1.1, M.1.4]

L.2.0.1.1 Include the proposed organizational structure with explanatory rationale.

Show outlined plans for each organizational element and defined responsibilities in support of requirements in the contract level PWS.

M.1.4 The Government will evaluate the offeror's outlined plans for each organizational element and defined responsibilities and business management practices, processes, and expertise to manage the contract.

1.1 Clear lines of responsibility and authority for controlling, reporting, and reviewing work [L.2.0.1.1]

L.2.0.1.1 Clear lines of responsibility and authority for controlling, reporting, and reviewing work.

1.2 Process for streamlining decision making while maintaining accountability [L.2.0.1.1]

L.2.0.1.1 Process for streamlining decision making while maintaining accountability.

5. Now you can go to the Statement of Work and find the paragraph relevant to the management section:

C.2.2 Management Process. The Contractor shall possess an innovative and efficient management structure. The management structure will be of sufficient depth to enable merging the operational requirements with the managerial controls that result in providing a seamless and integrated team capable of delivering quality products, reports, assessments, and/or services on time.

6. Add the Statement of Work language to the outline, finding an appropriate "home" for it:

1.0 Factor 1: Management Organizational Structure [L.2.0.1.1, M.1.4, C.2.2]

L.2.0.1.1 Include the proposed organizational structure with explanatory rationale.

Show outlined plans for each organizational element and defined responsibilities in support of requirements in the contract level PWS.

M.1.4 The Government will evaluate the offeror's outlined plans for each organizational element and defined responsibilities and business management practices, processes, and expertise to manage the contract.

1.1 Clear lines of responsibility and authority for controlling, reporting, and reviewing work [L.2.0.1.1]

L.2.0.1.1 Clear lines of responsibility and authority for controlling, reporting, and reviewing work.

2.1.2 Process for streamlining decision making while maintaining accountability [L.2.0.1.1, C.2.2]

L.2.0.1.1 Process for streamlining decision making while maintaining accountability.

C.2.2 Management Process. The Contractor shall possess an innovative and efficient management structure. The management structure will be of sufficient depth to enable merging the operational requirements with the managerial controls that result in providing a seamless and integrated team capable of delivering quality products, reports, assessments, and/or services on time.

---

7. Now that you have gotten all the requirements information from the RFP, your next step is to annotate the outline and create instructions for the writers. You can include anything that might be useful—from your notes as to what points you would like them to address, down to graphic concepts, tables, introductory sentences, references to other sections, win themes, and any other useful information you can come up with. Assign page count in parentheses. The annotations are in a regular font following each set of RFP instructions. Here is what the product for this step would look like:

1.0 Factor 1: Management Organizational Structure [L.2.0.1.1, M.1.4, C.2.2] (3 pages)

L.2.0.1.1 Include the proposed organizational structure with explanatory rationale.

Show outlined plans for each organizational element and defined responsibilities in support of requirements in the contract level PWS.

M.1.4 The Government will evaluate the offeror's outlined plans for each organizational element and defined responsibilities and business management practices, processes, and expertise to manage the contract.

Given multiple locations of work performance and travel requirements, Acme will manage this program using a central Program Management Office (PMO). Describe the PMO.

Figure concept: PMO graphic, functionally describing what it will do for the program, and how.

Discussion points:

- Discuss business management practices.
- State that we will use PMBOK processes.
- Refer to our past experience managing three other similar contracts at Ft. Huachuca, Pax River, and Charlotte.

Transition sentence: Sections below present our **outlined plans for each organizational element and defined responsibilities** in support of requirements in the contract level PWS.

(Ensure we address outlined plans for each organizational element, and defined responsibilities).

1.1 Clear lines of responsibility and authority for controlling, reporting, and reviewing work [L.2.0.1.1]

L.2.0.1.1 Clear lines of responsibility and authority for controlling, reporting, and reviewing work.

- Show a hierarchical organizational chart: who reports to whom.

- Show how the Task Order Leads/Project Managers are fully empowered.

- Discuss how we give this project the utmost importance so all the Acme managing partners are involved.

1.2 Process for streamlining decision making while maintaining accountability [L.2.0.1.1, C.2.2]

L.2.0.1.1 Process for streamlining decision making while maintaining accountability.

C.2.2 Management Process. The Contractor shall possess an innovative and efficient management structure. The management structure will be of sufficient depth to enable merging the operational requirements with the managerial controls that result in providing a seamless and integrated team capable of delivering quality products, reports, assessments, and/or services on time.

- Discuss how we will streamline decision-making, meaning that our people at the locations can make autonomous decisions and follow government's directions (given all the time differences); but what kinds of checks and balances do we put in place to ensure that they are accountable?

- To address section C.2.2, discuss the depth of management structure to merge operational requirements with the managerial controls to provide a seamless integrated team. (Note that this requirement could be lifted to a more general level and discussed in section 1.0 if it doesn't fit here as you develop content.)

---

8. Now that the section outline is done, it is ready to be handed to the section author. With such a detailed set of instructions, the section author doesn't have to know much about navigating the RFP, or guess as to what he or she has to write about. The likelihood of the author writing exactly what you need him or her to write is much higher—and your likelihood of having to rewrite everything the author has written is significantly lower. This should reduce your stress level, reduce the amount of work that you have to do, and raise your win probability.

Made in the USA
San Bernardino, CA
27 January 2013